GREEN LONDON

GREEN LONDON

A Handbook

ROY HAWKINS

PHOTOGRAPHY BY MILES MAIDMENT

SIDGWICK & JACKSON
LONDON

FOR MUM AND DAD

First published in Great Britain in 1987
by Sidgwick & Jackson Limited

Text copyright © 1987 by Roy Hawkins
Photographs copyright © 1987 by Miles Maidment

Designed by James Campus

All rights reserved. No part of this publication may
be reproduced, stored in a retrieval system, or
transmitted in any form or by any means, electronic,
mechanical, photocopying, recording or otherwise,
without the prior written permission of the
copyright owner.

ISBN 0 283 99728 1

Phototypeset by Falcon Graphic Art Ltd
Wallington, Surrey
Printed in Great Britain by
Hazell, Watson & Viney Ltd, Aylesbury
and bound by Dorstel Press Ltd, Harlow
for Sidgwick & Jackson Limited
1 Tavistock Chambers, Bloomsbury Way
London WC1A 2SG

Frontispiece: **The quality of life in London
is greatly improved by the city's wealth
of open spaces**

Contents

Introduction	6
KEW GARDENS	8
CHELSEA FLOWER SHOW	17
Other Activities of the RHS	
THE ROYAL PARKS	22
Greenwich Park, Hampton Court, Bushy Park, Hyde Park, Kensington Gardens, Regent's Park, Primrose Hill, Richmond Park, St James's Park, Green Park	
PARKS	52
Battersea Park, Golders Hill, Holland Park, Kenwood, Lesnes Abbey Wood, Osterley Park, Waterlow Park	
GARDENS	81
Chelsea Physic Garden, Chiswick House, Fenton House, Ham House, The Hill, The Tradescant Garden	
HEATH AND COMMON LAND	108
Hampstead Heath, Wimbledon Common	
THE SQUARES AND INNS OF COURT	120
The Squares: Fitzroy, Gordon and Tavistock, Russell, Grosvenor, Berkeley, St James's	
The Inns of Court: The Temple, Lincoln's Inn, Gray's Inn	
ROOF GARDENS AND LANDSCAPED OPEN SPACE	131
The Barbican Conservatory, Derry and Toms' Roof Garden, St Katharine's Dock, The South Bank	
EATING OUT	142
Restaurants, Pubs, Cafés, Picnic Places	
BUYING PLANTS	150
Garden Centres, Shops, Markets, Florists	
FOR CHILDREN	160
FOR PEOPLE WITH DISABILITIES	163
Information	170
Maps	176

Introduction

The trouble with guidebooks is that they tell you the 'where' and 'how' but do not give much explanation of the 'why'. Though comprehensive they do little more than list places and give brief descriptions which are just a list of features. 'Large lake, waterfowl, trees and shrubs' describes both St James's Park and my local ornamental gardens, but there is a world of difference between them. Places sound alike because there is no indication of quality; of what distinguishes the good from the bad and the indifferent. This handbook is intended to be a useful guide to only the best 'green' places in London, giving reasons why they are worth a visit.

It is well known that London is very fortunate in having so much open space; that has been documented many times. Here I hope to show how people can take full advantage of this most pleasurable aspect of the city's life. Or at least to make people aware of plants in London and how they can benefit from them to improve the quality of life. This handbook is for everyone who comes into contact with the city, whether they like plants or not.

I have only included what I consider to be the best 'green' places in London; those of interest to the majority of people. 'Green' is a blanket term I have used to cover anywhere that people and plants meet. The book covers not only open spaces but 'Chelsea' and other flower shows, where to buy things horticultural, the best places to take children, gardens specially designed for people with disabilities, where to eat and drink outdoors – not forgetting the Museum of Garden History.

The open spaces include some places like Ham House and Lesnes Abbey Wood, which deserve to be better known, as well as all those for which London is justly famous: Kew Gardens and the Royal Parks. (It is worth noting that most of them are free of charge and the others good value.) The Chelsea Flower Show is another reason why London holds such a prestigious place in the horticultural world. Some of the places to buy plants are sights in themselves, and who needs to be a gardener to enjoy a pub lunch in a garden? There are many ways in which people and plants can meet.

Please do not think of al fresco living as being confined to the summer. A fine day in any month is a reason to be out of doors. Nature, fresh air and a sense of space are essential in London at any season.

I hope this handbook will encourage people to get out and about and try new places. There is much to be enjoyed: the city charm of St James's Square, the surprising suburban calm of Wimbledon Common, the dramatic South Bank, bustling Columbia Road market, lunch at the amazing 'Gardens' restaurant high above Kensington – the possibilities go on and on. I also hope it will stimulate interest in everything else that is 'green' in London and the benefits to be gained.

I would like to thank the following for their interest and support: Marina Blodget, Diana Foster, Mike Fuller, Paula Harte, Mary, Michael and Mark Maidment, Eamonn Marshall, Gareth Morgan, Chris Moore, Rosemary Nicholson, Michael Pilcher and everyone at Boreham Wood Day Centre. And my special thanks to Bernard Morrish for his advice and practical help.

ROY M. HAWKINS

Kew Gardens

Kew, I am sure, is familiar to a lot of people who know London. For the rest, here is a taste of this magnificent garden which must be the best value in London – just fifty pence for admission to 300 acres of pure pleasure. What could be nicer on a spring day than to walk among masses of beautifully scented shrubs?

> Go down to Kew in lilac-time,
> In lilac-time, in lilac-time,
> Go down to Kew in lilac-time,
> (It isn't far from London!)

These lines from a poem by Alfred Noyes, popular between the wars, illustrate what Kew still means to the majority of people. I remember my mother reciting them to me when, at the age of eight, I was considered able to appreciate the splendours of Kew. I have wondered since if it was that first visit that sparked off my interest in plants and eventually made me decide to work with them.

But I am not the only one with a romantic view of Kew. Many people return to Kew again and again. On a recent visit I met a local woman with her two young sons, who referred to Kew as 'our garden'. An elderly woman from Worthing said she used to live nearby but now comes up three times a year 'because I miss it so much'. Kew relaxes everyone and it is easy to strike up a conversation. Others I have met include a professional photographer, two art students sketching the Temperate House, and an Australian girl travelling alone on the 'Grand Tour of Europe'. Kew is all things to all people; those who wish to enjoy its many pleasures are as welcome as the most learned plant specialist. Primarily, however, the garden functions as a scientific institution, and in this respect the world importance of the Royal Botanic Gardens, Kew, cannot be over-emphasized.

The work of the gardens includes the identification of plants from all over the world; acting as a quarantine station; distributing economic and decorative plant material, and conserving endangered species by growing them and storing them in a seed bank. Kew studies natural species before they have been altered by the hybridizing activities of plant breeders. This, by definition, excludes the majority of new garden plants; for these, the equivalent institution is the Royal Horticultural Society.

The land at Kew was first acquired by George II's son, Frederick Prince of Wales. In

1759 his wife Augusta started a botanic garden of about nine acres on the site, and in 1792 their son, George III, combined the Kew estate with the neighbouring Richmond estate, which he had inherited from his grandfather. In 1841 the garden was given to the State, along with further large areas of neighbouring land, which increased the size to over 200 acres. The first director was Sir William Hooker, who started the museums, library and herbarium – a collection of dried plants which now numbers 7 million and is the largest in the world. Sir Joseph Hooker, who succeeded his fathr, founded the Jodrell Laboratory in 1876; this undertakes all aspects of plant research. Further royal donations enlarged the site to its present size of 300 acres. Kew's latest developments – the new Exhibition and Reference Collection Building and the Princess of Wales Conservatory, with their futuristic designs – are in every way worthy of the gardens' international reputation.

It is a difficult task to describe Kew. To say the gardens are exquisite does not convey their immense variety or the range of plants to be seen. There are formal gardens and wild stretches, shady walks and a lake, giant glasshouses with jungles of palm and fern, tropical fruits and water-lilies. In addition to the amazing variety of flowers, shrubs and trees the gardens are full of unusual sights such as a pagoda, a Japanese gateway and several temples. Then there is a Wood Museum, the Marianne North Gallery, with brilliant paintings of rare plants, and Kew Palace itself.

These varied attractions may help to explain why Kew is all things to all people; they certainly help to make Kew worth a visit at any time of year. The enormous variety of plants grown here means that you are always going to see something at its best; that does not mean simply in flower – fruits, coloured foliage or ornamental bark may also be well worth a look. Even if it rains, the glasshouses, museums and other buildings can take a day to see. The best that can be done here is to describe briefly some of the gardens' most striking features. It must be stressed that Kew is best viewed as a whole and not as a series of sights to be seen. It is not only the individual features' ability to surprise and impress but also their surroundings and the way in which they merge which give Kew its charm – in 'lilac-time' or any other.

The formal gardens may be of most interest to the casual visitor used to seeing plants grown in organized groupings; they are all near the main entrance. It must be remembered that the educational purpose of the gardens takes precedence over any aesthetic design concepts: people come here to learn, rather than admire.

The Aquatic Garden is sunken, with a central tank of water-lilies and goldfish. Other aquatic plants are grown in nearby beds, as are marsh and bog plants – enough to inspire or dishearten anyone with a pond in their garden. The lilies are best seen in the morning, when the flowers are fully out.

The Cambridge Cottage Garden is, as its name suggests, a very English mix of trees, shrubs, bulbs, perennials and annuals. The Herbaceous Ground is a collection of approximately 2,000 species of annual and perennial herbaceous plants. The plants are arranged in their families, so related plants are near to one another, allowing easy comparison for botanical study.

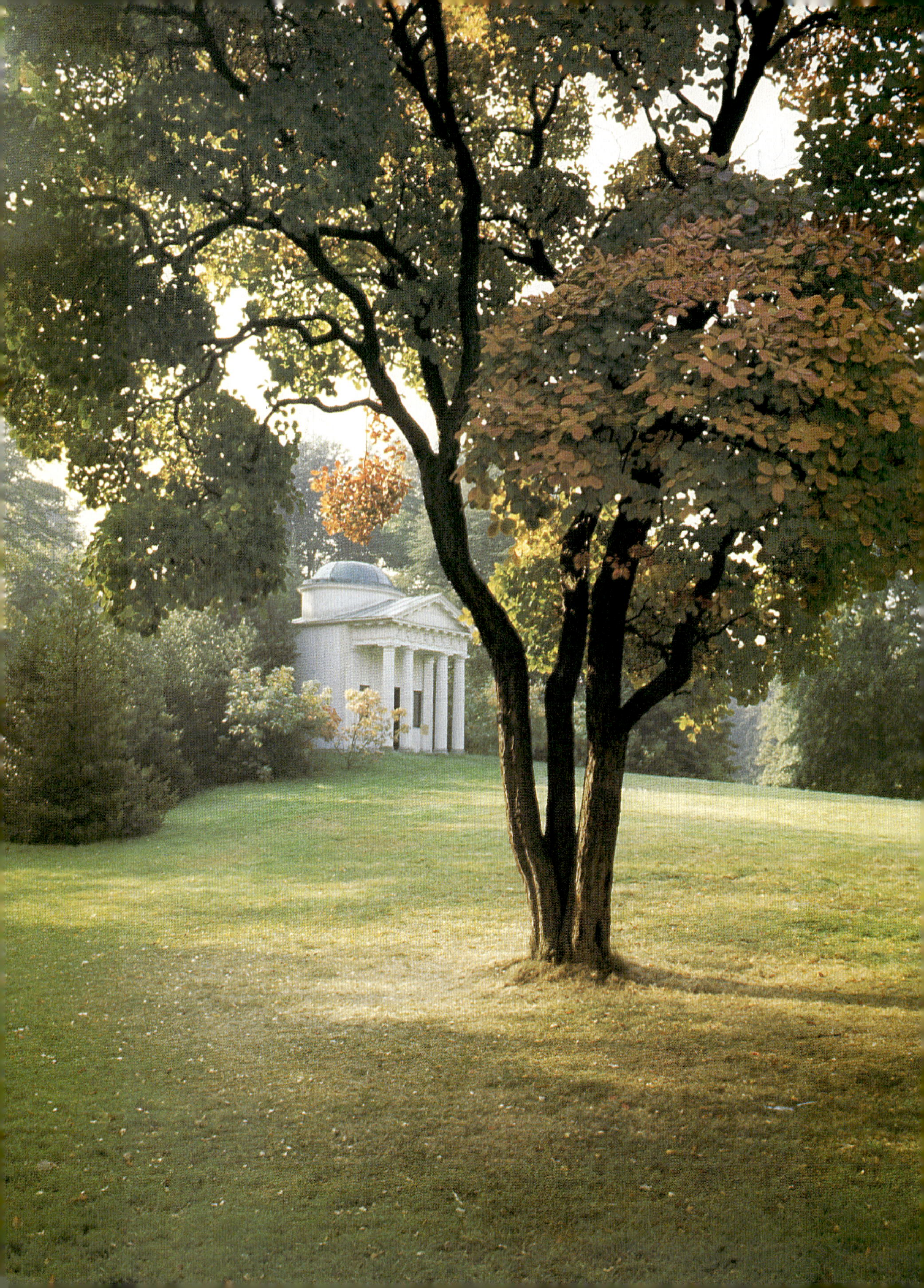

Opposite: Kew Gardens has many interesting buildings ranging from the pagoda and the Japanese gateway, to classical temples such as the one seen here

Above: Charming seventeenth-century Kew Palace has a formal garden with features of the same period. Here we see the sunken herb garden

Behind Kew Palace is the unique and lovely Queen's Garden. A careful replica of a seventeenth-century garden, to complement the house, it is really a collection of features of the period. There is a parterre (an ornamental arrangement of flower beds), a sunken garden, a gazebo (look-out turret) and a mound with a rotunda on top. Plants are also used to form a pleached alley (a hedge of lime trained to appear to be on 'stilts'), a camomile seat and an arched alley of laburnums, which is a superb sight in May. Care is taken to use only plants that were available in the seventeenth century. These include the many herbs used as medicines or to disguise the smell of stinking homes and clothes, and the flavour of bad meat. This is 'period' gardening and a good example of living history.

Then there is the Rose Garden, with old and new hybrid tea and floribunda roses laid out in a large formal design. The Rock Garden features a winding path between Sussex sandstone, waterfalls and streams, giving the impression of an Alpine valley in miniature. The alpine plants, bulbs, dwarf conifers and shrubs are best seen in late spring.

In contrast to the formal gardens are the vast collections of trees and shrubs in the beautiful walks around the Temperate House and lake at the southern end of the site. It is here that Kew is perhaps most idyllic, where fine avenues of trees combine with marvellous vistas of the lake, the pagoda, and Syon Park on the other side of the Thames. It is here that the Kew 'regulars' will be found, away from the formal areas where most 'first-timers' seem to congregate. Here are rhododendrons, azaleas, oaks, eucalyptus, magnolia, lilac, winter-flowering shrubs such as witch-hazel, heathers; the list is endless.

An unusual feature is the Bamboo Garden, first planted in 1892. This exotic plant soon became popular in other gardens at the time. Being surrounded by these tall erect stems with varying leaf colour and size is really quite a strange experience, particularly as they grow so densely and seem to form an impenetrable jungle.

The Heath Garden, planted in the 1960s, is worth a look at any time of year. These plants provide year-round interest, with gold and silver foliage and varied flower colour. Their carpeting effect contrasts well with the bolder forms of the associated dwarf conifers.

There are many collections of deciduous and evergreen trees in this part of the gardens, some with fine specimens. The tracery and bark of deciduous trees can be best appreciated in winter, when the eye is not distracted by flower, leaf or fruit. It is in winter, too, that the colours and forms of coniferous trees come into their own.

The lake was artificially created last century, and many water-loving plants thrive on and around its banks. Most of the conifers are near it. In the south-east corner of the gardens is the main café, a delightful spot in which to relax surrounded by trees and overlooked by the pagoda. Its year-round interest, the lake and the seclusion are what make this area of the gardens so deservedly popular with the 'regulars'.

The glasshouses are one of the most impressive features of Kew because of the range of plants displayed and the size of the buildings themselves. The Palm House is Kew's most famous and historic greenhouse; it is one of the first examples of a nineteenth-century iron-and-glass conservatory. In 1981 a detailed survey was begun to investigate the extent of corrosion caused by the warm, moist conditions required by the plants; this led to the house being closed for extensive restoration. Coffee, cotton, yam and bougainvillea are among the plants grown in the Palm House – and palm, of course.

The Temperate House, which originally took from 1860 to 1899 to complete, has recently undergone similar treatment, and has now been faithfully restored to the architectural concept of its designer, Decimus Burton. It includes collections from South Africa and the Mediterranean; there is a small exhibition space in the basement. Apart from the straight thoroughfares and meandering paths, the collection can also be viewed from spiral stairs and a gantry running around the roof of the central area of the house. From here, the plants seem even more exotic.

The new Princess of Wales Conservatory is an exciting development in both concept and design. This one building has ten environments, with plants ranging from cacti to those which grow under water; it replaces the ferneries and 'T-range', a jumble of twenty-six old houses. A microprocessor maintains the various temperatures and humidities in the interior, which is like the set of a sci-fi film with its sloping glass roof, water running throughout, the many strange plants, misters keeping the air moist, and slopes, paths and steps connecting the numerous levels. This is a fascinating building, one of the world's most sophisticated glasshouses; it can certainly be seen as taking Kew into the twenty-first century. It is interesting to note that the new conservatory is within yards of a pagoda tree (*Sophora japonica*), recumbent with age and planted in 1761 soon after the original nine-acre garden was opened by Augusta.

The Alpine House is another recent development. Shaped like a pyramid to reflect the shape of a mountain, it contains a rock landscape incorporating a large range of plants. A refrigerated bed, with controlled lighting, contains a collection of Arctic alpine plants. The Australian House has a collection of plants representative of lower rainfall areas in that country.

Kew also has a diverse collection of buildings in which to study the history of the gardens and the natural history of plants. Perhaps not high on the list of priorities for the first-time visitor, but certainly very rewarding for anyone who can forsake the beauty outdoors – and the buildings are ideal places to shelter from rain. The General Museum is basically a collection of economically useful plants, including those used for medicines, dyes and the like. Kew Palace was built in 1631 and acquired by George III in the eighteenth century. The house is used to display relics of George and his wife Charlotte, the only royal couple to occupy it. The Marianne North Gallery houses a stunning collection of 832 paintings. Marianne North, born in 1830, travelled widely in order to paint flowers in their natural habitat. After a successful exhibition in London in 1879 she gave her collection consisting of all her own paintings to Kew, together with the money for a gallery in which to house them. The Orangery, now housing an exhibition space and bookstall, was designed by Sir William Chambers for the original gardens. It was used as an orangery from 1761, when it was completed, until 1841. The exhibition space

The old and the new at Kew.
Above: The Palm House and *(below)* the Princess of Wales Conservatory
Opposite: The beautifully restored Temperate House

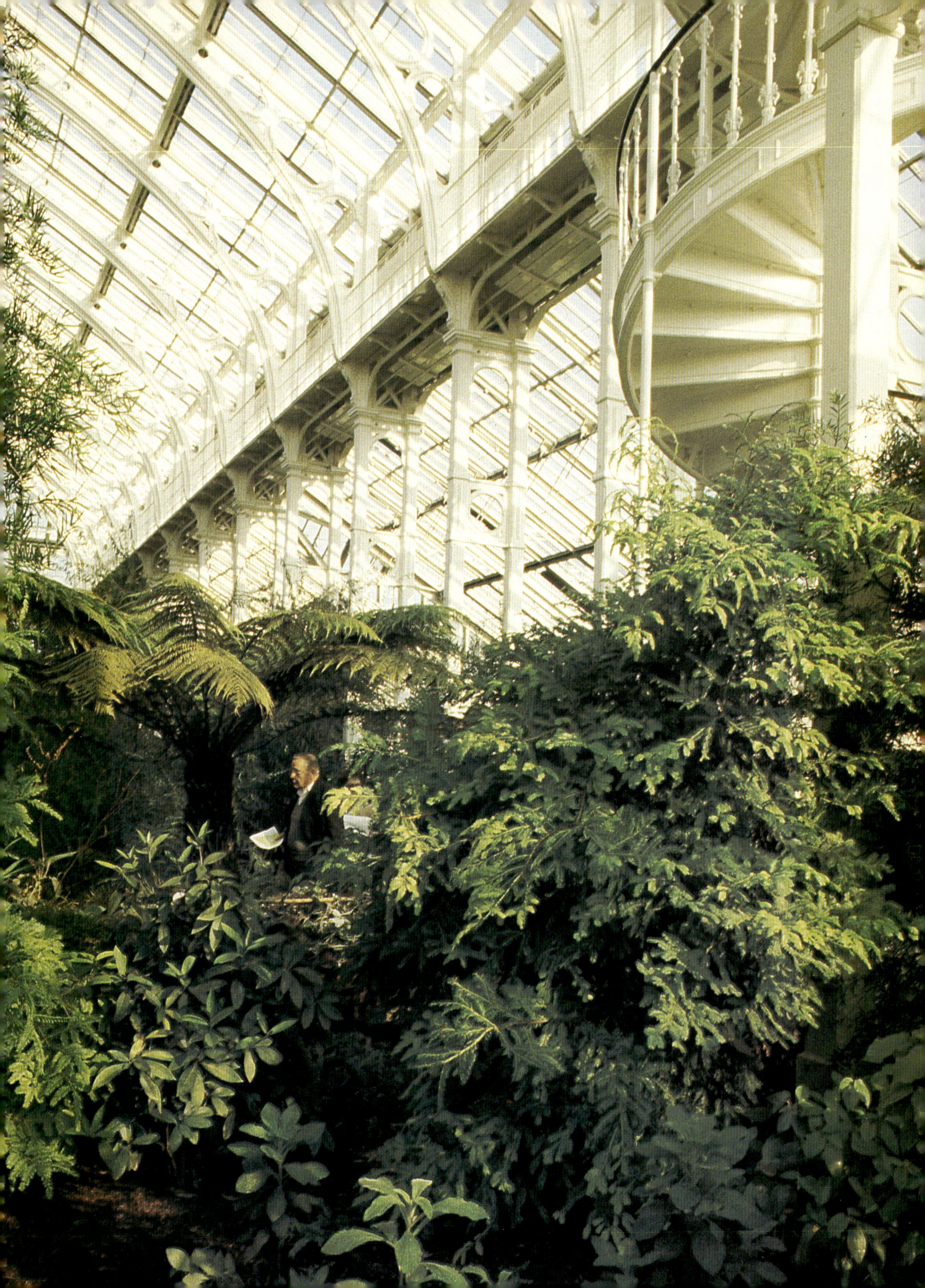

includes items on the scientific work of the gardens, as well as featuring plants of particular interest. The shop sells guides, books, postcards and gifts. The Wood Museum is a collection of woods from Britain and the Commonwealth, with their uses explained; it also gives examples of the uses to which wood is put.

The gardens' newest building is the Exhibition and Reference Collection Building, which has a theme of 'Plants for Man', showing our dependence on plants for survival. As fascinating and complex a building as the new conservatory, this design also features plenty of glass as well as a roof garden, lakes, and in all five acres of new gardens. It seems impossible, but Kew keeps getting better.

In fact the building most associated with Kew is probably the pagoda, another of Sir William Chambers' designs, dating from 1761. To the frustration of adults and children alike, it is not open to the public, for reasons of safety. The pagoda is 163 feet high. A more secluded feature is Queen Charlotte's Cottage, built for that lady as a picnic place in the 1770s; it was never intended for habitation. The cottage is surrounded by woodland, thickly carpeted with bluebells in May.

For gardeners, botanists and all who care about plants Kew is perhaps the prime reason why London is known as the hub of the world. The key to enjoying Kew is to give yourself plenty of time. You will never come away having seen everything, but at least go with the intention of doing it justice. Kew is a place to return to time and time again.

Chelsea Flower Show

The activity of the Royal Horticultural Society (RHS) most familiar to members of the public is known as 'The Chelsea Flower Show', or to gardeners simply as 'Chelsea'. It is one of London's great annual events; indeed, there is nothing like it anywhere else in the world. Held in late May in the grounds of the Royal Hospital, Chelsea, it attracts about a quarter of a million people. They go to see breath-taking displays of plants in the enormous marquee, complete gardens, flower arrangements, all manner of garden buildings, ornaments and furniture; they also have the chance to buy the latest equipment or get expert advice. It is a Mecca for the gardening world.

In May 1912 a very successful International Horticultural Exhibition was held on the same site, promoted by a small company with the support of the RHS. It covered twenty-eight acres and lasted for eight days, a much larger event than anything the Society had ever arranged. Observing the willingness of the public to visit such an exhibition, and realizing that its annual site at Temple Gardens was now too small for its requirements, the Society decided in 1913 to move to the Royal Hospital for its annual show. The event was a marked success and 'Chelsea' was established.

The 3½-acre marquee is erected on a lawn between the hospital building and the Chelsea Embankment. On its north and west sides are the exhibitors of machinery and garden buildings and also a smaller marquee of flower arrangements. Its south and east sides have the display gardens, furniture and garden ornaments. Eastern Avenue is a wide tree-lined path with all the sundries stands; it divides the hospital grounds from Ranelagh Gardens, where a band plays and there is plenty of room to picnic. Throughout the show-ground there are several places to buy refreshments and rest a while. Chelsea is a mix of horticultural bazaar and social event, frequented by plant-lovers of all kinds from experts through keen amateurs to weekend gardeners, with a sprinkling of British eccentrics in all these categories. There is always a marvellous festive atmosphere, no matter what the weather or how crowded it becomes.

All the plants at Chelsea are in first-rate condition – exhibitors would not consider using anything else – and there is an enormous variety. In the Great Marquee you can see daffodils that have long since finished blooming in gardens and roses yet to bloom outdoors – at Chelsea in May anything is possible. Certain stands are always popular. The large flowering begonias with their garish bright colours is one; the delphiniums is another – and not just blue but white, yellow and purple. Parks Departments regularly exhibit here, and the City of Aberdeen had a large stand in 1986, showing not heathers but cacti. The Belgians are usually present with their houseplants, and the South Africans with magnificent proteas and birds of paradise (*Strelitzia reginae*). Vegetables never look more delicious than when arranged by the National Farmers' Union. Several firms specializing in bonsai (dwarf trees) have been a prominent feature in recent years with their eye-catching displays of these elegant, ancient and expensive plants. There are small exhibitors who specialize in unusual plants, carnivorous plants, ivies, herbs, pinks – you name it. Then, there are the larger nurserymen with their displays of trees and shrubs. You really do not know where to look first; there is such a wealth of beauty and perfection. Also in the marquee are flower arrangements and exhibits by conservation

The Chelsea Flower Show is one of London's great annual events

19 · GREEN LONDON

At the Chelsea Flower Show in May you can see plants in season and out,
from home and abroad

groups, horticultural societies, colleges specializing in horticultural courses, and many others with an interest in plants.

The gardens outside are created by a variety of organizations. There is usually one from a horticultural college and one from a newspaper which is running a garden design competition; there is also a variety of commercial retailers, from High Street stores to nurserymen. The emphasis is usually on designs suitable for small urban gardens. The outdoor exhibitors have everything for al fresco living – furniture, barbecues, gazebos, summerhouses in all shapes and sizes. Eastern Avenue is a sort of gardening street market. All the latest labour-saving gadgets, pest and disease sprays, pressed-flower craft, pots, tools, dried flowers, books; it's all here. You can take out a subscription to a gardening magazine, join the National Trust or find out more about a host of other horticultural organizations. It seems that no aspect of gardening is not included somewhere, and everyone is having a good time.

The trouble with Chelsea is that it does get extremely crowded. I have found that the best time to visit is in the evening. Not only is it less crowded but the admission charge drops after four o'clock and you still have four hours' viewing time. The other trick is to get there very early and queue for opening at eight o'clock in the morning and get out by lunchtime.

Other Activities of the RHS

Though Chelsea may be the most familiar activity of the RHS, this is only one of many ways in which it promotes horticulture – as it has done for 183 years. Its international standing is shown by the fact that in 1985 it hosted the prestigious World Orchid Conference. Its two exhibition halls, full of these exotic plants, were a marvellous sight.

Begun as the Horticultural Society of London in 1804, one of its founder members, John Wedgwood, defined its aims as 'to collect every information respecting the culture and treatment of plants and trees, as well culinary as ornamental'. It received its Royal Charter in 1861. The Society's headquarters are in Vincent Square, London. Besides the administrative offices, the Lindley Library and Old Hall are situated here, with the New Hall just round the corner in Greycoat Street.

The two halls are used for the Society's monthly shows and competitions and those of kindred societies (Dahlia, Chrysanthemum and Rose). All these shows are worth seeing. Though not as big, they are less crowded than Chelsea, with floral displays of an equally high standard. Apart from the growers' stalls, there is an area set aside for the Society's competitions where its members may exhibit their achievements. These shows also feature flower arranging, educational exhibits and a few sundries stalls. Some shows are bigger than others, which means that both or only one of the halls may be used. The Lindley Library is one of the leading horticultural libraries in the world, containing over 35,000 books and other literature. It is primarily a reference library, but members of the Society may borrow books. It is situated on the third floor of the RHS offices in Vincent Square.

Mention must also be made of the Society's Wisley Garden, twenty miles from London in the countryside between Cobham and Ripley. They advertise it as 'one of the finest gardens in the world', which says it all. With plenty of colour and interest throughout the year, this is a great place for a day trip out of London.

Joining the RHS is well worth considering for London gardeners, who have the best opportunity to benefit from it. For the membership fee you get admission to Wisley and Chelsea and to the shows and lectures at the Society's halls, use of the library, a monthly journal called *The Garden*, and expert help with gardening problems. If you make full use of the membership it can save a lot of money, and you can become a better gardener in the process.

Whether or not you join the RHS, their Chelsea Flower show is a 'must' in Green London.

The Royal Parks

A park, my dictionary tells me, is a large enclosed piece of ground, usually with grass and trees. Well, that is true of all the Royal Parks but hardly does them justice, for they are immensely varied in style and content. What they do have in common is that they were all once in the possession of the sovereign – hence, 'Royal' – and are now administered by the Department of the Environment.

Personally, I find it is largely the historic associations of the Royal Parks which give them character and make them so appealing. In the same week that I was taken to Kew, I also saw Hampton Court for the first time. As an eight-year-old who loved history, I was overwhelmed by this magnificent and enormous palace, which brought Henry VIII to life for me. History is everywhere in the Royal Parks; Kensington Palace, the Albert Memorial, Whitehall, Buckingham Palace and the magnificent architecture at Greenwich and Regent's Park are all inseparable from them. Within these historic settings occur a multitude of activities, such as swimming and horse riding, which keep the Royal Parks very much a part of life in London. They are a great amenity for physical recreation. A theatre, bandstands, an art gallery and a host of nearby museums means that they are also caught up in the cultural life of the capital. Then there are London Zoo, Speakers' Corner, children's playgrounds, special events, deer, wonderful views, cafés, and space in which to sunbathe, read, walk, practise your Tai Chi and anything else you care to do. And finally there are the magnificent trees and beautiful gardens, for which the Royal Parks are justly famed.

Apart from anything else, the Royal Parks are largely responsible for London's being acknowledged as one of the world's 'greenest' cities.

GREENWICH PARK

It is impossible to write of this park without mentioning the 'village' from which it takes its name. Greenwich is a fascinating place and well worth exploring. A popular venue with tourists who dare to venture into south-east London, it is in fact only a few miles from Charing Cross. The journey by British Rail takes only a few minutes. An alternative, in fine weather, is the pleasant and leisurely ride by river-boat from Westminster Pier.

The park is inseparable from the elegant collection of buildings on its northern edge –

Opposite above: Greenwich Park offers spectacular views
Below: Hampton Court, with its splendid Tudor palace and elaborate gardens, is a popular day excursion

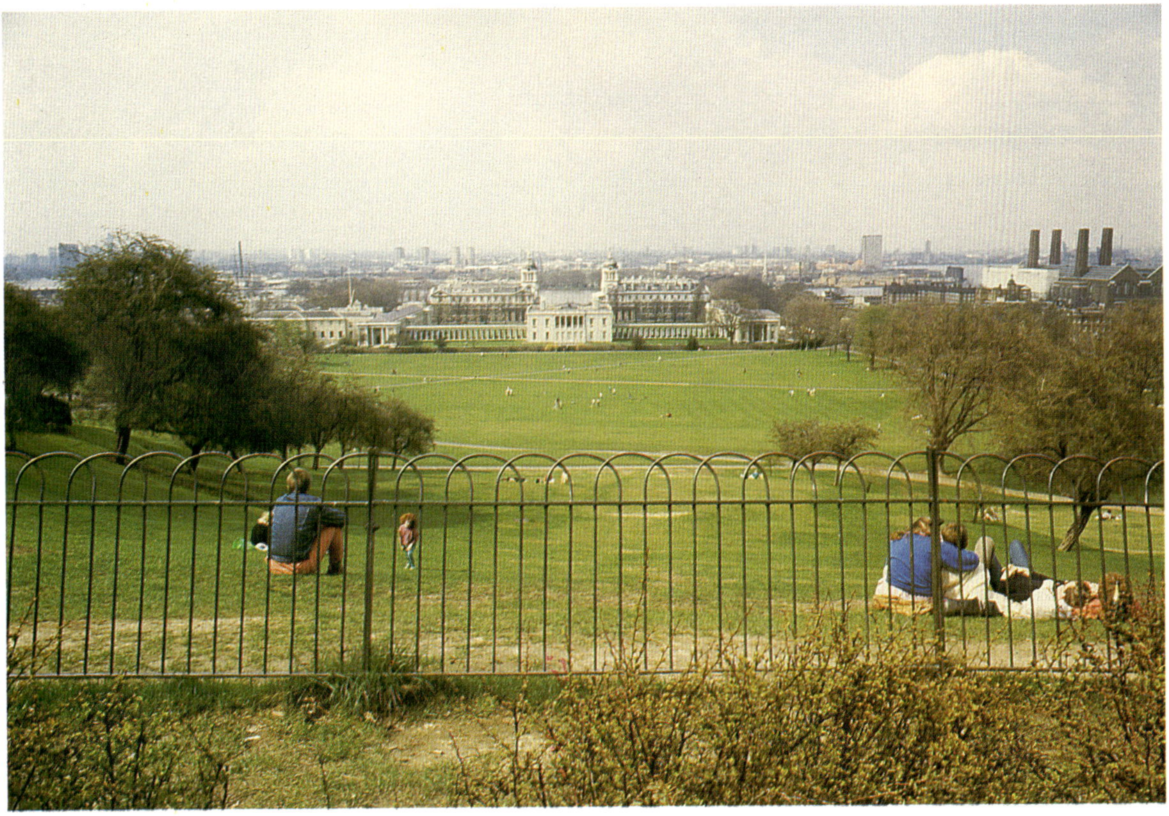

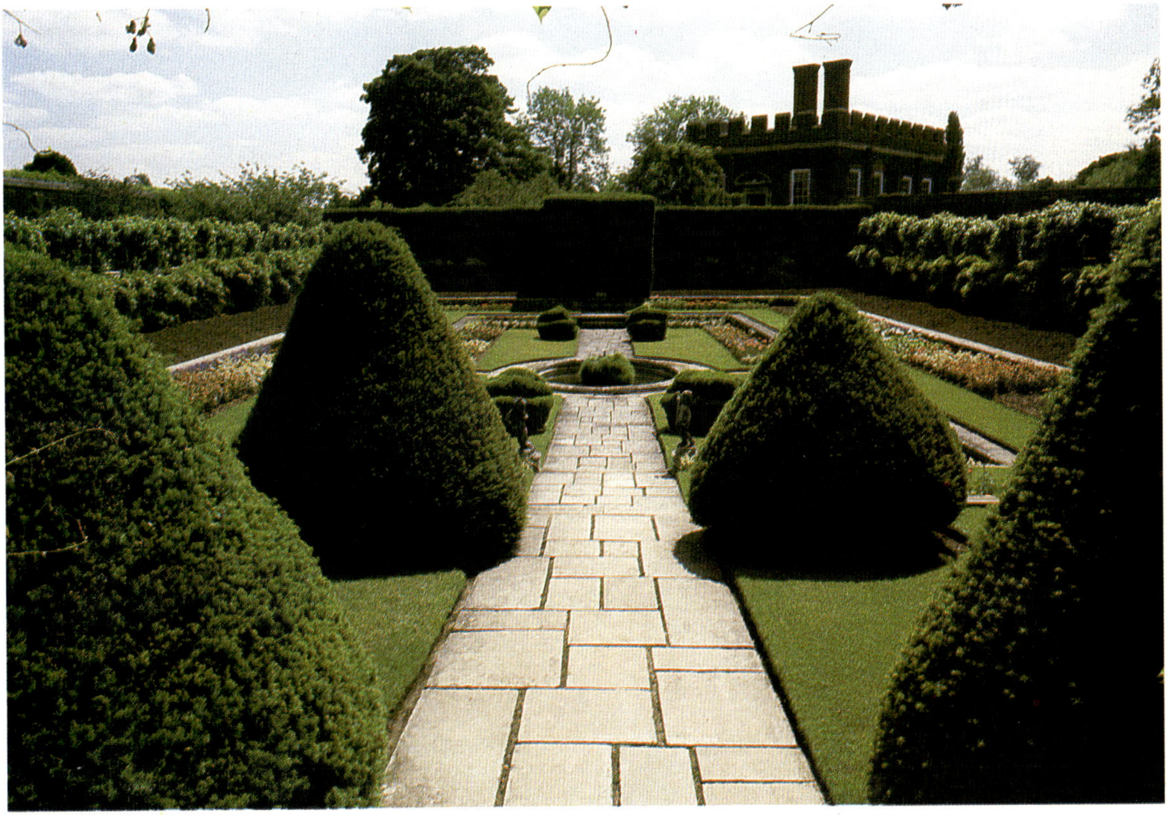

the Royal Naval College, the Queen's House and the Maritime Museum – to which it is a perfect foil. A familiar image of Greenwich is the view of these buildings from Island Gardens on the Isle of Dogs. This is reached by a foot tunnel under the Thames, the entrance to which is near Greenwich Pier. Close by are the tea clipper *Cutty Sark* and the yacht *Gypsy Moth IV* in dry dock; these, and river trips to places such as the Thames Barrier, add to the maritime atmosphere of Greenwich. Fine Georgian architecture, a prestigious professional theatre, craft stalls and flea markets are some of Greenwich's other attractions. When the sightseeing is done, the park has quiet corners in which to relax, although its many activities reflect the lively cosmopolitan nature of the whole of Greenwich.

Greenwich became the first Royal Park to be enclosed in 1433, when Henry VI granted a licence to his uncle Humphrey, Duke of Gloucester, to enclose 200 acres of the common land of Blackheath 'to make a park in Greenwich'. The basic design of the park remains much as it was in the reign of Charles II in the mid-seventeenth century. Le Nôtre, landscape architect to Louis XIV at Versailles, is said to have provided sketches for an overall design, but the work was probably supervised by his friend, Mollet. In Victorian times Greenwich was restored from privileged enclosure to public open space.

Today the park is a pot-pourri of features which makes a visit very pleasurable. Locals make good use of the tennis courts and pitches for rugby, hockey and cricket; visitors will enjoy flower gardens, deer, café, bandstand performances and – not least – the magnificent views from the Wolfe statue in the middle of the park. The college is in the foreground, then the sweep of the river and the bulk of suburban east London, with the City landmarks of the National Westminster Tower and St Paul's Cathedral on the far left. This is not a beautiful view but it is impressive. Not surprisingly, this is a popular rendezvous in the park; there are always people here, and it is worth joining them just to look. Being aware of a sense of space is one of the best reasons for visiting any park; a park with a view like this does lift the spirits.

General Wolfe, who lived in Greenwich, is commemorated for his victory over the French general, Montcalm, at Quebec in 1759, thus obtaining Canada for Britain. Beside the statue is the old Royal Observatory, Britain's first, built in 1675. It houses a baffling museum of astronomical instruments. Here can be seen the Greenwich Mean Time 24-hour clock from which world time is measured and the line of the Prime Meridian – if you straddle it you will be standing in both the east and the west hemispheres.

Le Nôtre's greatest legacy is the avenues of trees, a feature which shows his love of symmetry. Blackheath Avenue joins the Wolfe statue to the Blackheath Gate; this is a road which gives cars access to the centre of the park. From this, The Avenue leads down the hill to St Mary's Gate and the centre of Greenwich. The other avenues are primarily for pedestrians. The avenues are planted with horse chestnuts and sweet chestnuts. Many of the original trees survive, dating from 1664. In the autumn, the spiny burrs of the sweet chestnuts (*Castanea sativa*) – sometimes known as Spanish – begin to fall, revealing the edible red-brown nuts. The ground beneath the trees is smothered, so it is easy to gather a good supply. It is a lovely way to spend a long autumn afternoon – a walk in the park and then returning home to roast fresh chestnuts.

The major flower garden is in the south-east corner of the park. Enclosed by a fence, this is a more peaceful area where it is possible to escape the bustle of the rest of the park. The northern half of the garden is a vast lawn with specimen trees and large flower beds. The trees include many fine old conifers as well as the park's characteristic chestnuts. There are also groups of cherry trees and magnolias, which make the garden particularly attractive in spring. The flower beds are both large and numerous, and the displays of bedding plants are extremely good. Here in spring can be seen the traditional use of tulips, hyacinths, pansies and wallflowers, with dahlias, marigolds, petunias and stocks in the summer. This is 'parks bedding' at its best. The plants may change from year to year but the principle is the same, and achieved to perfection. To be fair, the bedding does include some more exotic plant species most years, but the bulk of the displays is always the tried, tested and true.

The other half of the garden is full of shrubs in large beds, separated by meandering paths; there is also a lake with an island. The lake area is at its best in the spring when the weeping willows, newly in leaf, make a very attractive display. Many of the trees here are underplanted with daffodils, which adds to the beauty of the scene. In early summer, rhododendrons, magnolias, cherries and azaleas come into flower. Later in the year, as winter approaches, several of the shrubs here colour beautifully, so the garden is worth seeing in the autumn as well. The lake attracts waterfowl, squirrels enjoy the trees and dense shrubbery, and deer can be glimpsed through a wire fence to the south-east of the garden. Behind this fence are thirteen acres of grassland, bracken and wild flowers called the Wilderness, inhabited by a herd of fallow deer first introduced by Margaret, wife of Henry VI. There are specific viewing points in the garden from which the deer can be seen. In fact, they are not very 'wild', as they come to the fence expecting to be fed and seem quite tame.

At the other end of the southern boundary is a large rose garden, which lies directly behind the Ranger's House; this is an early eighteenth-century mansion which was once the official residence of the ranger of Greenwich Park. The building now houses the Suffolk Collection of Paintings and the Dolmetsch Collection of Musical Instruments. The magnificent rose garden is best seen in June and is another example of the high standards to which the Royal Parks work.

The bandstand is situated near the junction of Blackheath Avenue and The Avenue; bands play here on Sundays throughout the summer. Many people wanting to listen sit on the deckchairs which are supplied close by; others use the park seating or the grass. Bands that play here are assured of a good audience because the park is usually very busy; even on dull days it seems to be bustling. Nearby is a popular café, so a cup of tea can be enjoyed during the programme interval; a good range of light meals and cakes are also available.

Literally just outside the southern gates of the park is another 275 acres of open space known as Blackheath. This is an area of open grassland used for cricket, football, rugby, kite-flying and a host of other recreational activities. There is usually a holiday atmosphere, especially on sunny weekends when organized sports rub shoulder with children just kicking a ball about, ice-cream vans and donkey rides. Blackheath is also used by funfairs and circuses. The village of Blackheath lies to the south. Here there is an assortment of shops and pubs, grouped between the church and the station (served by trains from Charing Cross). If you visit Greenwich Park, give Blackheath a look too.

HAMPTON COURT

The name Hampton Court immediately conjures up images of the splendid Tudor palace by the Thames; it is on most visitors' list of day-trips out of town, along with Greenwich and Richmond. The sheer size of the place and its historical associations with Henry VIII and Cardinal Wolsey make it a 'must'. The elaborate palace gardens are well worth exploring. While in the area you should also visit nearby Bushy Park, a vast area of open parkland.

Wolsey acquired the land to build the palace in 1514 when he was Archbishop of York; the following year he became a cardinal and Lord Chancellor of England. With his new

The Great Fountain Garden, Hampton Court, is magnificent in high summer

power and wealth he decided to build his home on a grand scale. Unfortunately it rivalled those of even the king. Henry became jealous of his most famous subject and Wolsey, aware of this, gave him Hampton Court, retaining only a small apartment for his own use. For a while this seemed a successful move, but when Wolsey failed to obtain permission for Henry to divorce Catherine of Aragon he was stripped of his wealth and power. He moved to York but was arrested soon after on a charge of treason; he died on the journey back to London.

The palace was popular with the Tudor monarchs, and in the seventeenth century it was enlarged and improved by Charles II and William and Mary, who also found it a pleasant country retreat with the advantage of easy river access to the capital. In 1838 Queen Victoria made the controversial move of opening the State Apartments, the gardens and Bushy Park to the public on Sundays. She was criticized as a desecrator of the Sabbath but persisted in her wish to allow working people the privilege, so for about 150 years Hampton Court has been a place of popular recreation. The hotch-potch of architectural styles and gardening tastes combine to make it an impressive, beautiful and highly enjoyable place to visit.

The 'musts' are the Great Vine to the south of the palace and the Maze to the north; it is easy to take in everything in between as there is nothing to the west. The world-famous Great Vine is grown in a greenhouse known as the Vinery, and may be viewed from the entrance. The whole roof is covered by its winding branches, some of which extend more than a hundred feet from the base, which has a diameter of several feet. An area immediately outside the Vinery is kept uncultivated but well manured to feed the roots of the tree, which must be extensive. Rumour has it that they extend down to the Thames. The vine, Black Hambro or Hamburg, was planted as a cutting in 1796; it produces several hundred bunches of good-sized grapes each year, which are on sale.

The two small enclosed Pond Gardens are richly planted with bedding, making a colourful display from spring to autumn. You cannot enter them, but they can be viewed through screens of lime, wistaria and hornbeam. They are both sunken and have several levels; at their centres they have ponds, hence the name. The larger garden has a fountain and the smaller a single jet of water. The hedges of box and yew make good backgrounds for the bright colours of bedding plants such as begonias, salvias and marigolds. Both gardens always draw the crowds because of their spectacular displays; such rich bedding in a setting like this is not often seen. Behind these gardens is the Banqueting House, a delightful building of 1700, the main room of which overlooks the river and is open to the public.

Opposite the Pond Gardens in a corner of the palace wall is the Knot Garden. Planted in 1924, the design is a typical Tudor pattern with interlocking bands of dwarf box, thyme, lavender and cotton lavender. The divisions are filled with low-growing bedding plants.

The Privy Garden is noted for its Tijou screen. This is twelve panels of the most splendidly intricate and beautiful wrought iron work, made for William III by the master craftsman Jean Tijou. Each panel is over ten feet high and thirteen feet wide; they are well worth inspecting closely. It seems impossible that wrought iron could be sculpted into anything so lovely. Their setting is perfect, for they act as a screen between the garden and the Thames. Along the east side of the garden is a raised terrace overlooking the Broad Walk; on the opposite side is a raised alley of wych elm, which is called Queen Mary's Bower. The dense shrubbery which is the heart of this garden is a lovely place to cool down on a hot day. The shrubs such as magnolia, lilac and the Judas tree (*Cercis siliquastrum*) provide shady walks, and at the centre of the garden is a fountain, the sound of which is always refreshing.

The Broad Walk, nearly half a mile long, runs from the Thames to the Flower Pot Gate. On one side is a herbaceous border where can be seen granny's bonnet, cranesbill, delphiniums, sweetpeas and many more. This is a lovely walk in high summer when these plants are at their best. Along it is the entrance to King Henry's Tennis Court, which makes an interesting diversion and can be visited free of charge. It was built by Henry VIII for his 'close tennys play', a game more like squash. He did also play 'open tennys', which was probably an early version of lawn tennis.

The Great Fountain Garden is an immense semi-circle of grass, clipped yew, flower beds and a central fountain, all bordered by a canal and lime trees. From this radiate three avenues of lime trees forming a gigantic '*patte d'oie*' or goosefoot design. The central avenue, or toe, edges a canal known as the Long Water.

Though not as elaborate as it was when created by William and Mary, the Great Fountain Garden is still one of Hampton Court's most impressive features. The flower beds are extremely well maintained; they are bedded out for spring and summer so the garden has colour for most of the year. The summer bedding includes some interesting plants such as plumbago, cordyline, canna, heliotrope and spider plants. There are also beds planted specifically with coloured-leaf plants such as coleus and ornamental cabbages, which seem to be increasingly popular in bedding schemes.

The Department of the Environment wishes to restore the semi-circular avenue of limes (*Tilia* x *Europaea*), which since the turn of the century have been replaced piecemeal with different varieties and ages, so that the overall effect is now lost. The plan, therefore, is to replant the avenue completely for uniformity and historical accuracy, for the benefit of future generations.

From the Great Fountain Garden there is a bridge over a small canal which leads to a tall iron gate, also designed by Tijou; beyond this is Hampton Court Home Park. It is basically just parkland, the domain of fallow deer, divided by the three avenues of limes, each about a mile long, and the Long Water of the *patte d'oie*. There are no flower beds – just the water-lilies on the canal – and there are never very many people, so it is a pleasant place in which to relax.

The Wilderness, to the north of the palace and entered through a gate off the Broad Walk, is another area of shrubbery divided by straight paths. Here are many spring-flowering shrubs such as azalea, and beech, chestnut, cherry and crab-apple trees underplanted with daffodils. The most attractive sight in spring is the Laburnum Walk, which is an arch of trained trees; they produce long racemes of brilliant yellow flowers in May.

The Maze is in a corner of the Wilderness, near the Lion Gate. As famous as the Great Vine and equally a 'must' for anyone visiting Hampton Court, it is extremely popular. It was first planted in the reign of Queen Anne, and consists of half a mile of paths divided by bushes. A small charge is made for admission.

The Tilt Yard Garden is where Henry VIII held his tournaments; a kitchen garden was later made there. The best feature now is an immaculate rose garden. All types of roses are grown, but with an emphasis on old-fashioned shrub roses. There are also tennis courts and a putting green here – and something which will probably be most appreciated, a restaurant and café.

Now it is time to escape the crowds; the peace and quiet of Bushy Park await.

BUSHY PARK

Bushy Park is divided from Hampton Court by the Hampton Court Road. The two places were linked together in the late seventeenth century when Sir Christopher Wren planted an avenue of chestnuts and subsidiary avenues of lime trees running from the Teddington Gate of Bushy Park right through to Hampton Court's Lion Gate. The Chestnut Avenue, as it is known, and two smaller avenues, are the only link with the palace. Bushy is a desert compared to its neighbour. It consists of 1,100 acres of open parkland, plantations and ponds with herds of roaming fallow deer – a natural open space in contrast to the rigid formality of the Hampton Court gardens.

The Chestnut Avenue is one mile long, and at its best in mid-May when the chestnut candles are in full show; visiting Bushy Park on Chestnut Sunday is a local tradition. Chestnut Avenue is a public road which gives motorists a short cut between Hampton and Teddington. It is broken at its southern end by the Diana Fountain and surrounding pool, which is appreciated by anglers; there are always some sitting on the edge.

Any walk through Bushy Park should at some point take in Waterhouse Woodland Gardens. As much an eyeful as it is a mouthful, this must be one of the Royal Parks' best-kept secrets. There is no car park especially for it, and a few hardly noticeable signposts are the only clue to its whereabouts, so it is not surprising that people are kept away. It is, however, well worth searching out; it lies to the west of Chestnut Avenue.

After walking over acres of rough grassland with isolated trees, deer, and only a couple of ponds to make a welcome break, it is quite a shock to enter this garden with paths meandering by the side of serene pools, wildfowl, mown lawns, flowering shrubs and herbaceous plants.

The water comes from the Longford River, an artificial stream channelled from the River Colne in the early seventeenth century. It runs through Bushy Park, feeding several ponds and the Diana Fountain, then on into Hampton Court and the Long Water. Water is present throughout this garden, and at Tries's Pond the expanse of water is sufficient to reflect the whole height of the trees and shrubs which line its banks. Among many fine oaks can be found rhododendrons, camellias and other typical woodland plants.

One of the most interesting plants in this garden is the swamp cypress (*Taxodium distichum*). It is a native of the southern United States of America and mostly associated with the Florida Everglades. In this garden it has a fascinating display of pneumatophores; these protruberances from the ground about the tree are commonly called 'cypress knees'. They are roots which grow up rather than down, allowing the tree to breathe. The expanses of water and lawns give space to this woodland garden, allowing the many fine specimen trees and shrubs to be seen to advantage. There are many wooden seats from which to admire the scene; it is a lovely place in which to linger.

HYDE PARK

Hyde Park, with its close neighbour Kensington Gardens, forms a tract of over 600 acres of open space in central London. It is surrounded by the capital's main office, hotel and shopping districts – Mayfair, Knightsbridge, Kensington, Bayswater Road and Oxford Street. In the eighteenth century the statesman William Pitt the Elder described Hyde Park as a 'lung of London', a description even more accurate today. An open woodland with extensive areas of grassland, Hyde Park is certainly a popular place to escape crowded streets, relax, and breathe fresher air. Kensington Gardens is more densely wooded, with flower beds and shrubberies. Because of their location and opportunities for recreation, both are busy all year.

Above: The Waterhouse Woodland Garden in Bushy Park makes a delightful contrast to the formality of its neighbour, Hampton Court
Opposite: Daffodils along the Broad Walk, Hyde Park, are a spectacular sight in the spring

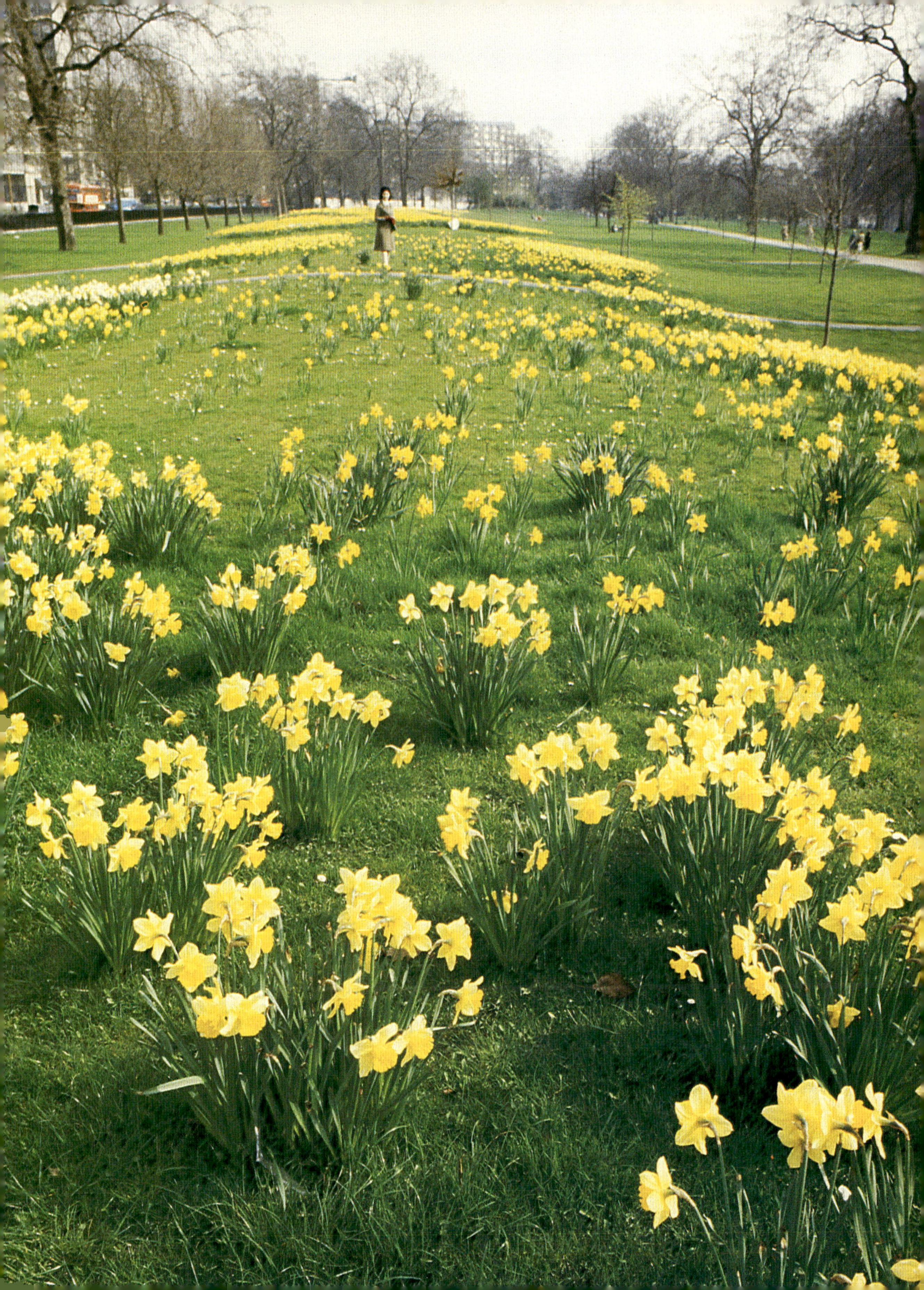

With the Dissolution of the Monasteries in 1536 the property was confiscated from Westminster Abbey by Henry VIII, who converted it into a royal hunting park by enclosing it and stocking it with deer. Charles I opened it to the public in the early seventeenth century and it soon became a fashionable parade ground. In the eighteenth century Caroline, wife of George II, instigated several changes, creating the park's two most famous features – the Serpentine and Rotten Row.

The Serpentine, a 32-acre lake, was made from a small string of ponds along the course of the River Westbourne. Beyond the Serpentine Bridge it becomes part of Kensington Gardens and is known as the Long Water, a further ten acres. The Serpentine is the heart of Hyde Park, and it is to this that everyone is drawn. Most people just enjoy a stroll around its shore but the more active can hire boats and go rowing. The boats are hired by the hour for a reasonable fee, plus deposit; it takes a full hour to do one leisurely lap. The Lido was first opened to the public in 1930 for people to swim and sunbathe in the summer months; a Christmas Day dip, even if it means breaking the ice, is a tradition adhered to by some stalwarts. At the eastern end of the lake is the self-service Dell Restaurant, where everything from a drink to a full meal can be obtained. There is plenty of seating indoors and out, overlooking the water. It takes its name from the park's best horticultural feature, the Dell, which is a small hollow planted with trees, shrubs and bulbs around a waterfall. The Serpentine Restaurant is at the western end of the lake; it has a waiter-service as well as a self-service restaurant. Both overlook the water; the latter has seating outdoors.

Rotten Row is a sand track for horse riders, to whom it is known as 'The Mile'. It runs along the southern perimeter of the park, pleasantly shaded by trees. The name derives from *Route du Roi*, meaning the King's Road. Last century Rotten Row was *the* place to ride or drive in one's carriage, to see and be seen. Today it is left to the riders, whose horses are either stabled privately or hired by the hour from commercial stables. Other users include the Household Cavalry.

One major event in the park's history last century was the establishment of free speech. At one time the police tried to stop all orators from speaking and mobs from gathering, whatever their purpose. In 1866 the Reform League was refused permission to hold a meeting in the park; they did so anyway, in an angry and violent demonstration against such rulings. The situation was reviewed and led to Speakers' Corner near Marble Arch being designated as a place where people had the right to speak their minds on any subject. The park is also a venue for national celebrations and a meeting place for marches and demonstrations. There was a mammoth tea party for 180,000 children to celebrate the Year of the Child in 1979, and in 1981 a firework display was held on the eve of the marriage of Prince Charles to Lady Diana Spencer. Rallies for the Campaign for Nuclear Disarmament, Gay Rights and other political causes all use Hyde Park.

Apart from the Serpentine, there is not a lot to see in Hyde Park; it is just a very pleasant open space for a walk. On a Sunday it is always entertaining to have a wander round Speakers' Corner. In spring a stroll from here down the Broad Walk to Hyde Park

Corner will reward you with the sight of a massive display of daffodils, which are guaranteed to dispel the feeling of winter. At Hyde Park Corner is Apsley House, for many years the home of the Duke of Wellington. It is now open as a museum dedicated to the 'Iron Duke'.

Beside the amenities already mentioned Hyde Park has cycling tracks, football pitches, a children's playground, and bowling and putting greens.

Though inseparable, Hyde Park and Kensington Gardens are quite distinct. Hyde Park had more space and thus gives people the freedom to do as they please and feel less inhibited. There is always a very relaxed atmosphere in this park.

KENSINGTON GARDENS

Though belonging to the same tract of land as Hyde Park, Kensington Gardens were created separately as the private gardens of Kensington Palace. William and Mary wanted to move away from the damp air of Whitehall Palace, which aggravated the King's asthma. To this end they bought Nottingham House and its twenty acres near the village of Kensington in 1689. Sir Christopher Wren was employed to convert the small Jacobean mansion into a more suitable home. Kensington House, as it became known, was a modest red-brick building which ideally suited the sober, domestic couple.

Their successor, Queen Anne, enlarged the garden by enclosing thirty acres of Hyde Park. The very fine orangery with carving by Grinling Gibbons, a highly praised craftsman, was built at this time. It was beautifully restored in 1977 and now contains statuary, but unfortunately it is not regularly open to the public. The garden was further extended by Queen Caroline, who took a massive chunk of the park, bringing the garden's total acreage to 275. It is her work which gives Kensington Gardens its character; the layout is more formal and artificial than that of Hyde Park, which she improved at the same time. The Long Water – an extension of Hyde Park's Serpentine – the Round Pond and many avenues, including the Broad Walk, were all created by Caroline. The house became known as Kensington Palace, and when Queen Victoria, who was born there, decided she would live at Buckingham Palace she opened the gardens to the public. They have remained open ever since.

Though smaller than Hyde Park, there is more to see in Kensington Gardens. Perhaps this is why it got a reputation for being full of nannies; they could easily find something here to keep their charges amused. Times change, and nannies today are more likely to be foreign 'au pairs', or Grandma. There do always seem to be a lot of children here, and the young-at-heart, especially around certain features. On the west bank of the Long Water is the Peter Pan statue, which must be the gardens' most popular sight. This delightful portrayal of J. M. Barrie's hero who could never grow up was commissioned by the author from Sir G. Frampton in 1912. The furry animals about the base of the bronze statue have been rubbed smooth by affectionate young children. More fairy folk can be found at the Elfin Oak, by a playground in the north-west corner of the gardens. This is the stump of a

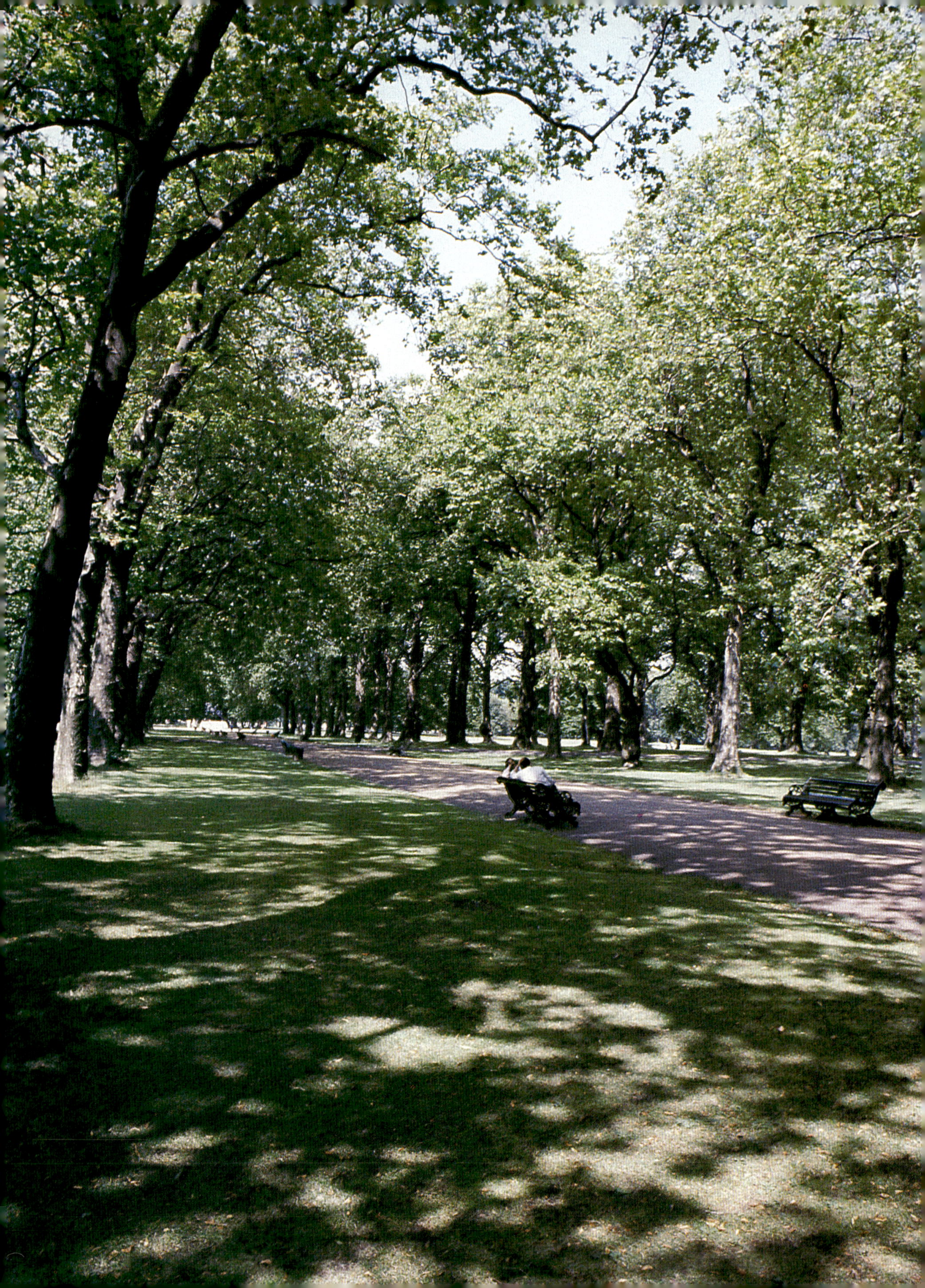

Opposite: Kensington Gardens has many avenues of fine trees
Above: The Sunken Garden, near Kensington Palace, bursts with colour from spring to autumn

tree from Richmond Park, carved by Ivor Innes in 1930 with figures of elves and more furry animals. Nearer the palace is the Round Pond, seven acres of water noted for its sailing boats, which are out in all seasons. Powered boats are not permitted as they frighten the birds which use the pond. Kite-flying is also practised around the pond.

Kensington Gardens is more interesting horticulturally than its neighbour, Hyde Park. Throughout the gardens are magnificent avenues and groups of trees, many of them hundreds of years old. The Broad Walk, a massive fifty feet wide, sweeps right through the park from north to south joining Black Lion and Palace Gates, passing close to the palace itself. This was one of Queen Caroline's creations, and when lined with its original elms must have been a magnificent sight. Unfortunately, these succumbed to the dread Dutch elm disease and had to be felled about thirty years ago. They have since been replaced with limes and maples. The orangery, to the north of the palace, is fronted by a terrace which is a marvellous sun-trap in the summer. Between here and the palace are some neatly shaped holly and May trees which border a path decorated with containers of bedding plants.

Nearby is the Sunken Garden, built in 1909 in the Queen Anne style and close to one of her gardens. This three-tiered garden around a rectangular pool fifty yards long is a real eye-catcher during the spring and summer when it is full of bedding plants. A cloister-like walkway of pleached lime trees, arched overhead, runs round the garden. Gaps cut in the foliage give views over the central display. On the Broad Walk between the palace and the Round Pond is a statue of Queen Victoria, sculpted by her daughter Princess Louise, who was obviously talented in this field. The State Apartments of the Palace are open to the public and it also houses the Court Dress Collection. Other parts of the Palace are still lived in by members of the Royal Family.

Further down the Broad Walk, just before Palace Gate, begins the Flower Walk, which goes east towards the Albert Memorial. This is one of the prettiest parts of the gardens, especially colourful in spring. It is a mixture of flowering shrubs, bedding plants and bulbs, all overhung by some of the gardens' fine trees.

The Albert Memorial is not just the symbol of the queen's grief for her dead husband; it is an assertion of Victorian wealth, knowledge and power. Queen Victoria's husband, Albert, died of typhoid in 1861, and the memorial to him was completed in 1872. It was designed by Sir George Gilbert Scott, who not only included a statue of Albert but also reference to four continents, over 150 people whom the Victorians thought of as great achievers, and the four highest human activities – agriculture, commerce, engineering and manufacturing. All this is elaborately executed in marble, coloured stone, mosaic and gilding, rising to 173 feet. The nicest touch is that on his knee Prince Albert has the catalogue of the Great Exhibition of 1851, of which he was the instigator and which was held nearby in Hyde Park.

Immediately opposite, on Kensington Gore, is the Royal Albert Hall, a familiar London landmark and home of the famous Promenade Concerts each summer. Both the memorial and the hall are remarkable examples of Victorian decorative art. To the north, from the memorial, runs Lancaster Walk; halfway along this is the Physical Energy statue by G. F. Watts, a striking bronze horse and rider.

North-east from here, at the head of the Long Water, is an Italian garden, which features four pools, fountains, balustrades, statuary and a shelter which was once a pumping station. The whole area is decorated with pots of bedding plants. On a summer's day this is a pleasant place to linger; the view down the Long Water is beautiful.

There is one other place of particular interest in the gardens, the Serpentine Gallery. This used to be a tea-room until the Serpentine Restaurant was built just across the road in Hyde Park. The gallery shows the work of contemporary artists, both names and unknowns.

Italian-style balustrades, statuary, pools and fountains in a formal area of Kensington Gardens

REGENT'S PARK

Regent's Park probably means London Zoo to most people. This world-famous collection of animals is in the north of the park and remains as popular as ever. But the park has a lot more to offer; an open-air theatre, a superb rose garden and other floral displays, a huge lake with waterfowl, and numerous sports pitches are some of the other reasons for visiting Regent's Park. It is, in fact, more than a park but rather a beautiful 'townscape' because of the villas within it and the terraces which surround a large part of it. These fine Regency buildings in the Classical style are inseparable from the park itself.

The land occupied by Regent's Park first came into royal possession in the reign of Henry VIII, who used it as an extension of his hunting chase around St James's Palace. In 1811 the Prince Regent and his favourite architect, John Nash, began to develop the estate. Unfortunately, Nash's ambitious scheme was never completed. A few villas within the park and the famous elegant terraces which surround it are the only evidence of what would have been a masterpiece of town planning.

The heart of the park, if not its centre, is surrounded by a road called the Inner Circle. It is called Queen Mary's Gardens, after the consort of George V. In high summer it is one of

Tucked away in Regent's Park is the garden of St John's Lodge, one of the park's quieter corners

the prettiest places in London with magnificent displays of roses, herbaceous plants and bedding. The rose garden is as much visited in the summer as the Isabella Plantation at Richmond is in the spring. It has a deservedly high reputation for the quality of the display and the care with which the plants are tended. There are at least 20,000 rose bushes here, set out in 100 rose beds. Bush roses are displayed in large formal beds of a single variety and the climbers up and along a circular arrangement of pillars, joined by heavy ropes. Many are scented, and on a calm day the air really is heavy with perfume; in the evening, even more so. Take time here to sit and enjoy the spectacle.

While speaking of roses, do not miss the garden at St John's Lodge. This is a hidden gem, best reached by leaving Queen Mary's Gardens at the gate facing Chester Road and turning left into the Inner Circle; just past the nursery on our right is one of Nash's villas, St John's Lodge. There is no signpost to the garden, but take the roadway between the Lodge and a small gatehouse. It is all a bit forbidding but ignore the 'private' signs and head for the four white columns, topped with cherubs supporting shields. The main door of the Lodge is on your left and the garden on your right. Because it is off the beaten track no one comes here unless they know of its existence; you cannot discover it by accident unless you are particularly nosy! It is never as busy as Queen Mary's Gardens, and though smaller is no less attractive or well maintained; it has to be seen in summer.

Through the entrance gate lies a wide immaculate lawn, edged with lush herbaceous borders; at the far end are a couple of steps, which lead to a circular garden, enclosed by privet. Here are the bulk of the garden's roses, planted one variety to a bed, around a pool with a statue of Hylas. This mythological figure – symbol of selfless service and fortitude – was better known to the Greeks as Heracles and later to the Romans as Hercules. Beyond this is a small oval garden, enclosed by pleached limes, where there are climbers grown on pillars as well as beds of bush roses. The garden ends in a leafy bower; here there is a seat from which the villa, fronted by the garden, looks magnificent. There are several seats throughout the garden on which to relax and enjoy the tranquillity. This garden really is worth tracking down.

Returning to Queen Mary's Gardens, there is much to see beside the roses. The attractive little lake has a Japanese feel to it, with the high-arched wooden bridge – straight off a black lacquered cabinet – spanning the water to a small island. Here, among a collection of slow-growing conifers, rockery plants and alpines, is a Japanese stone lantern. On the head of the island, overlooking the widest point of the lake, is a ferocious-looking bronze eagle, thought to have been made in Japan in the last century. This lake and the much larger boating lake are the only visible stretches of the Tyburn River on its subterranean route to the Thames. Near the lake is a group of fossil tree-trunks and a cascade from a hill which has winding paths through many fine trees and shrubs like azalea and acer; these create a good display in spring and autumn and cool shade in summer.

The Open Air Theatre had its first summer season in 1932. There are usually three plays each season; *A Midsummer Night's Dream* seems almost obligatory – quite rightly,

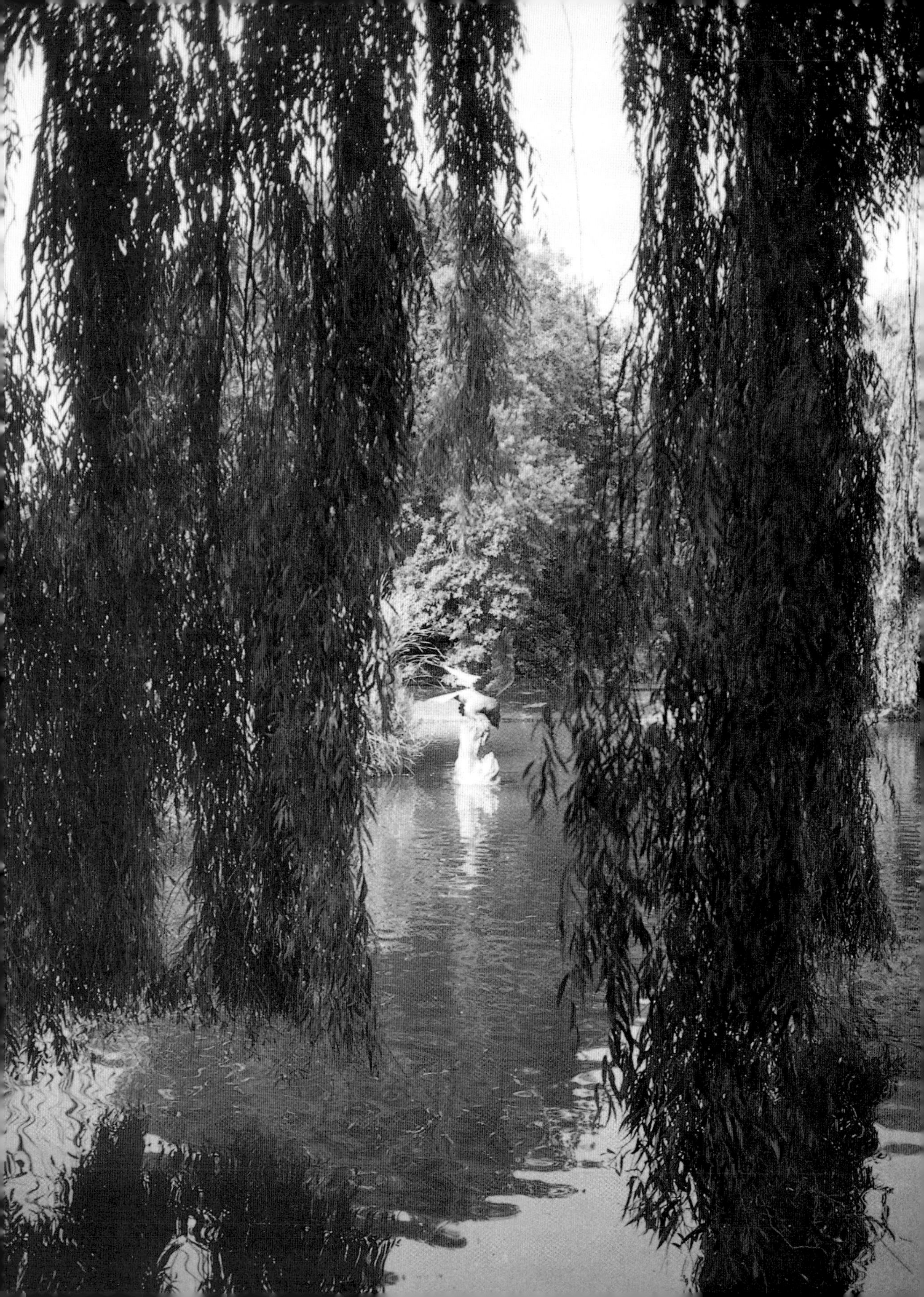

because the lawn, trees and shrubs which form the stage could not be better for this play. Recent innovations have been short lunchtime performances, usually one-man shows, and special Sunday events such as all-day readings of Shakespeare sonnets to raise money for charities. A bonus is the theatre's cold buffet and barbecue, which are open well before the evening performances, and the hot punch served in the interval. This has to be the most pleasant place in London for an evening's entertainment.

Opposite the theatre entrance, on the other side of the garden's central path, is a collection of herbaceous plants, alarmingly arranged up a steep bank; no traditional long, wide borders here. In mid-summer the display is magnificent. A path winds along the base of the mound through a rich mix of plants which tower above you – hemerocallis, polygonum, echinops, tradescantia, hollyhocks, sweetpeas, ornamental grasses; you name it, they have it here.

Near the Rose Garden Restaurant there is a gate on to the Inner Circle, and opposite that a gate into the rest of the park. Here a path leads towards the boating lake. The twenty-acre lake is a curious shape, with six wooded islands, some of which are bird sanctuaries. One has become known as the Heronry because in the early 1970s pairs of herons began nesting here for the first time; since then several pairs have successfully bred and reared young birds. The lake is home to mallard, Canada geese, moorhens and coots, and in winter black-headed and common gulls can be seen. The park has a reputation for being home to an unusually wide variety of bird species, and is famous among naturalists.

Boats are for hire at the eastern fork of the lake, near the children's pond and playground. A walk round the perimeter of the lake gives some lovely views of the park and its terraces. On the east side is a lawn with a fine bandstand; lunchtime concerts are a regular feature of summer in Regent's Park.

On the eastern side of the Inner Circle is the Broad Walk. This is the main pedestrian route through the park from Park Square in the south to the Zoo in the north. It is cut about a third of the way along by Chester Road, which joins the Inner Circle to the Outer Circle. This first stretch before the road is most decorative. Either side of the path are broad lawns with large, regularly spaced flower beds, and two handsome Victorian flower vases; each summer these are packed full of bedding plants. The imaginative use of the varied and colourful plants creates an impressive display, which is a credit to the park's gardeners. In terms of size this is certainly the best display in any Royal Park, and it is extremely popular. With its constant stream of passers-by and seats full of onlookers, the Broad Walk has been likened to a seaside esplanade, but I doubt if you could find one as elaborate or as well cared for. Beyond Chester Road the Broad Walk becomes more of a tree-lined avenue, surrounded by the bulk of the park's open space. On the right are some tantalizing glimpses of the fine architecture along the Outer Circle, notably Cumberland Terrace, with the bold white statues of the frieze contrasted against the blue background. Halfway along on the left is a refreshment pavilion, beyond which the land sweeps down towards a sports pavilion.

Opposite: **Regent's Park, in the heart of central London, offers space, calm and beauty**

There's more to Regent's Park than London Zoo. *Top:* Picnic areas abound
Above: The wooden bridge in Queen Mary's Gardens lends a Japanese
feel to this part of the park
Opposite: There are over 20,000 different varieties of rose in Regent's Park

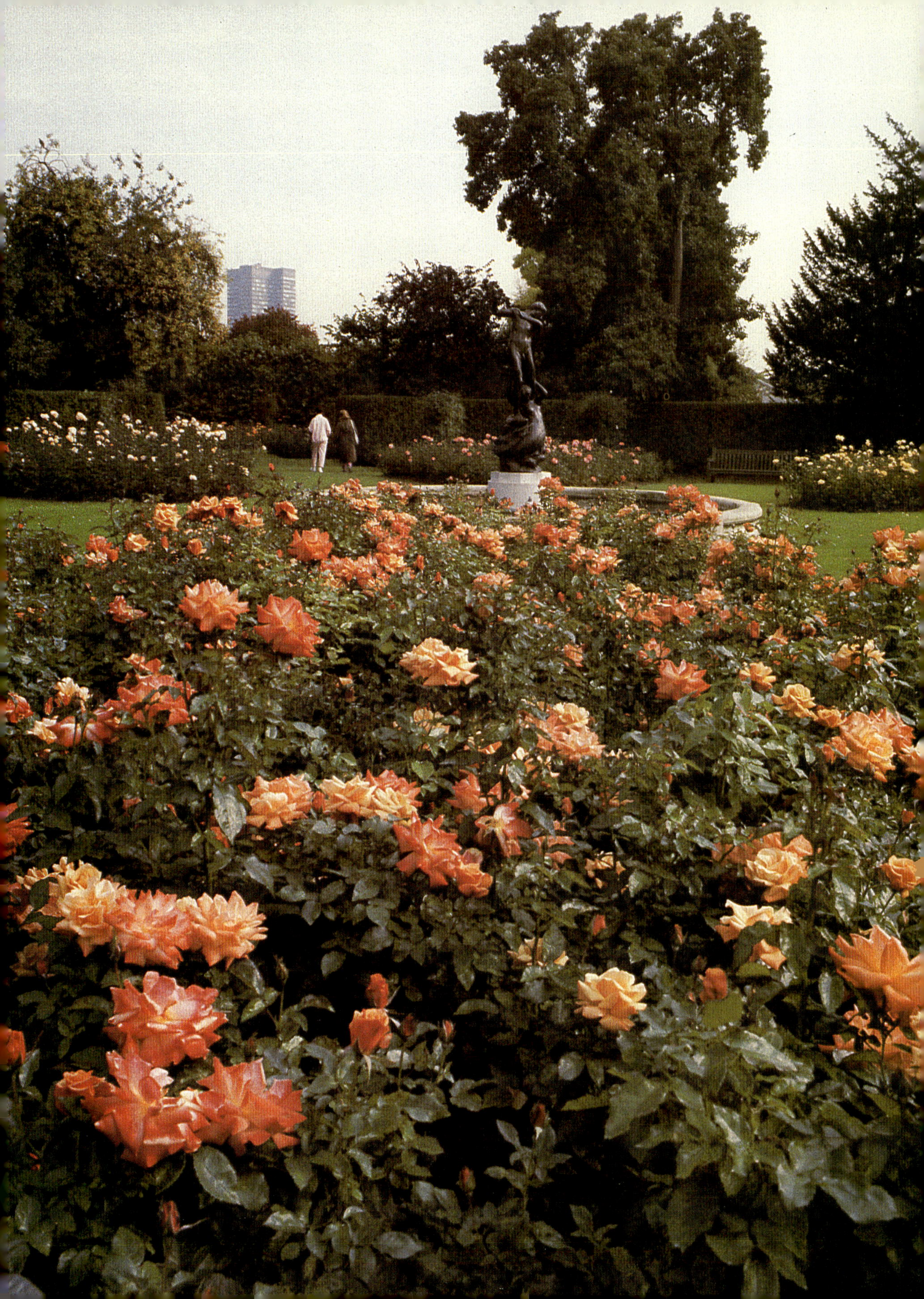

There are over 1,000 sports teams registered as using the park's football pitches, cricket pitches, hockey pitches and rugby pitch. There are also golf nets, tennis courts and an athletics track. The sports pavilion houses the changing rooms, toilets and a café. The café has also been serving as an art gallery for the past two years, although it is hardly known about because of poor publicity and its out-of-the-way location.

I have frequently referred to summer when writing of Regent's Park but it would be unfair to give the impression that it is only worth visiting in June, July and August. True, the roses, bedding and herbaceous plants are splendid then and the lunchtime concerts and evening theatre only take place in summer, but that is not to say that the park is dull during the rest of the year.

It is a beautifully landscaped park, attractive not only on a sun-scorched June day but also on a frozen January day when there is snow on the ground. Queen Mary's Gardens and the Broad Walk boast fine displays of spring as well as summer bedding, and there are April-flowering cherry trees throughout the park. October brings its own delights as the leaves of trees and shrubs turn to rich autumn shades, and some plants bear fruit. The terraces around the Outer Circle never look anything less than magnificent whatever the time of year or weather, and the Zoo is of course open all the year round. This is a park for a good day out, whatever the season.

PRIMROSE HILL

Primrose Hill is reached by crossing the busy Prince Albert Road, which is the dividing line with Regent's Park. It is a pleasant open space of about fifty acres, worth visiting for the excellent panoramic view of central London from the 219-feet-high hill. It is fun to pick out the landmarks and learn a few more from the panorama indicator. The City, St Paul's, the Post Office Tower, Westminster Abbey, Westminster Cathedral and Battersea Power Station can all be seen clearly.

Local residents take their children to the playground and use the recently constructed 'boules' pitch and 'gymnasium' of exercise bars and ropes; people also fly kites here. If, like most people, you enter Regent's Park from the south side then Primrose Hill makes a good objective for a walk. It is a fitting climax, too, as you can sit at the top of the hill and look down over the whole park and London beyond. Of course, it is most enjoyable on a fine day though the view from Primrose Hill probably looks better on a clear winter day than a hazy summer one.

RICHMOND PARK

Like Greenwich, Richmond Park cannot be written about in isolation from the place from which it takes its name. As Greenwich was once a Thames-side village, now enveloped by the urban sprawl of the city, so Richmond was a Surrey town which is now incorporated into Greater London.

The palace Henry VII named Richmond after his Yorkshire earldom became popular with all the Tudor monarchs in the sixteenth century, and the town which grew up around it became known by the same name. Although the palace was demolished in the seventeenth century Richmond continued to be a popular resort because of its attractive hilltop location next to the Thames, with fine views up and down the river, and for the hunting in the beautiful park. There is a rich legacy of fine architecture from the eighteenth and nineteenth centuries when the town had its heyday. It was during that period that the famous view from Richmond Hill was immortalized by Reynolds and Turner.

Being easily accessible from central London by District Line tube trains and British Rail from Waterloo, Richmond is now a popular place for day-trips. The town has many specialist shops, chain stores, a good theatre on the lovely green and a first-class ice-skating rink; nearby are Kew, Hampton Court and Ham House. There is always plenty to see and do in Richmond at any season.

Shene Chase, as Richmond Park used to be known, was for many centuries a hunting area; it was particularly favoured by Henry VIII because of its close proximity to his palace at Richmond. Charles I, who enclosed the area in 1637 as a hunting park, named it Richmond New Park – which it remained until the last century when the 'New' was dropped. It is the size of Richmond Park which is most impressive – 2,470 acres of parkland, two and a half miles across from north to south and east to west, with vast stretches of grassland, clumps of ancient trees, herds of fallow and red deer, plantations and ponds – a place where it is easy to avoid people even on the busiest summer's day.

There are roads within the park, joining all the major gates and forming a circuit of the whole park. A speed limit of thirty miles per hour is in force. There are several car parks at points of particular interest and at the two restaurants. Parking is permitted nowhere but at these car parks. A tour of the roads by car gives a good impression of the park, but the best way to enjoy it is to have a good long walk. Give yourself plenty of time to enjoy this vast open space with its splendid views, plants and wildlife. All the main features are well signposted.

The deer are probably as familiar an image of Richmond Park as the Royal Naval College is of Greenwich. Today there are approximately 250 red deer and 350 fallow deer roaming freely over the grassland and in the woods and drinking at the ponds. Feeding the deer is strictly prohibited, although the Royal Parks Constabulary have a thankless task trying to tell the public that this is so. Parking is not allowed on any of the roads, but wherever the deer are you will find parked cars with people feeding them and taking photographs. The deer can be dangerous if approached, especially during the mating season, so it is just as well to keep away.

The Isabella Plantation is one of the best reasons for visiting Richmond Park. In April, May and June, when the extensive collection of rhododendrons, camellias, azaleas and magnolias are in full bloom, it is a mass of colour. It is a 'must'. The Isabella Plantation, an area of forty acres, was first enclosed in 1831. It remained natural woodland until

1951, when the then Superintendent of Richmond Park, George J. Thomson, began planting informally along the banks of the stream, which runs through the plantation, to create a pleasant walk. There was no master plan and the garden just grew; it is a classic example of a woodland garden.

The season begins early with Chinese witch hazel (*Hamamelis mollis*), which has bright yellow flowers in January. More early colour is provided by the pinks and whites of heathers (*Erica carnea*) and the scented white tree heaths (*Erica arborea*). These are followed by the early-flowering rhododendrons and camellias. Spring brings masses of naturalized daffodils and bluebells. Then, from April, the azaleas and rhododendrons begin to overwhelm the whole garden. The streams are lined with these plants; indeed, there seem to be no other plants in the garden save for the trees, which provide a shady canopy. The magnolias are also good in May and June. The garden rests over the summer, with only a few heathers, primulas and Himalayan poppies providing any colour. But when autumn comes, the garden is again alive with the fiery reds, yellows and oranges of the deciduous azaleas as their leaves turn before falling.

The garden has three ponds as well as the streams. Around all these watery areas can be seen moisture-loving plants like *Primula denticulata*, with its drumstick-like flowers in spring, and the large buttercup flowers of *Caltha palustris*, also spring-flowering. Willows and swamp cypress – trees which like water – can be seen around the ponds. The ponds are also attractive to waterfowl; mallards and moorhens are often seen. Other birds seen in the garden include woodpeckers, kingfishers and nuthatches. In keeping with this natural wonderland, all seats in the garden are made from tree trunks. Make use of these seats; this is a perfect place in which to waste time.

Much of the character of Richmond Park is given by the small groups of trees and larger plantations which break the horizon of the undulating grassland terrain. The English oak (*Quercus robur*) is the dominant tree in the park, and some of the biggest specimens are hundreds of years old. Other trees in the park include the common beech (*Fagus sylvatica*), with its multi-stemmed trunks caused by pruning, the elegant silver birch (*Betula pendula*), hornbeam, chestnut and quickthorn. The trees in the enclosed plantations have an undergrowth of bracken and fern which provides cover for birds and animals.

Sidmouth Wood, the largest, is only partly enclosed; the rest is open to the public. An open ride bisects this wood, giving one of the park's finest views; on a clear day St Paul's Cathedral can be seen, eleven miles away. This wood has a fine display of rhododendrons in June. The ride through the wood is one of many used by horse riders, who are a common sight throughout the park. There are, in all, twelve miles of tracks for riding and a ring for teaching.

Spankers Hill Wood has some coniferous trees such as Scotch pine (*Pinus sylvestris*) and larch (*Larix decidua*) as well as oak, beech and chestnut. There are some good views from here over the park and beyond. This is the only other major wood open to the public.

Spankers Hill Wood *(top)* and the Isabella Plantation *(below)*, Richmond Park, provide areas of beautiful woodlands. In the spring the plantation becomes a riot of colour

The Pen Ponds are situated in the middle of the park. There are over two dozen ponds in the park, but these are the most attractive. They are both man-made, having been created in the eighteenth century. They are a good place for watching birds; the swans and Canada geese in winter are particularly fascinating. The ponds are stocked with fish and well used by anglers; a permit is required to fish. Near the ponds is White Lodge, a classic Georgian building, used as a hunting lodge by George II and now the home of the Royal Ballet School.

Richmond Park is a great place for exercise, whether walking, jogging, horse-riding, cycling (there are designated cycle tracks) or golf (there are two courses), because there is plenty of space in which to do these activities. The sense of space is the park's most appealing asset. It is large in itself, and its boundaries are extended by several magnificent views from places like Sidmouth Wood, Spankers Hill Wood and King Henry VIII Mound near the Richmond Gate. These are places to relax and escape from the city.

ST JAMES'S PARK

This park is always busy, being especially popular with visitors to London because it is right in the heart of the city and so close to Buckingham Palace. It is a charming park, more like a large garden, with a beautiful lake and brilliant displays of bedding plants among handsome trees and shrubs – all extremely well maintained, of course.

That busy monarch Henry VIII created St James's Park. He acquired the land as a deer park and garden for his new palace of St James's. But it was not until Charles II returned to England in 1660 that the park was properly landscaped, planted and opened to the public as a formal pleasure garden in the French style. In the early nineteenth century George IV decided to give the park a more romantic feel, as was the fashion of the time. His architect, John Nash, carried out the task; the park is very much as he left it.

It is no wonder that St James's Park is so popular with visitors; all around are buildings which symbolize the pomp and circumstance for which Britain, and especially London, is renowned. To the east is Buckingham Palace, home of Britain's last six monarchs, in front of which is the Queen Victoria Memorial at the centre of what must be London's most noble roundabout. The surrounding gardens are each year planted with vivid red geraniums, and the whole area is a classic image of London. To the west are the Houses of Parliament, Westminster Abbey and Whitehall. The northern edge of the park is The Mall, along which are St James's Palace – the official home of the Court – and Clarence House, home of the most popular member of the Royal Family, the Queen Mother. Somehow, St James's Park is the essence of what London means to people throughout the world, which is why you can walk around it on a busy summer's day and not hear a word of English being spoken.

The lake is the heart of the park; with its bridge, weeping willows and ornamental ducks, it is often said to have a Chinese style. It is a splendid feature, covering a large part of the park's ninety-three acres, and every visitor is drawn to it. Most end up by doing a lap of it on the encircling path; others spend time with the ducks or admire the views from the bridge. The bridge in St James's is famous for its views of Buckingham Palace and Whitehall, which have been likened rather romantically to Leningrad and Istanbul.

At the Whitehall end of the lake is Duck Island, a bird sanctuary. The park's most famous residents are the pelicans, which parade around in a very assertive manner – as well they might, having been favoured guests here since the Russian ambassador first donated a pair from Astrakhan in the seventeenth century. Birds are difficult to avoid in this park. Where the park touches the water's edge near the Cake House there are often scenes of chaos, with people feeding all manner of ducks as well as geese and swans in their hordes. The bridge near the centre of the lake is a favourite place for people to feed sparrows, gulls and starlings, which are all remarkably tame. In winter the lake is even busier with birds hassling visitors and each other for food. They know the flow of food does not freeze in winter, even if the lake does. John Evelyn, the diarist, wrote of a visit in February 1663: 'The park was at this time stored with numerous flocks of several sorts of ordinary and extraordinary wild fowl, breeding about the Decoy, which for being so near a great city, and among such a concourse of soldiers is a singular and diverting thing.'

Various fountains, as well as being attractive, usefully aerate the lake, thus providing oxygen for its large population of fish.

The park has a rich mix of trees, shrubs and plants which provide colour and interest all the year round. There are evergreen conifers, exotic cabbage palms (cordyline) and the obligatory plane trees. By Duck Island are two large fruiting figs (*Ficus carica*) and a medlar (*Mespilus germanica*). Near the exit from the bridge to Birdcage Walk is a black mulberry (*Morus nigra*), while the lake is edged with willows and swamp cypress (*Taxodium distichum*). The displays of bedding plants usually include not just geraniums, salvias and all the usual things but exotics like plumbago, eucalyptus, canna and abutilon. Colour is provided early in the year by crocus and daffodils, followed by azaleas and cherry trees. The rose beds on the north side of the lake were planted to commemorate the Queen Mother's eightieth birthday in 1980. In autumn many of the park's trees and shrubs colour well before the leaves fall, and some, like crab-apple and shrub roses, produce fruit, providing more interest. Winter has its own fascination in the tracery of the deciduous trees; the willows are particularly attractive. In winter, too, the naked trees reveal more of their splendid neighbours; the view of Whitehall, for example, presents an even more romantic image.

Mention must be made of the bandstand. During the summer there are concerts by brass bands and military bands, which are always popular. Unless the weather is really extreme the bands play on, and out of respect for their efforts there will always be people listening. In fine weather there is nothing better than to hire a deckchair for a few pence and sit in this lovely park, listening to live music. In the early evening, when the crowds have thinned, it is especially pleasant.

You may wish to stay here until the park closes at midnight – which is not as silly as it sounds. I have often walked through St James's Park late on a fine summer's night and found it just as attractive as during the day. There are underwater lights in the lake, and more light streams in from the lamps of Birdcage Walk and The Mall. There may be the odd splash of a duck or rumble of a taxi, but basically all is quiet. The smell of shrubs and bedding plants delicately scents the air, which is just a little chill – a very different way to enjoy London.

   The park used to be open all night but it now closes to discourage intruders, whether they are vandals, muggers or simply people wanting a place to sleep. The new rule means that the Royal Parks Constabulary have the right to chuck people out. If you are a night

St James's Park: the front garden of Buckingham Palace

owl, The Mall is of course open all night and is a pleasant place to walk. Stay out late enough and you can be at the park for morning opening at five. At dawn you will have the company of the park's regular birdwatchers, who have a quiet couple of hours here before going to work. There is more to London's Royal Parks than a Sunday afternoon stroll will show you.

GREEN PARK

Officially 'The' Green Park, but 'The' has been dropped from everyday usage, this is indeed a green park of fine grass and numerous plane, lime and hawthorn trees. There is little else. Created in 1688 by Charles II, its western boundary is Constitution Hill, so named because of the King's liking for walking among his people here. This park is popular for lunchtimes out of the office, especially in summer when its forest of trees provides cool shade. Unfortunately you cannot escape the persistent noise of traffic in Piccadilly and Constitution Hill. A little unfair perhaps, but the best that can be said about Green Park is that it joins St James's Park to Hyde Park. I used to enjoy visiting a friend in Notting Hill by walking from Charing Cross Station via three miles of Green London through St James's Park, Green Park, Hyde Park and Kensington Gardens, crossing only two public roads.

Parks

The definition of a park used in the introduction to the Royal Parks was 'a large enclosed piece of ground, usually with grass and trees', but the dictionary actually goes on to say 'attached to a country house; similar ground in towns for the public use and recreation'. The full definition provides a good description of the two kinds of park covered in this chapter. Kenwood and Osterley Park are the grounds of one-time country houses and have a suitably dignified atmosphere. Golders Hill, on the other hand, has lost its house, and, like Holland Park, where little of the house remains, has the feel of more urban parks like Battersea and Waterlow. Lesnes Abbey Wood does not fit neatly into any category but is included here because it is large and does have grass and trees. More importantly, it is a lovely open space which should be better known.

The seven parks described here are what I consider to be London's best, Royal Parks excepted. In them you will find flamingoes, an art collection, a peace pagoda, and an open-air concert bowl. These parks are much more than large pieces of enclosed ground with grass and trees.

BATTERSEA PARK

This 200-acre riverside park on the south bank of the Thames between Albert and Chelsea Bridges provides a special mix of sports and recreational facilities, horticulture and frequent entertainment events. It is one of London's great Victorian parks which proliferated from the middle of the last century, in recognition of the need to retain open space within the ever-expanding urban sprawl.

Unfortunately, Battersea is one of the few parks from this period – it was opened by Queen Victoria in 1858 – which contribute as much today as it did then. The magnificent new peace pagoda which crowns its beautiful riverside frontage, the garden specifically for the use of disabled people, the annual Easter Parade, the performances by the Bolshoi Ballet in 1986 – it is things like this which keep Battersea Park very much alive and an exciting part of London life.

One of the park's entrances is at Queen's Circus on Queenstown Road, which runs along the side of the park to Chelsea Bridge. This is at the south-east corner of the park, which is dominated by its neighbour, Battersea Power Station.

Carriage Drives North, South, East and West form a circuit of the park, the last two being joined by a central avenue. Carriage Drive South is particularly attractive as it is overhung by magnificent plane trees. This circuit of roads through the park makes it an ideal place for the Easter Parade, held every year on Easter Sunday.

The 13½-acre lake is a popular feature in the park. It is interestingly designed, with several islands and an outline which is richly indented so you can never see it all at once.

The formal gardens of Battersea Park, one of the capital's most lively parks

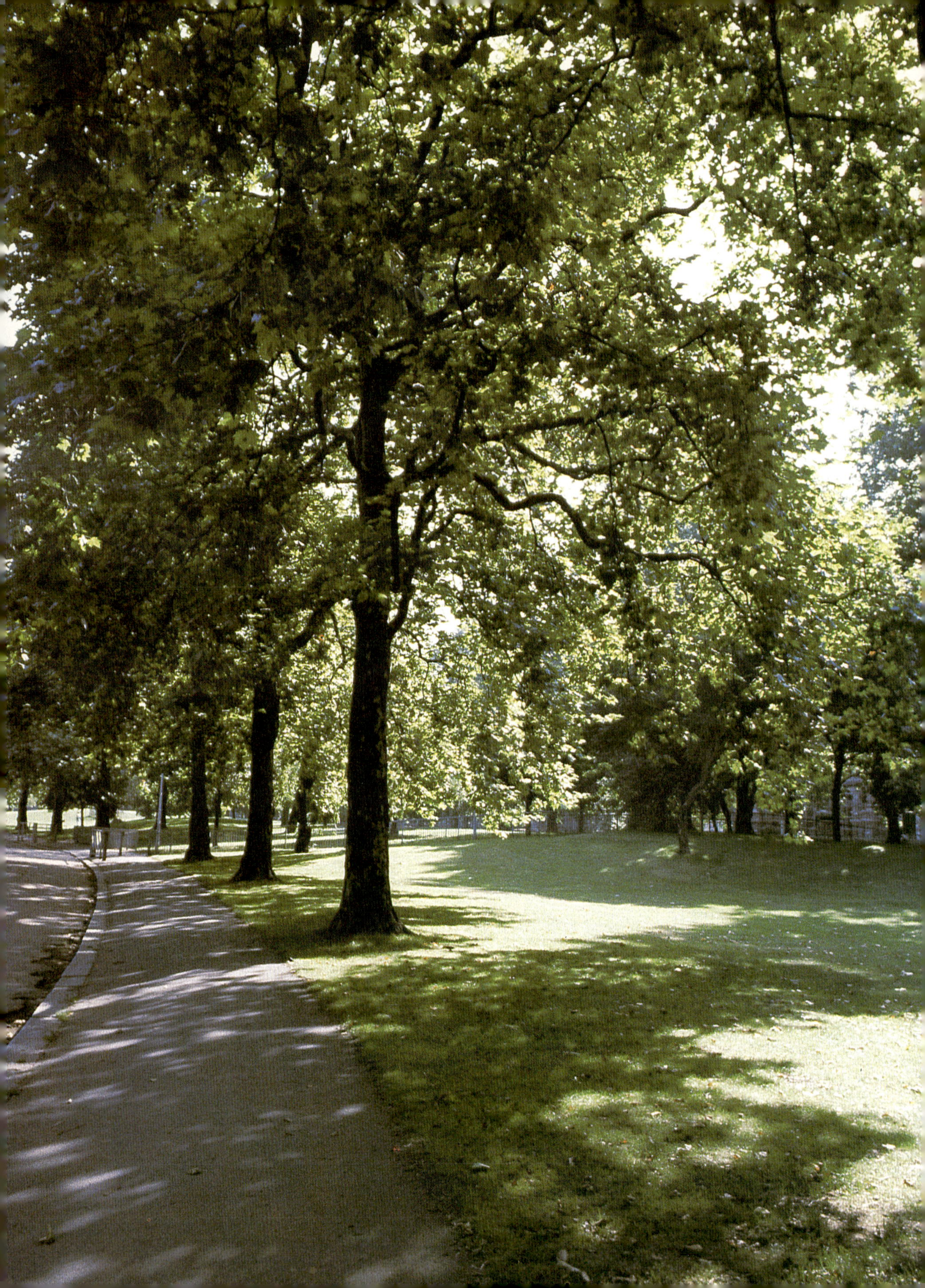

Battersea Park.
Opposite: The carriage drives are lined with many fine plane trees
Above: It is a great place to enjoy a quiet walk by the Thames

From the south-east corner of the park it stretches about half the length of Carriage Drive South and half the length of Carriage Drive East. At its western end its banks are smothered in willow and oak trees. This area looks more like landscaped gardens on a country estate than a park. There has been much new planting of willow and similar 'natural' species to maintain the lake's unpark-like look. This large expanse of water, protected and sheltered by all the trees, is a favourite place for wildfowl.

At the southern end of the lake is a large animal enclosure. Here, roaming over a huge mound dotted with plane trees, can be seen numerous deer, wallabies, crested cranes, rabbits and peacocks, all living happily side by side. I have never seen so many peacocks in one place; there must be ten at least. The animals are not shy, so they can easily be seen. They must not be fed.

Beyond the animal enclosure on Carriage Drive East the park begins to get busy. On the edge of the lake is a café; here can be found a good range of fresh rolls, sandwiches, cakes, pastries and drinks. There is plenty of seating indoors and out. Near here boats can be hired. A chalk board gives all the details in a chatty manner, including essential information such as that they close when the Boss says so; all very casual and friendly. Over the road is the well-used athletics ground; there is a small charge for use of the facilities.

Next door is the Horticultural Therapy Demonstration Garden, for the use of people with disabilities. Next to, and opposite, this garden are tennis courts. Like the athletics ground, the courts are always busy; there is again a small charge for their use. All these amenities are within a small area, carefully woven together among shrubbery and fine trees. There is always a lot going on in this corner of the park.

In 1986 the Bolshoi Ballet came to perform in England and Ireland. Their egalitarian aims led to the erection of what is claimed to be the largest tent in the world, in Battersea Park on the site of the old fair ground. Here the Ballet performed to 4,000 people at cheaper prices away from the élitist atmosphere of Covent Garden. Its owner and the Bolshoi's promoters hope there will be no objections to the tent's remaining in the park, as they plan to use it for pop concerts, dance festivals, circuses, championships and other large prestigious events. Performances of ballet in tents at Battersea Park are, surprisingly, nothing new. The Sadlers Wells Ballet and the Ballet Rambert have had tent seasons for years. A tent seating 4,000 people, complete with raked stage, orchestra pit, bars and restaurant, is an exciting addition not just to Battersea Park but to the arts and entertainments scene of London as a whole.

Another recent innovation at Battersea is the playing of 'boules'. This has been given prestige by the evening paper *The Standard*, which organizes the London Standard Boules Championships. As London takes more and more to the continental idea of outdoor living, this is becoming an increasingly popular activity at many of the city's pubs.

Walking to the end of Carriage Drive East, one is confronted by the river. The view is not spectacular – there are no sweeping vistas with famous landmarks as at the South

Bank – but it is certainly attractive. To your right is Chelsea Bridge, to your left Albert Bridge; opposite, on the Chelsea Embankment, are the grounds of the Royal Hospital and Ranelagh Gardens. The Thames itself is busy during the summer, with pleasure craft of all shapes and sizes plying their trade between Charing Cross and Westminster downstream and Hampton Court, Kew and Richmond upstream.

Walking towards Albert Bridge you begin to see through the trees the pagoda, or rather The London Peace Pagoda. This fanciful, exotic temple, sacred tower or whatever, certainly grabs your attention. To those of the Buddhist faith it is obviously a very meaningful monument, but as it is dedicated to world peace it should say something to all of us. Completed in May 1985, it is a gift from the late Most Venerable Nichidatsu Fujii and the Buddhist Order Nipponzan Myohoji, which he founded. It is based on ancient Japanese and Indian pagodas. The roof pinnacle, known as a kata, is gilded, as are the bells at the corners of the two octagonal roofs. North, south, east and west niches depict episodes of the Buddha's life. The pagoda is unique in London; it deserves a moment of your time for itself and, more importantly, for the meaning behind it.

Since May 1985, one of London's most unexpected sights has been the Peace Pagoda in Battersea Park

Further along the river frontage you may be able to distinguish the wrought iron gates of the Chelsea Physic Garden on the opposite bank. Reaching Carriage Drive West and walking south, there are signposts to the park's office. Here is a glasshouse packed full of interest, with an especially good collection of alpine plants. There is also a display of pot-grown conifers, climbing plants growing up the supports of the house, and annuals in baskets and a variety of other containers. Outside are two large beds of herbs, one of culinary herbs, the other medicinal and aromatic.

The centre of the park is the most 'showy'. There is a rose garden with fountains and arches of ornamental vines, flowering trees and shrubs, and bold displays of bedding plants. Here also are the rather sad remains of the entrance to the Festival Pleasure Gardens, largely a fun-fair, which was part of the Festival of Britain in 1951, and a familiar sight from the river and Chelsea Embankment afterwards.

Apart from the features described, there are numerous other recreational activities throughout the park. It seems that every sport which can be played in a park is played in this one. You would think that the park had not a spare inch left, but room has been found around its perimeter for conservation areas. Here are unkempt places where native 'wild' specimens are encouraged which attract insects, birds and small animals. It is not that the park is crowded, more that it is fully utilized and space is not wasted. As the Victorians were aware, open space in London is a valuable resource. There is room at Battersea Park for everything and everyone.

Battersea, we hope, will remain one of London's most lively public parks; it deserves to be better known.

GOLDERS HILL

Golders Hill is a charming, traditional suburban park. Like Kenwood and The Hill it is part of Hampstead Heath, but none of the three has the wild, natural character of the Heath itself. They are all cultivated places, to a greater or lesser extent. Golders Hill is probably the most trim. For several reasons it is a lovely place for a summer Sunday afternoon, not least because of its very individual café.

Purchased by the Metropolitan Board of Works in 1899 for £38,000, the park was created from the grounds of a manor house which was destroyed by a bomb in the last war; it covers thirty-nine acres. The main entrance on North End Road, at its east side, is nearly opposite to The Old Bull and Bush public house. There are a couple of entrances on its west side, where it is bordered by a suburban area known as Child's Hill; to the south, gates lead into West Heath. As at Kenwood and The Hill, it is easy to wander onto the Heath proper without realizing it.

Golders Hill is a gently undulating grassy park, liberally dotted about with interesting features like ponds, a highly decorative flower garden, animal and bird enclosures, a bandstand, a café, tennis courts, a putting green and golf nets.

Opposite: **Parts of Golders Hill are as wild as its neighbour, Hampstead Heath**

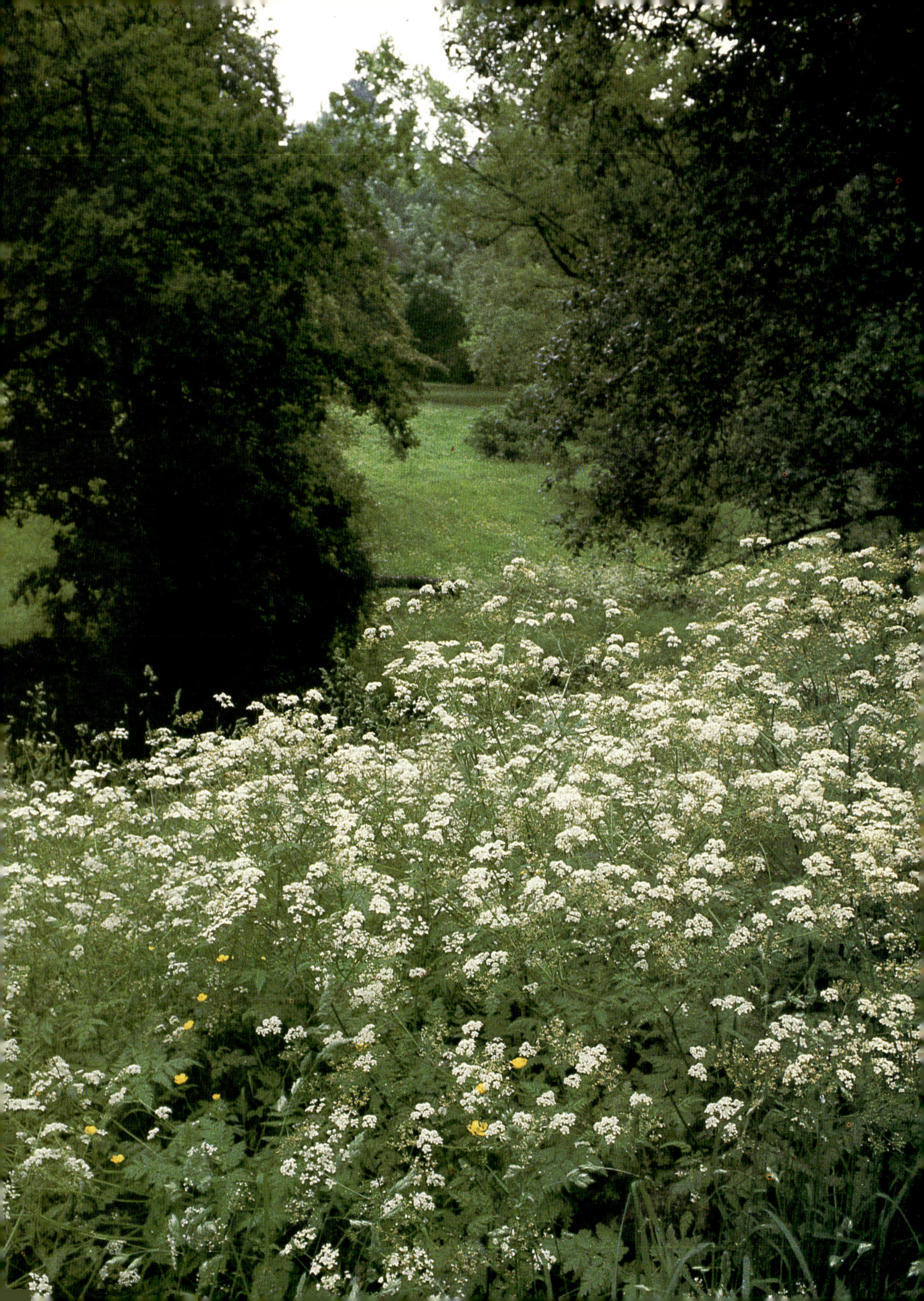

The charming flower garden is full to bursting with colourful plants from spring to autumn. A large fig tree against a west wall and one or two ancient pear trees suggest that this was once the kitchen garden which supplied the manor house with fresh fruit and vegetables. The garden could hardly be described as formal, but there are flower beds of varying sizes, laid out in a regular pattern and separated by flagstone paths. Some of the beds are given over entirely to bedding plants. A typical summer display might be a massed bed of geraniums of a single colour with spider plants as an edging and canna as dot plants to give height and contrast. Some of the beds are edged with low box hedges. There are also larger beds of mixed herbaceous plants; those that need it are supported in the traditional way by peasticks.

Through a door in the north wall is a series of glasshouses; these are open to the public between two and four o'clock on Saturdays and Sundays. The bedding plants raised here are used in the garden. The garden has some fine specimen trees, such as eucalyptus and magnolias; there is also a collection of mixed shrubs and wall plants. There are seats throughout the garden, strategically placed for people to enjoy the floral displays. The most shaded seat is 'within' a yew tree, which has surrounded the seat on three sides and above. The garden also has a charming ornamental pond with a central fountain of a young boy playing with two fish. Nearby but not actually in the garden is more water, known as the lily pond, but popular more for its pink flamingoes. Other less unusual waterfowl also use this pond.

Next to the flower garden, on its western side, is an orchard-like area of cherry and pear trees. This area is especially worth seeing in the spring, both for the blossom and for the daffodils which are planted around the trees.

The animal enclosures have been likened to the type of menagerie which was a common feature in private parks of the eighteenth century. The larger enclosure has a background of beech, oak and rhododendrons, and is indeed reminiscent of the type of landscape found in the grounds of many country houses. Goats and deer laze, apparently content, only stirring as visitors – possible sources of food – approach the fence. Nearby is a smaller enclosure, subdivided and roofed with mesh to house a collection of birds. These exotic animals include guinea fowl, Sarus crane, rhea and – most beautiful of all – the ever-popular peacock. They have a white one here which seems to be everyone's favourite.

Apart from the animals, younger children will enjoy the specially enclosed play area. Free from dogs and attendant problems, this grassed area has wooden animals to climb and ride; there is also a sandpit to play in.

The fine bandstand atop a slight rise is near the main entrance and just across from the café. Sunday band concerts are a popular event in the park. Organized by the London Residuary Body since the demise of the GLC, the concerts are free and take place every Sunday from the end of May to the end of August.

As far as sports amenities are concerned, the park has golf nets, hard and grass tennis courts, and a putting green. There is also plenty of room to kick a ball about.

In the extreme west of the park, here much wilder and more akin to its neighbour, West Heath, is Swan Pond, which is surrounded by dense shrubbery and overhung by birch, oak and may trees. Between the pond and the boundary of the park is a cinder track. This weaves uphill beyond the pond and follows the line of a stream, which is barely visible through a fine crop of cow parsley, eventually emerging near the animal enclosures.

The flower garden at Golders Hill could once have been the kitchen garden belonging to the now demolished manor house

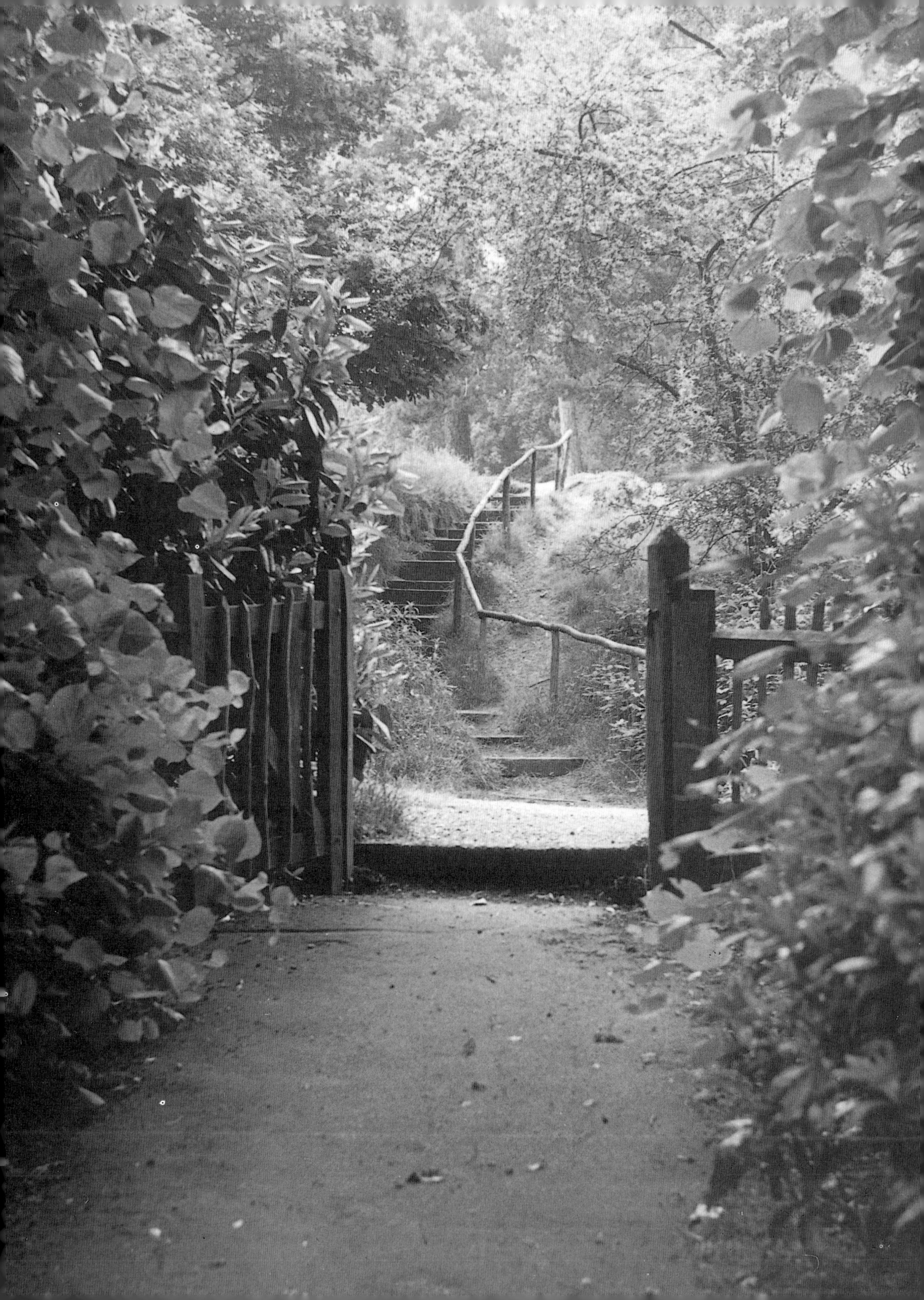

Large copper beech and Scots pine trees mark the park's southern boundary. There are one or two gates on to the Heath between these trees, and large beds of rhododendrons and foxgloves, a fitting introduction to the wilderness beyond.

The café is one of the best in any London park, so is included in the 'Eating Out' chapter. Perhaps the café is the reason why Golders Hill always seems busier than any other suburban park during the week, even when the children are at school. Locals certainly go to the park just for the café.

HOLLAND PARK

Twenty-eight acres of peaceful woodland in central London seems unlikely, but that is what you can enjoy at Holland Park. When walking here it is hard to believe that Kensington High Street, one of London's busiest shopping districts, is literally just down the road. It is a perfect tonic for anyone who is fed up with being in the city.

Opposite: **A stairway on West Heath from Golders Hill**
Above: **The Napoleonic Garden at Holland Park, so named because a bust of Napoleon once stood here. Today a sculpture by Eric Gill is the centrepiece**

In total, the park covers fifty-five acres and is as valuable an open space as any of the central Royal Parks. Though it is less well-known to visitors, it is not surprisingly very popular with local people. The 'Friends of Holland Park' do much to promote its use, and work hard on its upkeep. Peaceful as the woodland is, the rest of the park is always very lively because it seems to pack such a lot in. There is a restaurant and café, two exhibition spaces, an open-air theatre, numerous sports facilities, children's play areas, exotic birds – and all this set among decorative gardens and unusual trees. The casual visitor will always find something of interest.

The park was once the estate of Holland House, a grand red-brick mansion begun in 1605 by Sir Walter Cope. The property was inherited by the family of his son-in-law, Sir Henry Rich, who as the Earl of Holland gave his name to the house. It was bought by Henry Fox, the first Baron Holland, in 1768. The third Baron Holland was responsible for the layout of the grounds we see today. The property belonged to the Earls of Ilchester when in 1940 the house was bombed and all but destroyed. In 1952 it was bought by the London County Council, who opened the woodland to the public immediately and the rest of the park in subsequent years. The one undamaged wing of the house was incorporated into a youth hostel.

The decorative gardens in Holland Park are to the west of the old house, with the restaurant, café, orangery and ice house exhibition spaces all set among them.

The formal garden is the largest, and was laid out in 1812 to a design by Buonaiuti for the third Baron Holland. It is an area of geometric beds, edged with low box hedges. The beds are full of colourful bulbs and bedding plants from early spring until late autumn. Towards the house is a terrace with seats which give you a perfect view of the formal layout. Beside the formal garden is the Napoleonic Garden; the name refers not to any style of garden design, but to a bronze bust of Napoleon which once stood here. The Emperor made a gift of it to his friends, the Hollands. This small enclosure is, like its neighbour, richly planted with bedding; at its centre is a statue of a maiden by Eric Gill. Nearby is Rogers' Seat, set in the fireplace of the original stable buildings. Samuel Rogers, banker and poet, wrote a book of poems entitled *The Pleasure of Memory*. Baron Holland commemorated his friend with the words which are inscribed above the seat:

> Here Rogers sat, and here forever dwell
> With me those pleasures that he sings so well.

These gardens are floodlit, making them a pleasant place for a summer night's stroll.

The open-air Court Theatre, used during the summer for a variety of entertainments, has its stage in front of the house, the façade of which is particularly effective if the right opera or play is being performed. The seating is a tiered temporary structure. With the abolition of the GLC in 1986 the management of Holland Park passed to the Royal Borough of Kensington and Chelsea. Their Libraries and Arts Service instigated a series of weekend jazz concerts with well-known musicians in the theatre, and on the north

The two styles of Holland Park: the grand and the informal. The orangery *(top)* reflects the former, the woodland *(below)* the latter

lawn, on the other side of the house, there is street theatre on Sunday afternoons. So entertainment in Holland Park will, we hope, continue to flourish.

To the south of the Napoleonic Garden is a restaurant called The Belvedere. This is an attractive place to eat, being almost, with plants inside, as green as the park its large arched windows look out upon. It is known as a fish restaurant but meat is always on the menu too. The food is delicious, the surroundings luxurious and spacious, but it is expensive. The restaurant is easily reached from the park's Abbotsbury Road entrance, which conveniently leads straight into a car park.

Adjoining the restaurant is the orangery, which was built by the fourth Baron Holland in 1850. A long, elegant building with huge windows and doors and an end wall that is completely mirrored, it houses two statues of classical wrestlers. Outside, along its western front, are some fine large camellias, which flower profusely early in the year. The orangery is frequently used for exhibitions; one I remember was 'Brideshead Revisited', which had photographs and costumes from the television series. It seemed particularly suited to this space. Concerts have also been held here.

The rose garden is at the southern end of the orangery, and is best seen in June. Close by is an area of lawn dotted with trees, a large children's sandpit, and tennis courts. At the orangery begins a roofed arched walkway, lined with mosaic tiles, which leads to the house. The walkway passes the iris garden, which has beds crammed full of irises, a white marble fountain and several seats. It is a lovely place to stop and rest, especially in late spring when the irises are in full bloom.

Further along the walkway is the ice house. Originally built to store ice in the winter for use in the summer, it is now in regular use as an exhibition space. Outside is a statue of a 'Boy with Bear Cubs' by John Macallen Scott, lent by the Trustees of the Tate Gallery.

A convenient last stop is the café; this is popular with local people for its friendly atmosphere and good food. Toasted sandwiches and spaghetti bolognese are available, as well as the usual assortment of rolls, cakes and drinks. There is plenty of seating indoors and outside, in the shade of some large trees.

All these features are very close together but do not seem cramped. There is space in and around them for interesting trees such as the Judas tree (*Cercis siliquastrum*) and flowering shrubs like azalea, lilac and mock orange, which form a very pleasant background for everything else.

Walking northwards from the house, there is a gentle introduction to the woodland via the north lawn with its ancient Indian bean tree (*Catalpa bignonioides*) and the rose walk. This leads to a pond, fronted by a statue of Henry Richard Fox, third Baron Holland, by G. F. Watts and E. Boehm. Watts was a protégé of Baron Holland. Four paths converge at this point; any one of them will lead you into the delightful woodland of pine, oak, May and poplar. There are two main routes through the wood – one lined with lime trees, the other with chestnuts. The lime-tree avenue was planted by Lady Holland, wife of the fourth Baron, in 1876. Both walks are on a slight hill, of which the statue seems to be the top. Lower down the hill from Baron Holland, to the south-west, is a

Opposite above: Holland Park rose garden is best seen in June
Below: The Lime Walk, Kenwood, is an extension of the terrace in front of the house.
Beneath it is the source of the River Fleet, from which Fleet Street takes its name

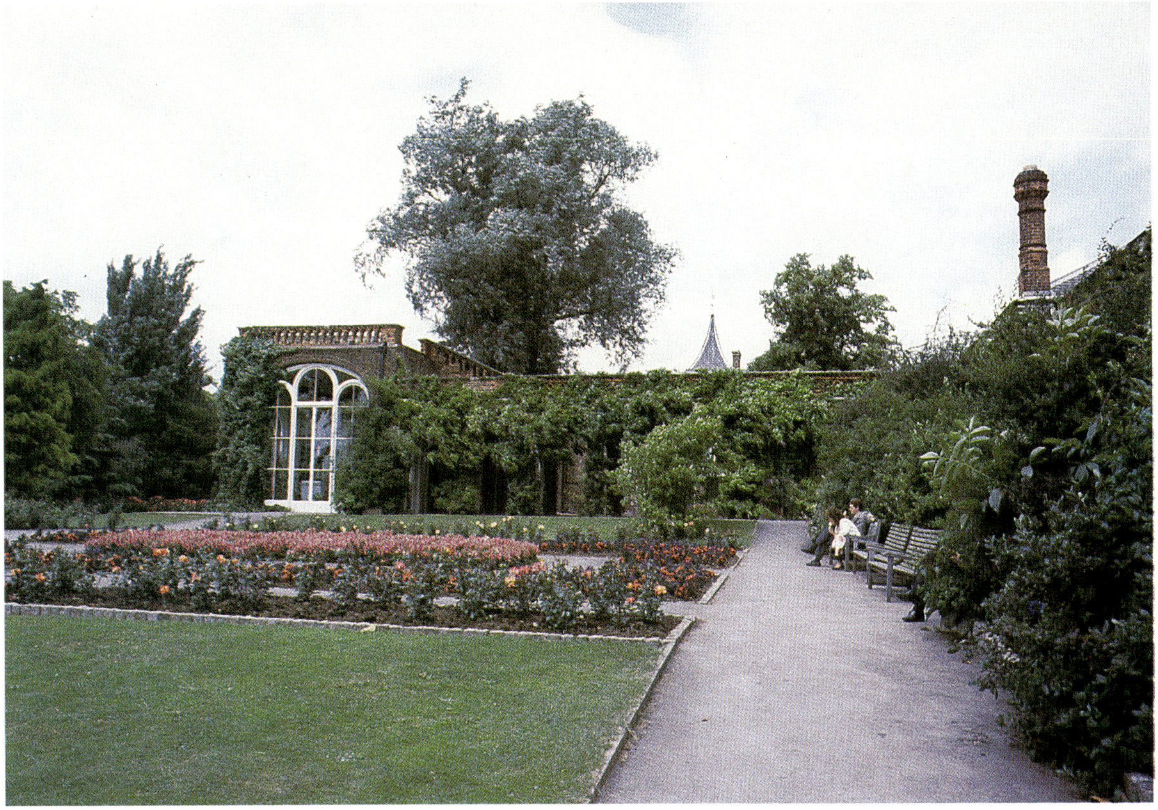

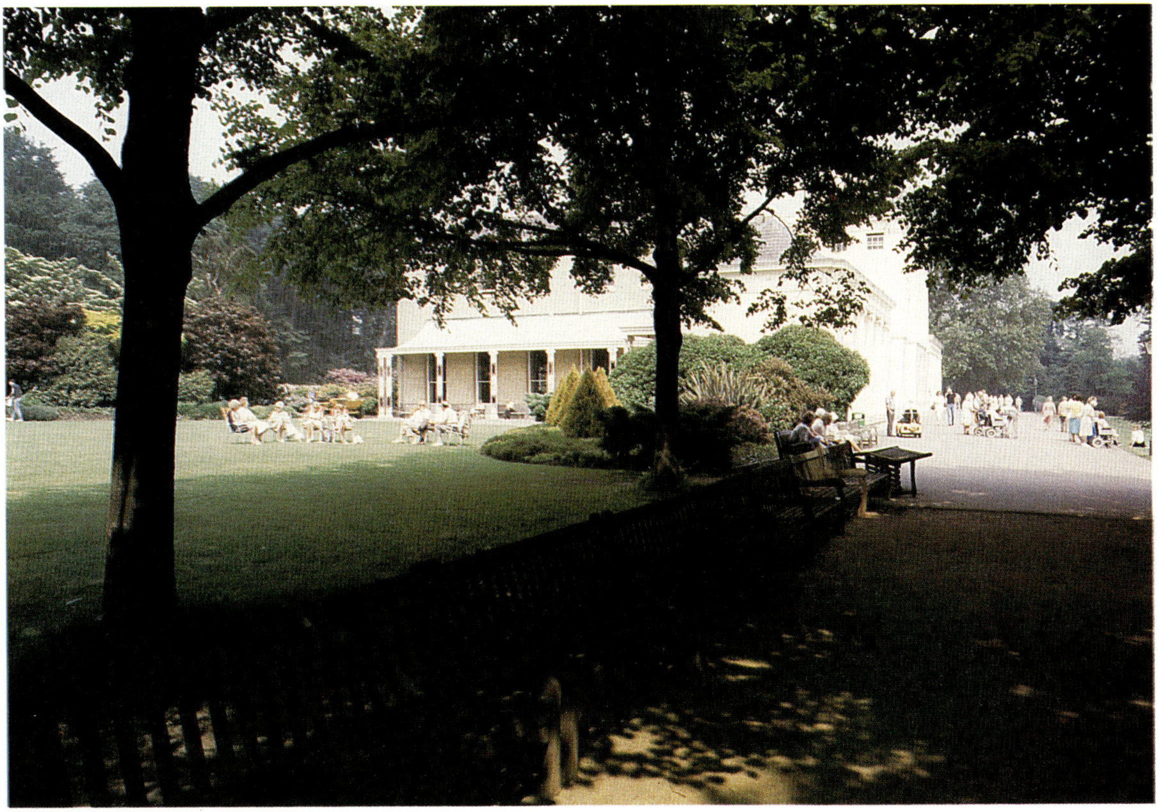

fenced area called the yucca lawn. This does have some grass but is really more a densely planted shrubbery. Bamboo, holly, pampas grass, birch and, of course, yucca unite in a rich mix of form, colour and size. It is here that you will find one of the park's most popular attractions: its collection of exotic birds, such as rhea and ornamental pheasants. Peacocks hop in and out, having the freedom of the park.

The park also contains facilities for cricket, tennis and squash, as well as cricket and golf nets. There is a club for the under-fives, a play area with sand and climbing frames for the under-twelves, and an adventure play-park for 5–16 year-olds.

KENWOOD

Kenwood consists of about 200 acres of Hampstead Heath. Like The Hill and Golders Hill, it is indivisible from the rest of it – although quite different in character. It has the atmosphere of a country estate, which is exactly what it was. Kenwood House is one of London's most delightful country houses; its parkland is characterized by sweeping lawns and blowsy shrubbery. There is a main entrance at the north on Hampstead Lane, and on the Heath at the south are Hampstead and Highgate Gates. In fact the area does not seem to be properly fenced, so it is easy to drift into Kenwood at several points. If entering from the Heath, you will soon notice the change in environment to dense shrubbery, with exotics like rhododendrons, after the Heath's comparatively open scrubland of native flora. Walking northwards you will find the lakes, lawns, gardens and terraces, and the house itself. Kenwood makes a pleasant objective for a walk on the Heath, particularly as it has a very good tea room!

The present house was remodelled by Robert Adam in 1764 for its owner Lord Mansfield as a country retreat. It remains virtually all Adam's work, a building of fine proportions and restrained decoration. The garden façade, facing south, is the most impressive, standing white and stately on the crest of a hill. The interior has some beautiful rooms, the breathtaking library being Adam's masterpiece.

The property remained with the Mansfields until bought by Edward Cecil Guinness, first Earl of Iveagh, in 1925. On his death in 1927 he bequeathed the part of his art collection which he kept at Kenwood, together with the house and park, for the benefit of the public. His will decreed that the atmosphere of an eighteenth-century gentleman's home, which he had created at Kenwood, should be maintained. The Iveagh Bequest, an extensive collection of works by artists such as Gainsborough and Reynolds, is perfectly displayed in the fine Adam rooms. Kenwood House must be the most handsome art gallery in London and well worth a visit. Admission is free.

To the west of the house is a well-kept lawn, informally planted with beds of rhododendrons and surrounded by shrubbery. In a clearing on the lawn is a piece of sculpture by Barbara Hepworth called 'Monolith Empyrean' dated 1953, which gives a focus to this part of the garden. The shrubbery is mainly rhododendrons. There are several shady walks with seats, where it is nice to stop a while and admire these showy plants, which are at their best in late spring. Almost concealed by the shrubbery is a humble building made of rough wood, known as Dr Johnson's Summer House. It is said to have been used by the great man on visits made to some friends, Mr and Mrs Thrale, in Streatham. It was saved from destruction, to be re-erected here in 1967.

Towards the car park at West Lodge there is a track through the shrubbery which leads to North Hill, in North Wood. Here there are good views over the house and grounds. Among the magnificent oak and beech trees can be found tombstones marking the graves of dogs which belonged to the Kenwood household. The track continues to Eastern Drive, which leads back to the house.

A sculpture by Barbara Hepworth stands in the garden of Kenwood House

Along the west side of the house a path leads to the garden façade. There is a wide terrace along the whole front of the house, from which there are fine views over the lawns to the woodland beyond. The Lime Walk is the western extension of this terrace. Here an avenue of mature lime trees overhangs the terrace and borders beds of rhododendrons and azaleas. Below the Lime Walk are two springs, the source of the River Fleet which flows underground through London and out into the Thames. It was from this river that Fleet Street took its name.

On the east side of the house are the kitchen and coach house, which are accessible from the terrace. Here is the tea room, serving a good choice of hot and cold meals, cakes, drinks and ice cream. From the terrace the ground slopes away across undulating lawns to lakes and woodland; in spring there is a marvellous display of daffodils immediately below the terrace. On the lawn near the springs is a colossal sculpture, for which the plaque reads 'Two Piece Reclining Figure No. 5 Henry Moore 1963–4'.

The lawns lead south-eastwards towards two expanses of water which might be called lakes, but are known as ponds. The Lily Pond is the largest; at one corner it is crossed by a stone bridge which leads into South Wood. The other is the Concert Pond, and on its far side is a concert bowl. A summer season of open-air concerts was begun here over thirty-five years ago by the London County Council and continued by the GLC. English Heritage is now responsible for organizing the traditional classical concerts; in 1986 it also introduced concerts by brass bands, a wind ensemble and jazz musicians. The concerts have always been very popular, attracting large crowds. The arena opens long before concerts begin so many people enjoy a picnic before the performance. Seats, or rather deckchairs, are bookable in advance, or you can just turn up on the night, which most people do.

The scene across the water to the concert bowl is enhanced by a bridge on the left which looks real enough from a distance but is in fact only a 'prop' of wood – not stone – and just two feet wide, of no practical use. But no matter; this sham adds to the setting. This is a delightful place, and going to a concert here a lovely way to spend a summer evening.

Backing on to the ponds is South Wood. It is much larger than North Wood – a maze of walks which it is fun to explore. Most of it is shady as the shrubbery is quite dense. The main types of trees are beech, oak and sweet chestnut. The undergrowth is mainly the wild purple-flowering rhododendron (*R. ponticum*), although there is also quite a lot of holly. Where the wood opens out on its southern edge to Hampstead Heath there are some good views towards London.

Kenwood has been likened to a Royal Spa like Baden or Marienbad; this is not so surprising. It has the cultured and genteel air associated with such places. The house is both beautiful and imposing in its location. The Iveagh Bequest is a superb collection of paintings, which perfectly suit the house. The gardens are well kept and have some charming features, such as the summer house. The terrace is a perfect place to promenade before going down the slope of the vast lawns towards the lakes and a concert at the bowl.

Opposite: Lesnes Abbey Wood in south-east London is a magnificent sight in spring with its twenty acres of massed wild daffodils

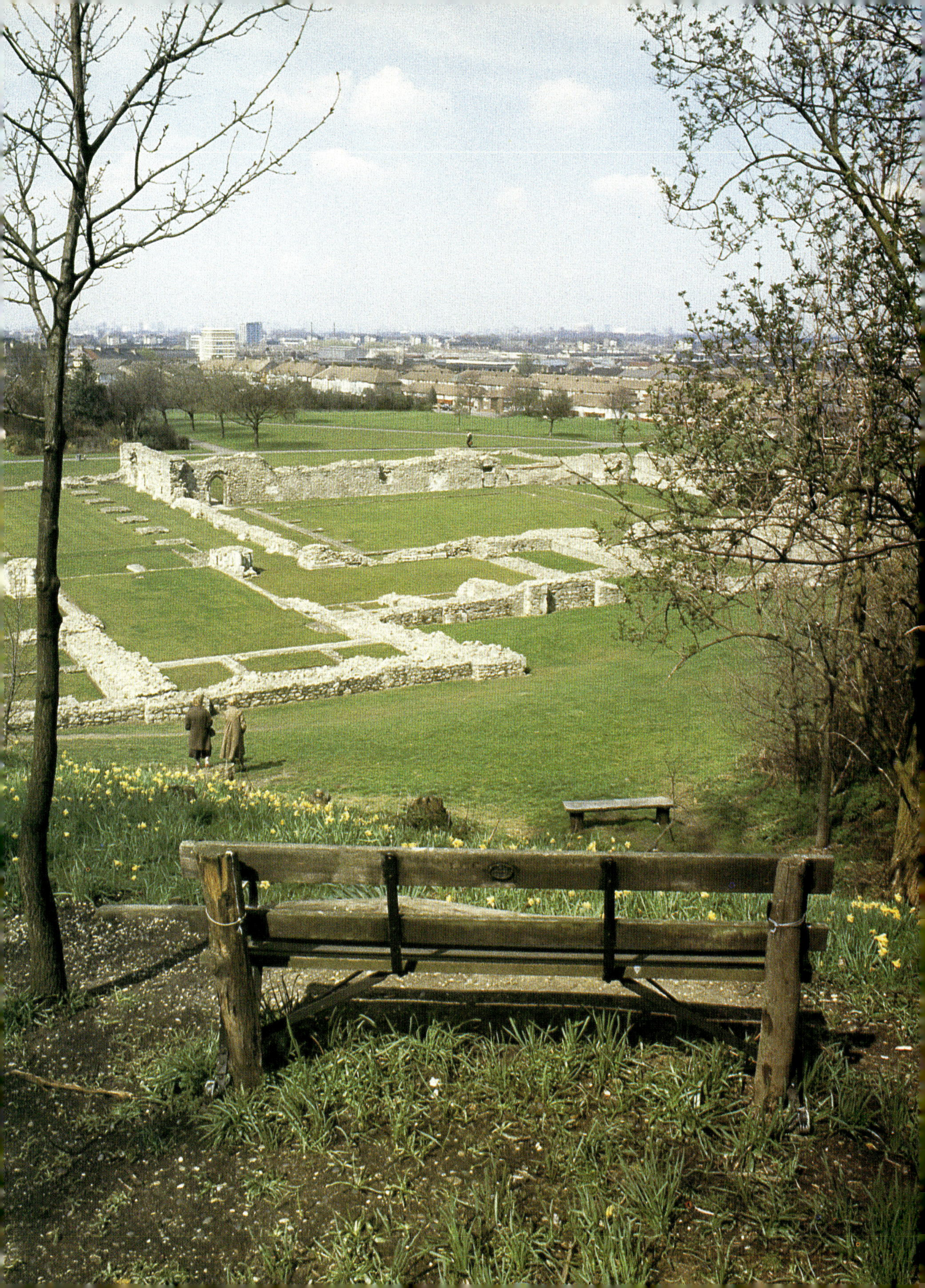

And what could be finer on a hot summer's day than a cooling walk through the shrubbery of South Wood?

It is pleasing that Lord Iveagh's wish that Kenwood should retain the atmosphere of a gentleman's private park is still being adhered to in such style.

LESNES ABBEY WOOD

One of south-east London's little-known open spaces, Lesnes Abbey Wood, is included here because it deserves to be better known than it is, and fits more comfortably under the heading of 'park' than 'garden'. A good example of how pigeon-holing always fails, this 'open space' is probably little known because this area of London has little to recommend it. But Lesnes Abbey Wood is worth making the effort to find. The fact that places like this are relatively unknown makes them even more appealing, and visiting them can be very rewarding.

The suburb of Abbey Wood is only half an hour's train journey from Charing Cross. Lesnes Abbey Wood is an area of 215 acres, most of which is taken up by the wood that gives this suburb its name; the remainder is a formal park around the abbey ruins. Lesnes Abbey, an Augustinian foundation, dates from 1178. It was built by Sir Richard de Lucy, Chief Justicer of England, probably in reparation for the share he took in the murder of Thomas à Becket in 1170.

The abbey cannot have been well run because by 1336 it was ruinous and in debt. In 1525 it was closed by Wolsey and the buildings dismantled or demolished. In 1909 the site was excavated, and in 1930 it was purchased by the London County Council and made into a park. Between 1956 and 1959 the ruins were skilfully cleared, to show the complete plan of the abbey church, its cloister and domestic buildings. Though unimpressive in height, the ruins are worth seeing; a vivid imagination can make much of small features such as a stairway to the reader's pulpit in the refectory and a serving hatch from the kitchen to the refectory.

The formal park which surrounds the ruins is full of colour all summer. Two long beds of mixed trees, shrubs, herbaceous plants and bedding echo the straight lines of the abbey church; in fact, the whole garden seems very right and proper and in keeping with an ecclesiastical setting. This is reflected again in the maintenance, which is very thorough, everything kept neat and tidy.

The garden has several fine ornamental cherry trees, which look lovely in April, when the many tulips, hyacinths and daffodils are also flowering. Throughout the summer there are shrubs such as buddleia and weigela in flower, as well as bedding plants.

Lesnes Abbey Wood's great attraction, however, is the large area of beautiful mixed woodland. The land is quite hilly and the woods extensive enough to make any visitor unaware of the surrounding suburbs, once you enter them. In fact, the wood has its own orienteering circuit, as if it were true countryside. A map and instructions are available at the park café. But unless this is a particular hobby, the wood is best enjoyed by wandering aimlessly along its many paths. Occasionally there is a feature such as a pond or viewpoint, but the charm of the place is its silvan serenity. The best time of the year to visit is in the spring, because large areas of the trees bordering the formal gardens are underplanted with wild daffodils. Throughout the woods there are over twenty acres of daffodils. From the edge of the wood, on the slope overlooking the abbey ruins, can be seen the new town of Thamesmead, built on the Erith Marshes. Not an attractive view, but a strong reminder that you are in suburban London.

To the south-west, the woods meet Bostall Heath and then Bostall Woods, another wooded public park. From the broad clearing at the top of this wood can be seen the Thames, the Tower of London, London Bridge and the river's dockland.

The café is run by an ex-army caterer. The snack food is good, cheap and filling – his speciality being bread pudding. The café is open during the day from April to September, and sometimes in winter after a fall of snow, when the slopes at the base of the hills are popular with children for sledging. There is seating indoors and out. The café is the best place from which to enjoy Lesnes Abbey Wood; it faces south and overlooks the gardens and abbey ruins, with wooded hills in the background. The view is especially attractive in spring, when these hills are covered with wild daffodils. On a sunny day in April, when the air is fresh and the buds on the trees are just opening, this is a lovely place to be.

OSTERLEY PARK

Osterley is a fine example of an informal park, with a series of lakes, large trees and extensive grassland. These 120 acres are a much needed 'green lung' in the heavily built-up western suburbs. The Great West Road (A4), a masterpiece of 1930s urban and industrial development, with its monolithic art-deco factories, is just to the south. Inter-war 'semis' encroach all around, and Heathrow is just down the road. Worst of all, the M4 motorway cuts the park almost in half. Land both north and south of the motorway is leased to tenant farmers, but a large area around the house is kept as a public park.

Considering the location, it is remarkable how Osterley Park manages to preserve the character and tranquillity of the countryside. There is enough space to give the illusion of being far from London – aircraft overhead excepted – the illusion being increased by grazing cattle and horses, and ploughed fields about the edge of the park.

The park surrounds a Tudor house, much altered in the eighteenth century; they complement each other well. The park is simple and natural, the house grand and carefully designed; each seems better for having the other. The perfect symmetry of the house is made all the more striking by its rural setting; in contrast, the park is refreshingly free of design. The beauty of Osterley Park lies in its simplicity. The lakes and fine trees, particularly the cedars, set in the extensive grassland are attractive at any time of the year.

The house owes much of its appearance to the architect Robert Adam, who undertook to redesign the house in 1762. Not only did he alter the external appearance of the house but he changed the interior decoration of all but two of the State Rooms and designed much of the furniture. Fortunately his work at Osterley remains largely complete and is open to view. He was employed by Sir Francis Child, whose family had owned the property since 1711. Through marriage the Earls of Jersey became owners and in 1949 the ninth Earl presented Osterley Park, the house and grounds, to the National Trust.

The main entrance for cars and pedestrians is in Jersey Road, opposite Thornbury Road. Passing through the main gates, one enters an avenue of large sweet chestnut trees set in a wide grass verge. Beyond a railing, on either side, is pasture land with grazing horses and cattle. About halfway down the avenue is a house which sells fresh eggs, flowers, fruit and vegetables in the summer. After approaching Osterley through inter-war suburbia, these suggestions of rural life make a refreshing change. The car park is at the end of the avenue on the right. A path leads between two lakes and brings the east side of the house into view. The park is very informal; it is not the sort of place which needs a guide so you do not miss anything. This is just the place for idly wandering and enjoying the open space.

First-time visitors will probably make a bee-line for the house, which is very eye-catching with its bright red bricks, four towers and large white portico atop a flight of steps; do go in and have a look. To the right of the house is the Tudor stable block, a

The chain of lakes is a beautiful feature of Osterley Park

red-brick building with an eighteenth-century clock-tower. Inside is a café, which opens at noon during the summer months for the sale of drinks and light lunches, cakes and sandwiches, all freshly made. There is seating indoors and outdoors on the large forecourt. Behind the stable block is the old walled vegetable garden, built by Mrs Robert Child – sister-in-law to Sir Francis – in the eighteenth century. It is now used as a service area for the park's gardeners.

Backing on to the walled garden to the north-west is a semi-circular garden house, designed by Robert Adam and built in 1780. Its curved shape meant that plants stored in it would receive maximum sunlight. Adam also incorporated a flue for heating in the back wall; his design plans are on view in the house. Adam also designed an orangery, which was built nearby but unfortunately destroyed in the last war. The only other garden building is a Doric temple, which faces the garden house across a wide lawn. This was built in 1770 to a design by John James of Greenwich. The interior is said to be of a later date and probably the work of Sir William Chambers. The classical interior decoration has representations of the four seasons, Art and Science. These elegant buildings are perfectly framed by huge trees, copper beech, oak, sweet chestnut and cedar.

To the north-east are informally planted decorative shrubs and trees such as rhododendrons, cherry and acer. The lawns are roughly mown but easy to walk on. A rough road leads to Osterley Park Farm, at the entrance to which is a track which follows the perimeter of the park. Follow the track for a pleasant walk through shrubbery and fine trees, with glimpses of the farmland beyond. At the beginning the track is bordered almost exclusively by holly, which comes into its own over the winter months – when wellington boots are a good idea for this walk. Further along yew predominates, scenting the air sweetly. In June the flowers of mock orange add their own heavy perfume. This is one of the remotest parts of the park, less frequented than areas nearer the house.

The track continues through a more densely wooded area to the end of the southernmost of the series of lakes. An overgrown bridge links the bank with an island in the lake. The water around the island is sluggish and hardly visible through thick scrub. The track continues along the western side of the lake and ends just past a mound, covering an old ice house, where ice cut from the lake was stored for summer use. The lake is broader here, and has more movement.

The house is now visible on the right, with some magnificent cedar trees growing in the grassy area between the house and the lake. They were planted by Mrs Robert Child in 1785 to commemorate the birth of her grandchild, Lady Sarah Sophia Fane. The west side of the house has a subtly curving horseshoe staircase, ornamented by iron balustrades with gold rams' heads. Around the base of the building are planted several evergreen magnolias which have large creamy-white and yellow flowers in high summer, and camellias which flower in spring. The southern lake is at its widest near the house, where its banks are planted with willows and alders. This lake and the park's two others were all created from ponds by Mrs Robert Child. She must have been a busy woman because, besides the lakes, cedars and walled garden, she was also responsible for creating a garden called the Wilderness, which unfortunately no longer exists, to the west of the house.

To the east of the house can be seen further evidence of Mrs Child's skill. Here the level ground has been cleverly landscaped so that the flatness is not apparent, with trees planted singly and in copses to break the lie of the land still further. It should be said that Mrs Child was assisted by her steward, Mr Bunce, in the creation of this informal parkland. The remains of avenues, planted by them, are also visible in this part of the park. The lakes here are very popular with anglers, and an island in the furthermost lake is home to several species of waterfowl.

The Doric temple at Osterley is surrounded by a fine collection of specimen trees

A little to the north and west is an old lodge and pedestrian exit on to Osterley Lane; this lane is a simple gravel track bordered by wild hedgerows. In contrast, looking northwards one can see the M4, with its constant flow of traffic, curiously sandwiched between fields – a reminder to anyone who may have forgotten that Osterley is trapped in Greater London. But the park still has an air of a private country estate – which it once was.

Osterley is well maintained, a pleasant place to take a walk and perhaps have a picnic. Or it could easily be combined with lunch at The Hare and Hounds in Wyke Green, a pub with an attractive garden.

WATERLOW PARK

This park is named after its creator, Sir Sidney Waterlow, who is remembered for wanting to create a 'garden for the garden-less'. He believed that besides being provided with good housing, the working class should have access to fresh air and areas for recreation. Proving himself a man of action as well as ideas, he presented his estate in Highgate to the London County Council in November 1889. Waterlow Park was opened to the public two years later.

The park is beautifully maintained with fine lawns, excellent displays of bedding plants and a chain of three lakes. It also features a popular café. What makes this park so attractive is that its twenty acres are richly covered with fine trees. There are some very secluded parts, and the whole is very shady; it is a lovely place to be on a hot summer's day. The few larger open spaces serve only to highlight the profusion of trees.

The best way to see Waterlow Park is to start at the top, work your way down one side of the lakes to the bottom, then back up the other side to finish at Lauderdale House, or rather the café at Lauderdale House. The main entrance is to the north of the park on Highgate High Street, which is at the top of Highgate Hill. A statue of Sir Sidney Waterlow presides over the park from near here, so it is a fitting place to start a walk. The inscription informs us that he served as Lord Mayor of London from 1872 to 1873.

Beneath the statue a path forms a terrace on which is a row of seats, always popular with people enjoying one of the best views over the park. Before them a lawn sweeps away down the hill, liberally dotted with good specimens of chestnut, lime and beech. The Post Office Tower is visible in the distance between the trees, which also reveal glimpses of the buildings surrounding the park. The park's sloping site gives it a great deal of character, which distinguishes it from many suburban parks. You can tell that some of the older people admiring the view are not casual visitors but locals, who get a great deal of pleasure from just being there.

Further up the hill are several well-used tennis courts and the highest and smallest of the chain of lakes. The park has numerous paths, which you are not obliged to stay on, so just wander down the hill towards the second and largest lake. Like the other lakes, this is a haven for wildlife; its banks are quite densely planted with all manner of trees and shrubs, though there is a preponderance of willow, oak and rhododendron. There is plenty of space for birds to nest undisturbed. An unlikely feature here is a piece of sculpture by Naomi Blake. A waterfall from the lake flows into the third and lowest lake. This too is very tranquil and shady.

If you go as far down the hill as the park's southern boundary you will come to some railings, the other side of which is a forbidding collection of overgrown monuments and gravestones. This is the newer eastern half of Highgate Cemetery. The old West Cemetery is on the other side of Swains Lane; a gate in the south-west corner of the park leads out to it.

Walk along the park's southern boundary around the bottom of the lake, and then begin to climb up the hill. Towards the gate on to Dartmouth Park Hill are aviaries and richly

Waterlow Park has fine herbaceous borders and is famous for its bedding plants

planted flower beds. Waterlow Park has a good reputation for the quality of its bedding schemes. There are large flower beds at key points throughout the park, but the largest and best are here on the eastern side. The aviaries are well stocked with small colourful birds, from distant continents, which are always a popular attraction. Apart from the bedding schemes there is a double herbaceous border with a collection of traditional cottage garden plants such as heuchera, iris, foxglove, peony and geum.

On this side of the park is one of the largest open areas, a quite steep slope which reaches down to the edge of the middle lake. This is a popular place for sun-worshippers to catch the midday sun. The area is equally well used after a snowfall in winter by children with sledges. Further up the hill mixed shrubbery surrounds Lauderdale House.

Lauderdale House was an earlier home of the Duke of Lauderdale, before he moved to Ham House at Richmond. It was later occupied by Nell Gwynne while she brought up her illegitimate son by the King. The building, which has a front door facing Highgate Hill, dates from the Tudor period, but its elegant white plaster façade gives it more of an eighteenth-century appearance. In the garden at the back of the house is a sundial, the plate of which is said to be on a level with the top of the dome of St Paul's Cathedral.

Waterlow Park has some very secluded corners

The house is now a community arts centre, providing a wide range of classes in art, dance and drama as well as space for theatre, concerts and art exhibitions. On the ground floor at the back of the house is the café. This has an attractive room indoors, and the garden provides extra space for tables and chairs during the summer. It is run by Italians, so very good pizzas, lasagne and the like are available as well as simple snacks and cream teas. Not surprisingly, wine and cappuccino are also available. The café is always well used because of its good, reasonably priced food and pleasant location.

While in the area you should have a look around Highgate. The centre of this north London suburb is full of eighteenth- and nineteenth-century houses with charming gardens and handsome trees everywhere. The shops mainly serve the local community but there is a sprinkling of art, craft and book shops. The most famous pub is The Flask, where Dick Turpin is supposed to have hidden to avoid capture and William Hogarth sketched the locals. They serve good food, which can be enjoyed indoors or on the large forecourt. The most unusual place to visit is Highgate West Cemetery, full of overgrown mausoleums, tombs, catacombs and effigies; it is a fascinating place which has a beauty and atmosphere all its own. In the newer East Cemetery is the famous bust of Karl Marx, which surmounts his grave. To the west, Highgate merges with Hampstead Heath.

Gardens

Described here are six of London's most beautiful and interesting gardens; they vary greatly in size. Chelsea Physic Garden and the garden of the Tradescant Trust both preserve the past, while the former also experiments for the future. The fine gardens of Chiswick, Fenton and Ham complement these historic houses. The Hill is delightfully unkempt, London's most romantic 'secret' garden. All are different in style but surprisingly none of them is very well known. They deserve to be.

> The size of the garden has nothing to do with it; twenty acres or one acre or half an acre, it is all the same.
>
> *Vita Sackville-West*

CHELSEA PHYSIC GARDEN

The Chelsea Physic Garden is a Mecca for plant-lovers, botanists and horticulturists; for anyone without their expertise it is a delightful walled four acres, crammed with colour and interest. It is open from spring to autumn, and it is well worth the price of admission for a chance to see some of the most unusual plants in London, lovingly cultivated in one of the city's most attractive gardens.

Chelsea Physic Garden is in fact a botanic garden like Kew. Since its foundation by the Worshipful Society of Apothecaries of London in 1673 its function has been educational and scientific. The garden's great benefactor was Sir Hans Sloane, who in 1712 bought the Manor of Chelsea, which included the garden's freehold. In 1722 he granted a lease for the gardens to the Society at five pounds per annum in perpetuity, on condition that it was forever maintained for educational and scientific use.

Seventeen twenty-two was also a good year because Philip Miller was put in charge of the garden. Miller became the greatest horticulturist of his day and made the Chelsea Physic Garden the most respected botanic garden in the world. Among his achievements were successfully propagating and cultivating species which had previously never been grown in England, and writing a book which became a gardening bible. During Miller's time at the garden, cotton seeds were sent to Georgia which became the foundation of the cotton industry in the southern states of America, which shows how influential he was.

The garden has not always flourished; indeed, at some points it has struggled to survive. Today it is an important centre for the study of horticulture and botany and a pleasant garden to visit. The staff are always cheerful, especially the guides who wander round the garden keen to help and answer questions whenever approached. An information desk has literature about the garden, and other places and events of horticultural interest in London. There are also booklets, gifts and plants for sale; on Sunday a great bonus is that tea is available. One thing to remember if you are planning a visit is that the garden is only open on Wednesday and Sunday afternoons from April to October.

The garden is entered through the old Students' Gate in Swan Lane. A main path straight ahead leads to the imposing statue of Sir Hans Sloane. Standing here, you get a good impression of the richness of the garden. It is a Noah's Ark of plants where one, if not two, of every species appears to have been crammed in. A small area of lawn seems an intrusion, but even that is planted with trees. This must be one of the most intensively cultivated pieces of land in London. The many gravel and grass paths are busy with people, who really seem to appreciate these plants. The garden is respected by its visitors and, crowded as it sometimes is, there is always a calm, dignified atmosphere which makes it very relaxing.

At the centre of the Chelsea Physic Garden is a statue of its benefactor, Sir Hans Sloane

A large part of the garden to the south-east of the statue is devoted to botanical family beds. Here, in long narrow strips of ground, plants are displayed family by family. It is interesting to see plants side by side which you would never think were related. There can be a great variety of habit, form and growth within a family. Some gardeners say plants should be treated like people: they need food, water and a rest now and again. It seems that plants have another similarity in that members of their families can be as varied as our own. These beds are arranged in a workmanlike manner but that is fair enough because, like Kew, Chelsea Physic Garden is primarily a working garden. Aesthetic considerations take second place.

Near the entrance gate in a corner of the family beds is one of the garden's most beautiful trees, *Koelreuteria paniculata* from north China. As its common name, 'Chinese willow pattern tree' suggests, this is supposed to be the type of tree represented on so much eighteenth-century porcelain. Sandwiched between the family beds and the perimeter wall along the Chelsea Embankment is a group of plants from South America, a collection of ericaceous plants (rhododendrons and heathers) and a large bed of mixed shrubs. Among these are some lovely wild peonies, which flower from April to September. Near the Embankment Gate is a pool, barely visible for large clumps of bog and aquatic plants which have grown rampant within it.

A path leads from the Embankment Gate up to the statue. Either side are some specimen trees, notably deciduous conifers – the maidenhair tree (*Gingko biloba*), dawn redwood (*Metasequoia glyptostroboides*) and swamp cypress (*Taxodium distichum*). Near the statue is a black mulberry, the fruits of which ripen in September. The main path to the western perimeter wall passes to the south of a woodland garden and more botanic family beds. At the end of the path is a small glasshouse with a collection of ferns. North of this are Australian plants and the Miller Display. Philip Miller is commemorated at the garden by these beds of plants, arranged according to geographical origin, which were mostly given their modern scientific names by him. The main buildings in the garden line its northern wall and include the lecture room, glasshouses, toilets, information desk and shop, through which there is an exit. It is here that you will find tea on a Sunday.

North-east of the Sloane statue are a herb garden, a rock garden and a pool. The herbs grown are divided into culinary, current medical and historical categories, and are displayed in beds around a large bay tree. There are two trees worth looking at in this part of the garden: a cork tree (*Quercus suber*) from the Mediterranean, which has the most fascinating bark, soft and spongy like that used by florists as a base for arrangements, and an olive tree (*Olea europaea*) which lays claim to being the biggest in Britain. It fruits remarkably well, and they even ripen so far from home.

Also in this corner of the garden is a research area. The experiments change from year to year but labels keep the visitor informed of what is happening. On a recent visit, Imperial College (part of London University) was researching into the effects of acid rain on a group of plants and King's (Chelsea) College was growing the herb feverfew to use in tests on its alleged migraine-relieving qualities. It should be said that everything in the garden is well labelled, which I suppose is not surprising considering that it is an educational establishment and a lot of the plants are rare.

Near the main building there are two beds devoted to the subject of rarity. Labels explain that a plant may be called rare for several reasons: it has been superseded; it is difficult to propagate or cultivate; it is slow to grow and increase; it has been neglected; it is only of botanical interest; it is new to cultivation, or it is rare in the wild. The garden is full of rare plants and it pays to read labels as otherwise you miss them.

CHISWICK HOUSE

The gardens of Chiswick House have a style all their own. Nowhere else in London is there such a silvan landscape adorned with a serpentine lake, classical temple, statuary and monuments, and all laid out in an informal manner with many delightful avenues and walks. This was the achievement of William Kent, an eighteenth-century designer who tried to recreate a vision of Italy to complement the perfect Palladian villa conceived and built by his employer, Lord Burlington, as a gallery and a place where he could entertain his friends. The lives and works of these two men make a fascinating slice of history. Chiswick House and its garden ensure that this history is kept alive, and serve as a great memorial to them both.

The Chelsea Physic Garden's research area is used for experiments by London colleges
Opposite: **Chiswick House from across the lake**

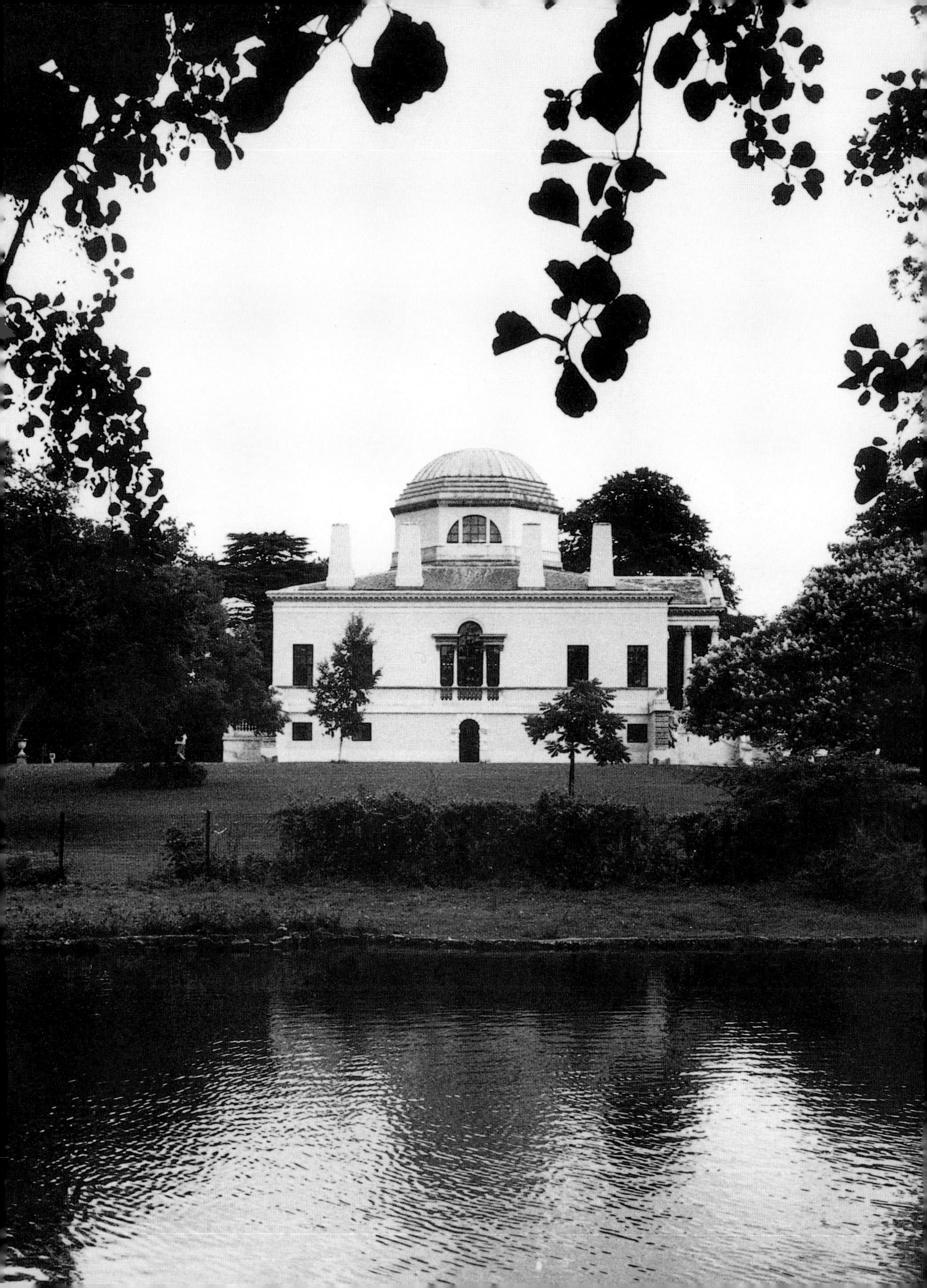

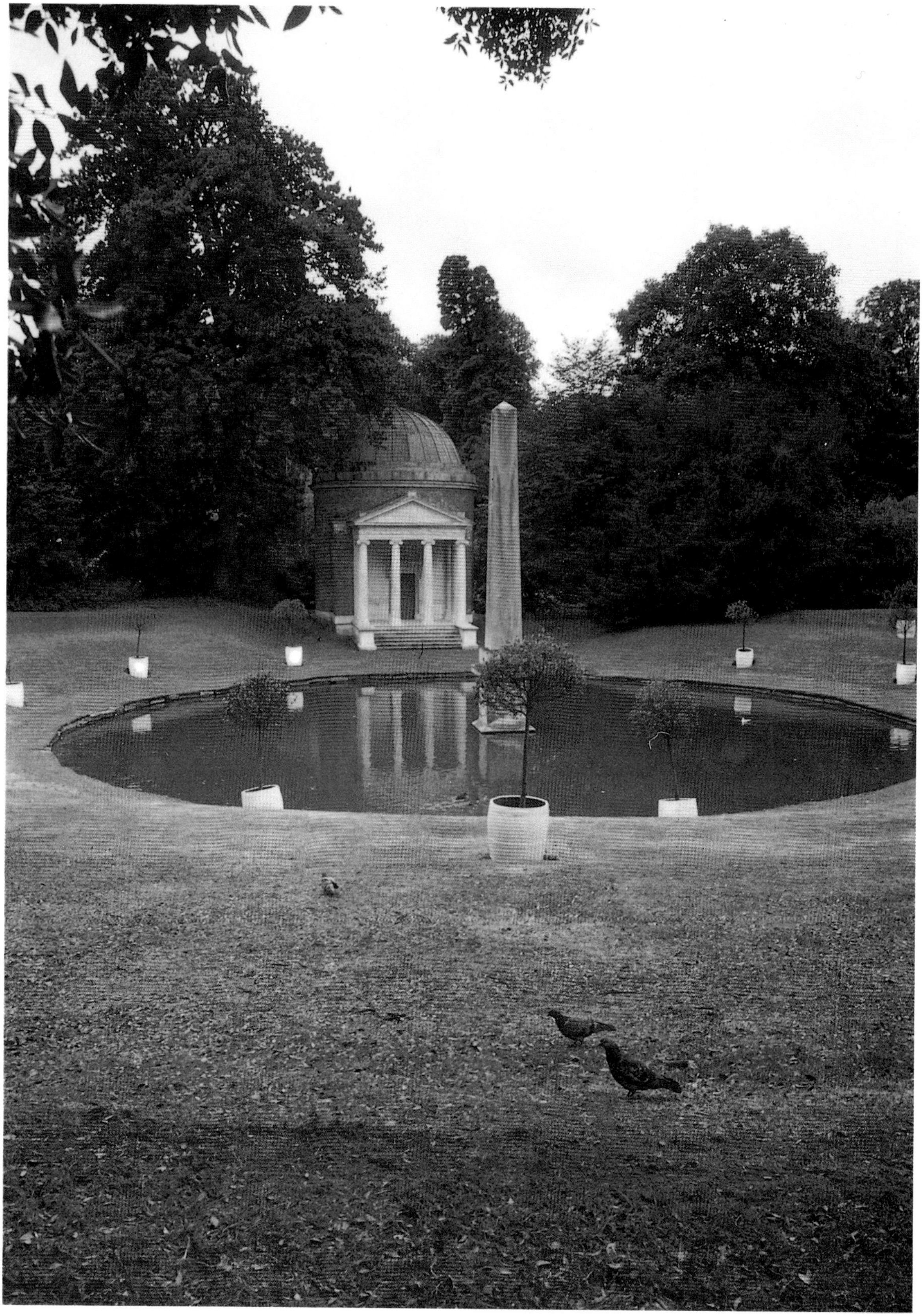

Like Burlington, Kent was enamoured of Palladian architecture, and of the picturesque paintings of Claude and Poussin, of half a century earlier. In his great garden designs, like Chiswick House, these influences are strongly felt. Kent created idealized Italian scenes in the English countryside, using water, grass, trees, statuary and temples. These were all strategically placed, so a walk through a Kent garden became a series of surprises. He succeeded in removing much of the stiffness and formality which characterized gardens of the time, with their knots and Dutch topiary, and added a note of romanticism. This natural style, created by Kent, and its influence over succeeding generations, has led to his being acknowledged as the first true landscape gardener – a title later taken by more famous names, Lancelot 'Capability' Brown and Humphry Repton.

The gardens at Chiswick were the first in England that were inspired by the Italian landscape. As such, they did not entirely escape the formality associated with the age of Sir Christopher Wren, as seen, for example, at Hampton Court. The canal-like lake and avenues are formal features, but here softened by a serpentine margin and a less geometric arrangement. The various buildings and statues are also more freely arranged; they are not necessarily focal points but are just 'happened upon', the element of surprise thus being introduced.

Any tour must begin with the house; this small but beautifully proportioned building is best approached from the main entrance on Burlington Lane. A broad avenue flanked by cedars leads through two fine gate-pillars into a courtyard enclosed by box hedge, and lined at intervals with busts on pedestals. The house is open to the public and worth the small charge for admission. The interior is elaborately decorated with ornate plaster ceilings and much sumptuous gilding.

On the other side of the house the garden front looks over a lawn of urns and sphinxes in the shade of magnificent cedar trees. At the end of this lawn is a feature called an exedra. This is a semi-circular expanse of turf with a hedge forming the curved boundary. Some of the statuary which was originally placed here is now sadly missing. Parallel to the lawn is a path which splits into three avenues next to the exedra. The avenue straight ahead, once known as the 'Grande Allée', used to lead to a grand domed pavilion; the one to the left to a pavilion by the bridge over the lake. Neither of these buildings survives, and the avenues have become indistinct. The right-hand avenue which runs to the north-west is largely intact and terminates at the Rustic House, a small building whose three niches once contained statues. There were originally two other vistas from the end of the path, one of a Doric column, the other of the Deer House. Both these structures remain but are now not approached by straight avenues but by winding paths through shrubbery. It is interesting to imagine what the garden must have been like when first completed; it is certainly not how Kent left it. Apart from anything else the trees have grown. But it has a great deal of charm, and is certainly full of the romance he intended.

Taking the left-hand avenue towards the lake, one of the garden's most attractive features comes into view. This is the Ionic temple, beyond a circular pond from which rises a small obelisk; around the pond is a turf amphitheatre. This dramatic feature is

Opposite: **The Ionic temple and pool, typical of the classical splendour of Chiswick House**

occasionally put to good use during the summer as a venue for concerts and plays. On a misty autumn morning this is a most magical place. Continuing down the avenue, on the left is a lawn which is home to several types of waterfowl. The lawn borders the lake, which is crossed by a bridge at the end of the avenue. James Wyatt designed the classical stone bridge in 1788 to replace a wooden one which had deteriorated. By this time the property was owned by the fifth Duke of Devonshire, who employed Wyatt to demolish the Jacobean mansion and enlarge the villa. Two wings were added, the north one completely engulfing the link building. The building was restored to its original proportions in the 1950s when it was discovered that the later additions were in such a bad state of decay that it was not worth repairing them.

Three more avenues once radiated from the west side of the bridge. Two have completely disappeared but the third leads to a large obelisk, the base of which incorporates a Roman tombstone. From here two more avenues point towards the temple across the lake and the cascade at the end of the lake. The cascade once had an engine which pumped water over the rocks and back down to the lake. Just beyond the cascade is the courtyard of the house, our starting point.

The lake is 2,000 feet long and sixty feet wide; it thus has the dimensions of a canal. Unlike the Long Water at Hampton Court, however, it is not a regular shape nor has it grass right up to its edge. Trees, shrubs and wild herbs grow naturally round it, making it an informal feature as Kent intended. The whole of the garden just described is a woodland area of trees and shrubs, quite dense in places. The avenues are the main routes through it and the buildings and other structures its clearings. There are also many small winding paths through the shrubbery where it is a pleasure to lose one's bearings as there is a surprise around every corner.

Returning to the garden front, walk past the house. Ahead is a gateway by Inigo Jones, salvaged from Beaufort House in Chelsea by Lord Burlington and re-erected here. To the right of the gateway a path leads to the café. To the left a path leads into the Italian Garden. With the return to formality in garden design during the last century the sixth Duke of Devonshire had this area of regular flower beds, path and statuary constructed. This garden is large and the beds boldly planted in spring and summer. There are two particularly fine trees here, a maidenhair tree (*Gingko biloba*) and a monkey puzzle (*Araucaria araucana*), both popular Victorian plants.

On a terrace facing the display of bedding plants is a large conservatory; this, too, was constructed during the nineteenth century. The entrance takes you into a central rotunda, two long wings of which stretch off to the left and right. Both wings have beds on the side of the back wall and tiered stone slabs on the side of the glass. The beds are full of magnificent camellias, all named, which make a superb display in March and April. On the slabs are kept fuchsias and geraniums, which are at their best in summer. There are hanging baskets containing these plants throughout the conservatory. The central rotunda also has plumbago, cordyline and other typical conservatory plants. At the rear of the rotunda is a large bay with brick walls and ceiling, in which there are some benches.

At a summer Saturday event, organized by the dedicated Friends of Chiswick House, I was fortunate enough to chance upon a trio playing classical music in this bay to an appreciative audience, sunning themselves in the rotunda. Chiswick is full of surprises and a good place to visit at any time of year. Because of their design the gardens never look dull. The extensive evergreen shrubbery, the magnificent cedars and the other coniferous trees provide interest even in the middle of winter; likewise, the buildings and statuary.

FENTON HOUSE

Fenton House is a gracious mansion in the heart of Hampstead. It was given its name by either Philip Fenton or, more probably, his son James, who made changes to the building in the early nineteenth century. It dates originally from 1693. Lady Binning bought the house in 1936 and on her death in 1952 left the house and a collection of furniture, paintings and porcelain to the National Trust. The house also contains the Benton Fletcher collection of musical instruments, which was given to the Trust in 1937. If you are lucky you may hear a harpsichord, spinet or virginal being played. This adds to the informal atmosphere of this delightful house, which is regularly open to the public.

The garden of Fenton House: a charming oasis of greenery in Hampstead village

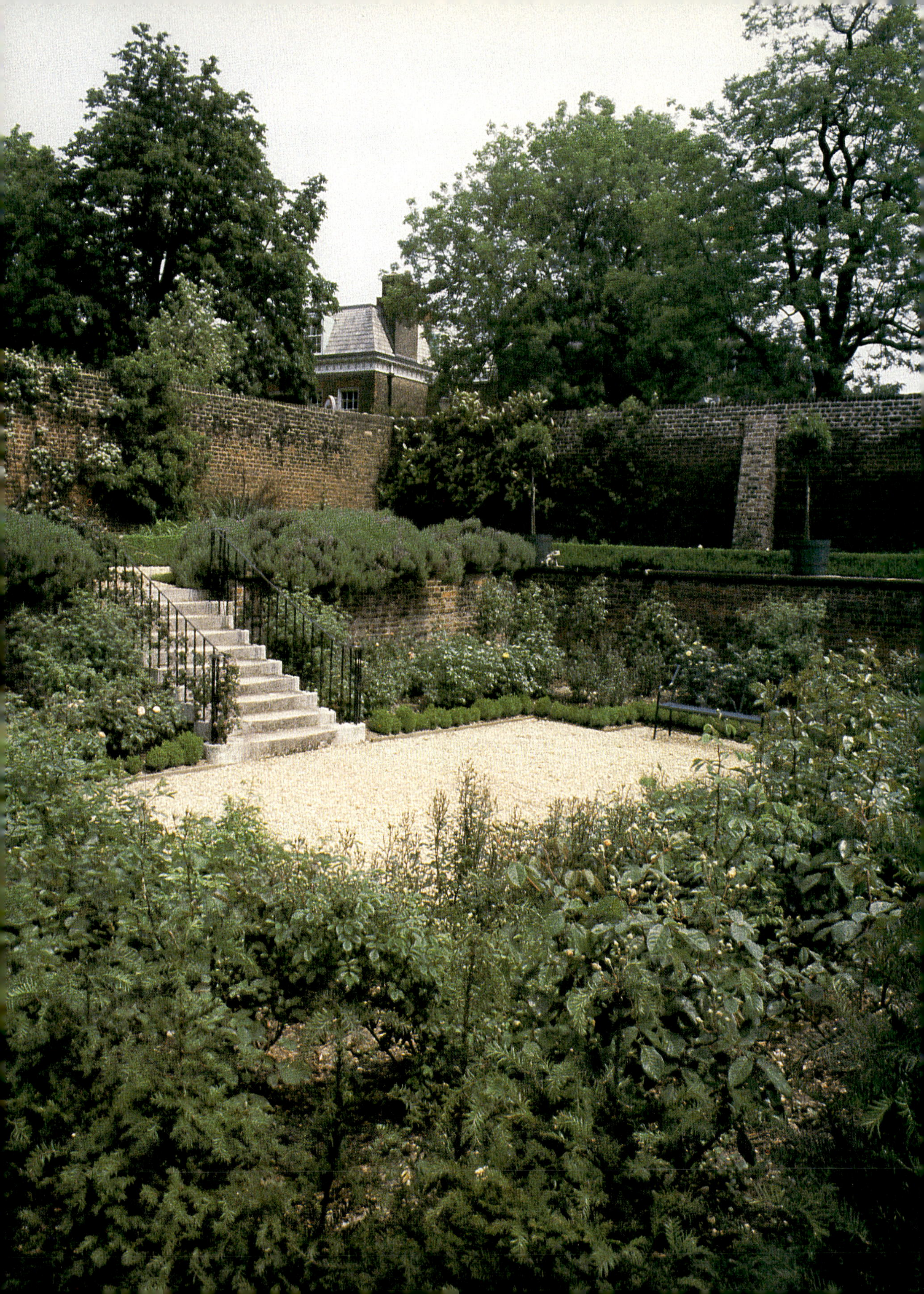

The garden is just as charming as the house and makes a worthwhile excursion when visiting Hampstead Heath. It is in Hampstead Grove, a short walk up the hill from the tube station. The original main entrance to the house was through the wrought iron gate on Holly Hill. This gate, dating from 1707, is of exceptionally high quality and may have been made by Jean Tijou or one of his pupils. Tijou was the craftsman of the screens at Hampton Court. From this gate you cross a lawn with some trees to reach the south front of the house. The alterations to the house made by James Fenton in the early 1800s made the east front into the main entrance. The front door is now reached through a wrought iron grille on Hampstead Grove.

The garden, which extends to the north of the house, is enclosed by high brick walls. Above the walls can be seen many large trees and glimpses of typically attractive old Hampstead houses. On entering, turn right and you are immediately on a gravelled terrace. This runs the length of the eastern wall and was probably part of the original seventeenth-century layout, made to overlook a sunken parterre. Spaced along the edge, overlooking the lower garden, are ten standard ball-headed *Prunus lusitanica*, grown in tubs. They immediately give the garden an impression of elegance, as befits the house. But, like the house, the garden is never formal, and the further in you go the more it becomes like a country garden; in fact, it ends in a vegetable patch. The garden is large for London and so can accommodate a series of features and a good variety of plants without seeming cluttered.

The wall which shelters the garden from Hampstead Grove is covered in a variety of ornamental climbers, including honeysuckle. The bed at its base is edged with low box hedges, and filled with dianthus and rosemary. All these plants are scented; the whole garden smells delicious throughout the summer.

The terrace walk turns left along the northern wall and is here edged with lavender – more scent. A flight of steps with wrought iron handrails leads to the lower level, below the terrace. At the base of the steps is a neat group of rose beds edged with box – again, more scent. Beyond the roses and stretching up to the house is a lawn. To the right of the rose beds a path leads to some more steps and, through a wall, into an even lower area of the garden. Here the garden is less formal, with a greater mixture of plants. A bed below a south-facing wall is planted with evergreen shrubs such as *Garrya elliptica*, herbaceous plants and roses.

The main part of the garden is taken up by a lawn planted with mature fruit trees. Gravel paths run either side of the lawn; parallel to one is a bed of lily-of-the-valley. There is also more box in this part of the garden, the smell of which seems to be particularly intense here, as though trapped by the walls and trees. The nostalgic smell of box seems to be either loved or hated. Queen Anne hated it, and had every plant of it removed from Hampton Court. Oliver Wendell Holmes in *Elsie Verner*, published in 1861, viewed it more romantically as 'one of the odours that carry us out of time into abysses of the unbeginning past; if ever we lived on another ball of stone than this, it must be there was box growing on it'. Like it or not, it is perfect in this garden.

Opposite: The garden of Fenton House is on several levels and features many scented plants

At the end of the lawn is the small but carefully planned vegetable patch. A cottage in the south-west corner completes this charming rural scene; London seems far away. Retracing one's steps back to the rose beds, a gravel walk parallel to the raised terrace leads to a small group of trees near the house. At the centre of the trees is a crumbling statue. The path turns left between a group of standard holly bushes and leads to a flight of steps up to the terrace and the garden entrance.

The garden of Fenton House is not a place you will want to leave in a hurry. It is a peaceful haven away from the hustle and bustle of Hampstead, with its trendy shops and restaurants crowded into narrow streets carrying too much traffic. The garden is extremely well maintained, as are all National Trust properties. The Trust advertise the house, but little mention is made of the delightful garden. This is fortunate, because not many people know of its existence and hence it is never very crowded. There is a charge for admission to the house but the garden is free and anyone can make use of it. At lunchtimes in the summer there are often some office workers enjoying a peaceful break. The garden is best seen in June, when the roses and many of the other plants are in full flower.

HAM HOUSE

Ham House is a Baroque villa on the Thames near Richmond, owned by the National Trust. The garden is one of the finest in London – fine, in that it is a stately design, and immaculately maintained. As with Fenton House in Hampstead, advertising concentrates on the house and little is made of the garden; both gardens deserve to be seen. They are very different, but both perfectly complement their houses.

The South Garden of Ham House, based on a central axis, is bold and immense. The chairs are replicas of the seventeenth-century originals

It is particularly important to view the garden at Ham in terms of the house. It has been restored to its seventeenth-century appearance, as has the fabric of the house, the interior decoration and the furnishings. The National Trust claims that the property gives a better view of life in the seventeenth century than any other in the country; the garden is therefore best appreciated from an historical perspective. The geometric design is predictable and possibly boring in isolation, but as living history one expects to see its seventeenth-century creators round every corner.

The East Garden at Ham is geometric and impressive in its simplicity

Ham House was built in 1610 but owes its present look to the Duke and Duchess of Lauderdale who, on their marriage in 1672, doubled the size of the building and decorated the interior sumptuously. It was inherited by the Duchess's son by her first husband and remained in the family until given to the National Trust in 1948. Surprisingly, the building was little altered after the Lauderdales and, more surprisingly, much of the original furniture never left the house because it was stored away. Inventories made in 1677, 1679 and 1683 still exist, and it is these which have made it possible to decorate the house and re-position furniture as it would have been in the time of the Duke and Duchess. It would be a pity to leave Ham without seeing the interior of the house; the Baroque decoration and furnishings are magnificent. Throughout the house are fine English tapestries as well as textiles and embroidery. The paintings include work by Sir Peter Lely, John Constable, Sir Godfrey Kneller and Sir Joshua Reynolds. It is a fine display, and well worth the price of admission.

What the visitor to the garden sees today is not so different from what John Evelyn, the diarist, saw on his visit in 1678:

After dinner I walked to Ham to see the House and Garden of the Duke of Lauderdale, which is indeed inferior to few of the best Villas in Italy itself, the house furnished like a great prince's; the Parterres, Flower Gardens, Orangeries, Groves, Avenues, Courts, Statues, Perspectives, Fountains, Aviaries, & all this at the banks of the Sweetest River in the world, must needs be surprising.

In 1975, as a contribution to European Architectural Heritage Year, the National Trust decided to restore the gardens to the south and east of the house to their late seventeenth-century appearance. Just as the house and its contents had remained little changed since this time, the 'bones' of the original garden could still be identified, although overgrown and planted with inappropriate species such as rhododendrons. The restoration, completed in 1979, has been meticulously carried out. The garden today is a fascinating indication of the taste and style of the late seventeenth century.

The house and garden are entered on the north front. The visitor is immediately confronted by a melodramatic statue of a river god, made of Coade stone. Coade is a name often mentioned in guides to historic houses, without explanation. It is in fact an artificial stone invented in 1769 and made at Lambeth.

The river god is the centrepiece of a walled forecourt to the house. Oval niches in the walls contain busts of Charles I, Charles II, Roman emperors and other noteworthy people. The busts continue on the front of the house – a rather unusual form of ornamentation, but one which links the house and garden. Here, too, are well-manicured lawns and closely clipped shrubs, emphasizing the architectural nature of the whole forecourt. This strong, bare style is even more evident in the gardens to the south and east of the house. Plants are used as the building blocks of the design, which is definitely not geared to display plants to their best advantage. Straight lines, gravel paths and rigorous clipping and pruning of plants is very much the order of the day.

The South Garden is entered by a small gate in a wall on the west side of the house.

Opposite: The gardens at Ham House are stately in design and immaculately manicured

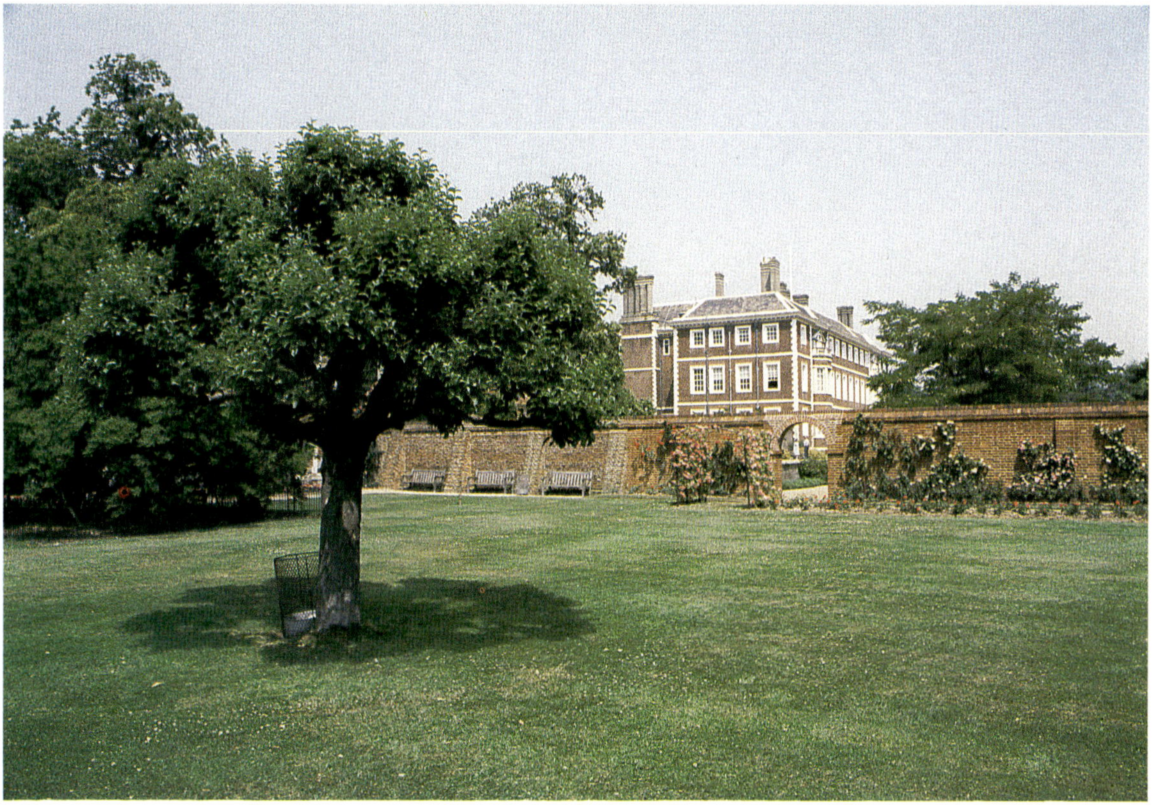

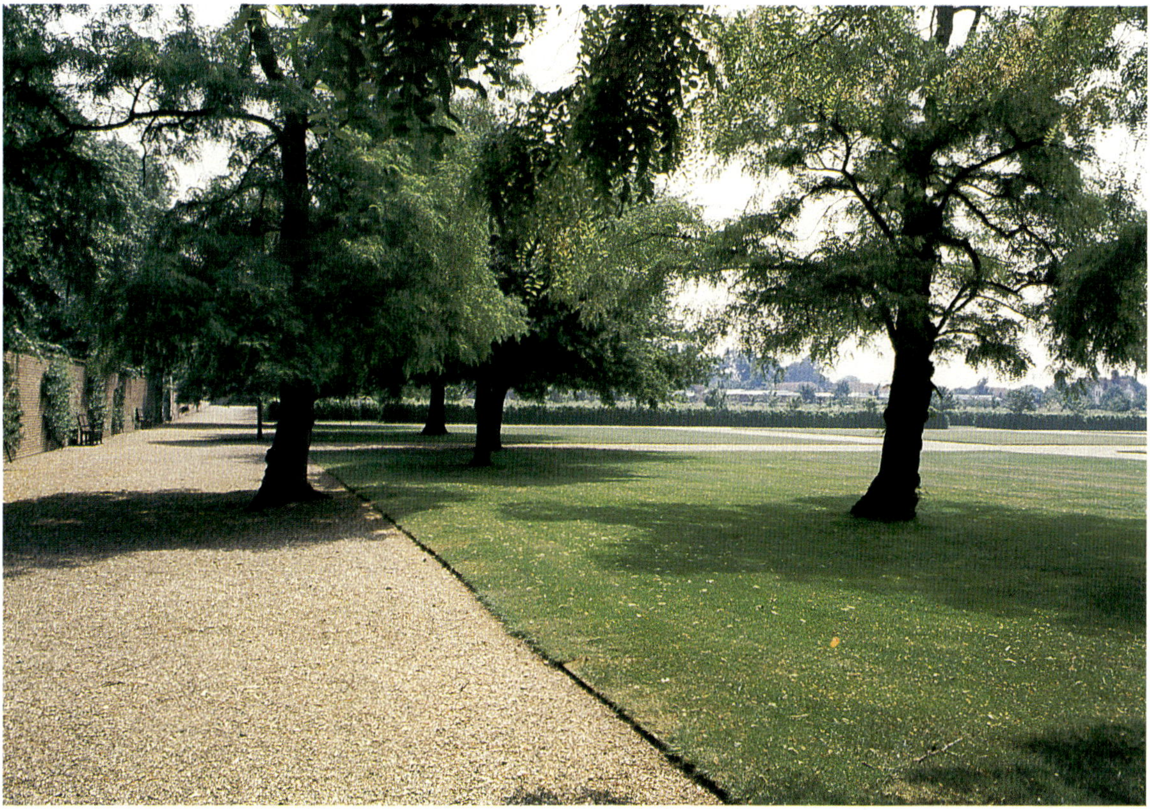

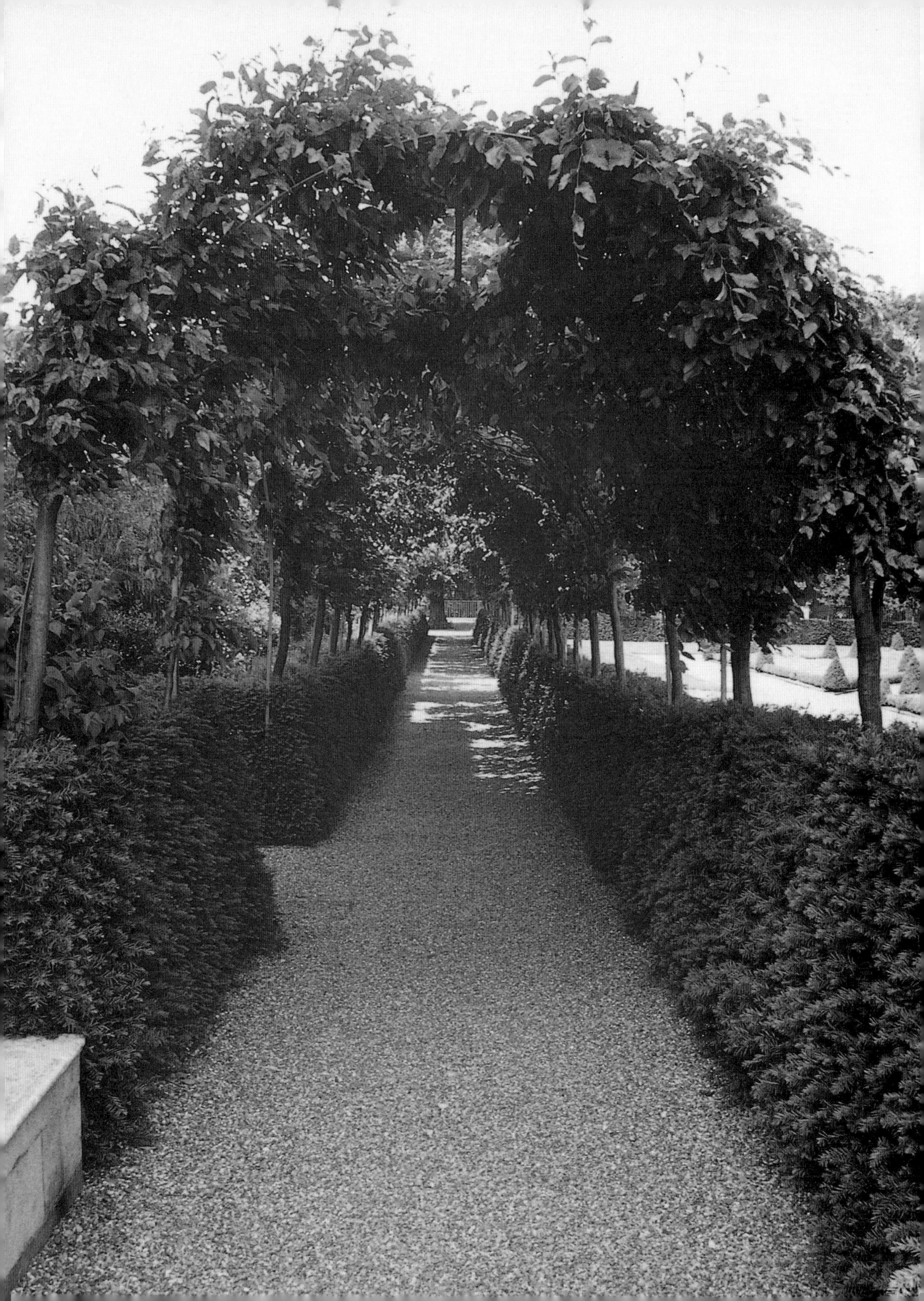

Immediately the bulk of the garden is before you, bold and immense. Below a wide gravel terrace which fronts the house are eight square lawns or plats divided by gravel paths, and beyond this the Wilderness, which is hardly wild at all. It is a geometric pattern of grassy paths and enclosures of hornbeam hedging (*Carpinus betulus*). Surrounding the whole garden is a high brick wall.

Baroque planning was based on a central axis, and this applied to both the house and the garden. From the terrace, at the centre of the house, the garden is laid out symmetrically, on either side of the central axis – through the plats, the Wilderness and its clearing, and beyond through the south gates in the wall to an avenue of trees and Ham Common beyond. The central clearing in the Wilderness has eight chairs and eight complementary square tubs with bay bushes clipped into rounds. The high-backed chairs are replicas of those that stood here in the seventeenth century. Also here at that time were eight statues. A painting in the White Closet of the house shows the formal garden very clearly. It is entitled 'Ham House From the South' and is attributed to Henry Danckaerts (c. 1675).

The hornbeam hedges in the Wilderness are planted with standard trees of field maple (*Acer campestre*). Four of the enclosures formed by the hedges contain summerhouses, reproducing those in an engraving of 1739. The engraving, in *Vitruvius Britannicus* by Colin Campbell, gives a bird's-eye view of the house and grounds. Except for grass paths through the enclosures, they are left unmown to encourage wild flowers; this is as wild as the garden gets.

The wall surrounding the garden is broken by south, east and west gates, all dating from 1675–6. The south gates have an overthrow with the Tollemache coat of arms and motto, '*Nemo Me Impune Lacessit*' – No Man Can Harm Me Unpunished. Tollemache was the name of the Duchess's first husband. Along the south wall is a line of large clipped holly bushes. On the east wall are several trained fruit trees, including apple, plum and fig; all are labelled, and all the varieties date from the seventeenth century.

Returning to the house below the gravel terrace is a border mainly of different sages and rosemary, and also ornamental vines. A border edging the gravel terrace and along the front of the house contains massed lavender, dianthus, aster, phlomis and hibiscus. These all add welcome colour and scent to the garden, and are all in keeping with the policy of stocking the garden with plants known in the seventeenth century. On the terrace and throughout the garden are high-backed plain wooden benches of a type contemporary with the garden. On the north front of the house are two such benches c.1675, listed in the inventory of 1679 – a good example of how Ham remains unchanged.

The East Garden is entered from the gravel terrace. On two sides of the square are arbours of hornbeam, the trees forming an arch overhead. The central area, a parterre of box hedges, is surrounded by a larger hedge of yew (*Taxus baccata*). The beds are filled with cotton lavender (*Santolina chamaecyparis* 'Corsica'). There are also cones of box (*Buxus sempervirens suffruticosa*). A designer's garden, the plant material could not be more limited. The effect is very striking; individual plants do not matter.

Opposite: **A formal arch of hornbeam beside the East Garden at Ham House**

Back to the South Garden and through the gateway in the west wall. Here is the Ilex Walk, at the centre of which is a naked Bacchus, dating from 1672. This walled garden, now principally roses, is the site of the former kitchen garden. The walls are covered in a variety of climbing roses, and there are beds of bush roses too. At the base of the climbers are some beautiful peonies. This garden is best seen in June. There are some fine old trees here too – Christ's thorn (*Paliurus spina-Christi*), Judas tree (*Cercis siliquastrum*) and a western red cedar are the best. At the north end of this garden is a pleasant tea room in part of the old orangery. In summer tables and chairs are placed on the finely cut lawn, facing the roses and Bacchus. A lovely place to end a tour of this most elegant of gardens.

The garden of Ham House is a fascinating piece of history, its design, plants, statues and even furniture contemporary with the house. In terms of formality one thinks of Hampton Court, just down the river. But here there are no bedding plants, fountains, canals or royal associations to draw the crowds. Ham has a stylish simplicity which is very relaxing. It is a mystery why more people do not take advantage of this garden. It is never very busy at weekends and almost deserted during the week, even in the hottest June weather.

But of course it is not necessary to visit this garden in high summer. Its strong architectural design makes it just as stunning when there are no flowers out or leaves on the trees. Indeed, the hornbeam leaves turn brown in the autumn but remain on the trees until the new foliage appears in the spring, so the Wilderness looks much the same all year, as does the East Garden which is mainly evergreens. But visiting in summer one cannot help feeling superior, knowing that Hampton Court is seething with thousands of visitors.

What makes Ham even more attractive as a place to visit is its location. It is on the south bank of the Thames, between Richmond and Twickenham, surrounded by meadows, playing fields and many fine trees, which give it a very rural appearance. It is accessible by car but the most pleasant way to approach it is along the towpath by the side of the river from Richmond through Petersham Meadows. This is a beautiful stretch of the river and it is easy to spend time idling on its banks; but make Ham your objective. Admittedly, the garden may not be to everyone's taste; it could not be called pretty, but it is striking and deserves to be seen at least once.

THE HILL

The most impressive part of this Hampstead garden is overgrown and neglected, and I hope it always remains so.

The long classical pergola walk, raised high above the ground with its balustrades and pavilions, is swagged in a profusion of climbing plants. Weeds grow through the paving; iron gates are locked and rusting; below is a kitchen garden, uncultivated for decades; a greenhouse with broken glass becomes each summer more shrouded by the leaves of sycamore trees, which are growing out through it. The whole place has a great

An imposing pavilion on the pergola walk at the Hill

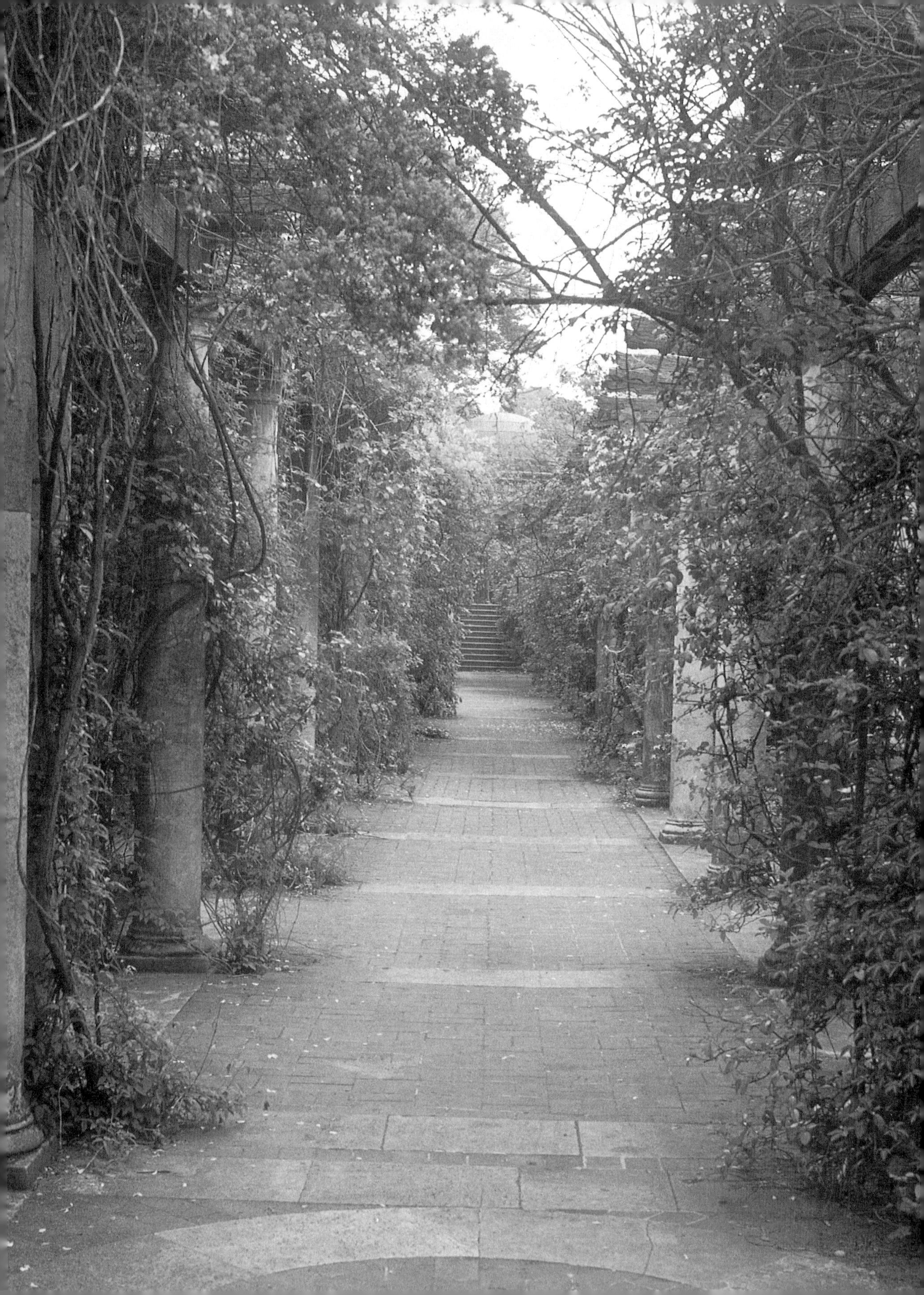

atmosphere of Time Past, and it is easy to be overcome by its romance. A Victorian poet such as Tennyson could have had a field day. One thinks of his images of decay in his 'Mariana':

> With blackest moss the flower plots
> Were thickly crusted, one and all:
> The rusted nail fell from the knots
> That held the pear to the gable wall.

But Tennyson could not have visited this garden: it was built in the 'golden afternoon' of the Edwardian era. It is a pleasure to imagine how it would have looked in the first decade of the century and to think of the lives of the people who created and enjoyed it. The Hill must have been a superb garden in its day. It still is, but not in the way originally intended, for it is now London's most romantic and 'secret' garden – a romantic notion in itself.

The Hill is part of Hampstead Heath, and one of the best reasons for visiting it. Like Golders Hill and Kenwood, it is quite distinct from the rest of the Heath – a pleasantly cultivated, or rather semi-cultivated, few acres in the wilderness and isolation of the West Heath. Like almost everything else in Hampstead, the garden is on a hill – and, rather unimaginatively, that is how it got its name.

Opposite: **The Hill's pergola is covered in many kinds of climbing and wall plants**
Above: **The pergola walk is reminiscent of the Alhambra or an Italian villa**

The Hill was created at the turn of the century by Lord Leverhulme, begetter of Sunlight Soap, who owned the adjoining house, now a private hospital. He employed an architect, Thomas A. Mawson, to design the garden, which may explain why its most important feature is an architectural one, the wood-and-stone pergola walk. The classical design of the garden has been likened to the Alhambra or an Italian villa. Lord Leverhulme died in 1925, and the gardens became part of the Heath in 1959.

The garden is reached from Inverforth Close, a small leafy road which turns off North End Way, one of the main roads over Hampstead Heath which joins Hampstead village, to the south, with Golders Green to the north. A gate leads into an unremarkable area of shrubs and herbaceous plants, but beyond is a tantalizing view of the garden as it opens out beyond a formal pool and the pavilion at the beginning of the pergola walk. This is the part of the garden any visitor should make a bee-line for. Take the wide gravel path, edged with yellow yew and balustrades, towards the pool; already the garden is 'architectural'. The path becomes a terrace, and steps lead down to the large oblong pool which is surrounded by a stark area of paving. Growing in the pool itself are some yellow iris and pink water-lilies, which provide colour during the summer.

Approach the pavilion, and climb its stairs. From here there are lovely views over the pool and immediate garden; the Heath and Harrow-on-the-Hill are in the distance. At the back of the pavilion is the first lengthy stretch of the pergola walk, inviting the visitor to see where it leads and what is at the end. The Doric columns seem barely able to support the honeysuckle, wistaria, roses and other climbing plants, which look as if they have remained unchecked for years; now, they almost completely cover the pergola, making it dark and mysterious in parts. The wistaria positively strangles the columns with its thick grey stems; some are almost as big as the columns themselves.

There is only one way to go along the walk, although there are a couple of dead-ends which may frustrate you. But it does not matter; this is the sort of place which it is fun to explore. Where did that gate lead to? There must have been a statue in that niche; what happened to it? What were all the greenhouses and buildings below used for? One inevitably looks at the present and thinks of the past.

There is a great variety of climbing plants and wall plants along the walk including chaenomeles, ceanothus, clematis and solanum. One of the most delightful is *Cytisus battandieri*, which has pineapple-scented flowers in summer. Most of the plants here flower in summer, so this is the best time to visit the garden.

The walk continues up and down steps and through a stone pavilion which provides seats and shelter. This first stretch of the walk eventually leads to the garden at the front of the house; here it turns sharply to the right. The house lies in its own private garden, which is never open to the public. It contains some lovely features, such as a double stairway with balustrades, terraces, and an empty and decayed pool. But the clipped privet is now out of proportion and the rest of the plants look a little sad. The only 'survivors' are the cedars and other specimen trees, which seem only to improve with age and neglect. Did the garden's creators have tea on the terrace or the lawn?

Opposite: **The Hill, London's most secret garden**

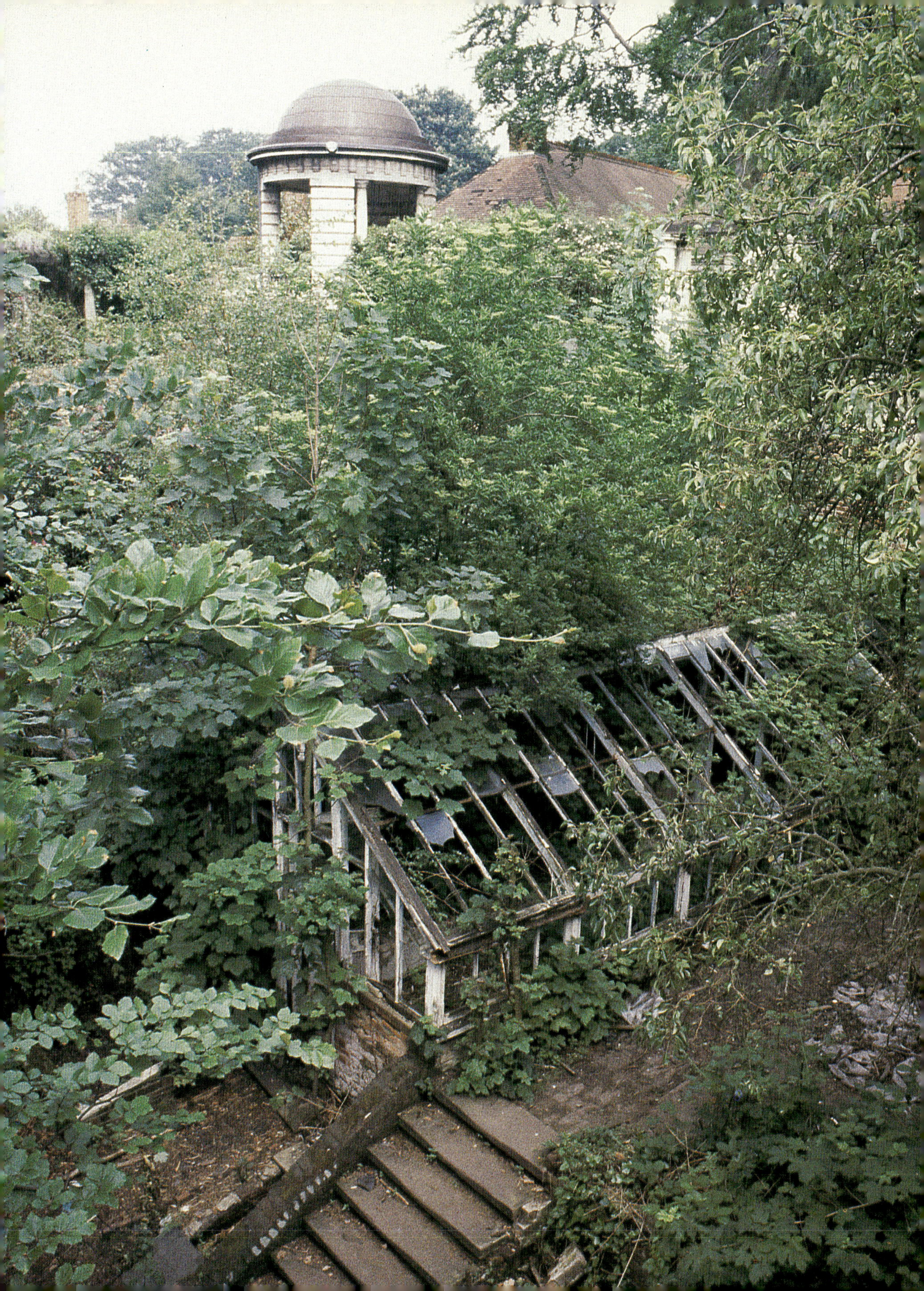

On along the walk; below on the right is the former kitchen garden, where nature has taken over with a vengeance. Carrots, potatoes and cauliflowers have given way to sycamore, nettles and brambles; the Heath is reclaiming its own. There are cloistered arches here, below the walkway, which look very strange and invite speculation. Presumably some of these covered areas acted as sheds for the gardeners – hardly a romantic use. Never mind, the pergola walk continues to surprise with ever more different types of plants. *Hydrangea petiolaris*, jasmine and pyracantha are here, each an enormous specimen with a multitude of blossoms. No pruning has been carried out here either to encourage growth or to keep them from choking each other. There is the odd unfortunate which has succumbed to pressure, but nowhere do dead plants seem more in keeping with a place. They honestly do not look amiss, and neither do the nettles, ferns and ivy which have taken over odd corners.

In places where the beams of the pergola are not entirely concealed by climbers, detailed carving is revealed – a reminder of the attention to detail which was a characteristic of life at the turn of the century. Even a pergola merited decoration in

The Hill has a large formal pool and a rich variety of flowering shrubs

Edwardian England. At the end of the pergola walk are some half-concealed steps which lead down to the West Heath. But you will want to walk back the way you came, and soak up the atmosphere once again. I suppose no London garden is truly 'secret', but it is a lovely idea that you can have a place as beautiful as The Hill all to yourself. If you visit here during the week it is possible not to see another living soul. You can walk under the beautiful scented plants and rest in the pavilions to dream of a better age, undisturbed.

Retrace your steps back to that first pavilion above the pool. Beneath it, to the south, is a flight of steps overhung with rhododendrons and other evergreens, a feature typical of many Edwardian gardens. From here a path leads round the edge of a gently sloping lawn which stretches down the hillside from the pool. Here is a dense shrubbery, planted with as rich a variety of plants as the pergola walk – *Cercis siliquastrum*, camellia, mahonia, ilex, pinus. . . the list is endless. The path reaches the southern limit of the garden where gates lead out to the West Heath; then it turns northwards towards the entrance gate. Hydrangea, cotoneaster, rhus, azalea and more edge the path, while there is a large bed of herbaceous plants near the entrance. Among the hellebores, bergenias and tradescantias is an abstract sculpture by Stephen Gilbert. Throughout this part of the garden are many fine trees, notably copper beech.

On sunny days there are usually a few people enjoying this south-facing slope. One elderly couple regularly collar a seat below the sculpture, which has a fine view over the pool and toward that enticing first pavilion of the pergola. They may not thank me for writing about this peaceful garden, but some secrets are meant to be shared. The Hill is one of them.

THE TRADESCANT GARDEN (The Tradescant Trust)

This pretty little garden in the churchyard of St Mary-at-Lambeth is part of Britain's first Museum of Garden History, an exciting and imaginative venture which is the work of the Tradescant Trust. John Tradescant was a seventeenth-century plant collector who travelled to Russia and North Africa – no mean feat in those days. He returned to popularize his own as well as other people's discoveries in gardens belonging to the Earl of Salisbury and Charles I. His son, also John, worked with him from the age of fifteen and succeeded his father as Keeper of the Royal Garden. He inherited his father's passion for plant hunting and made three trips to North America. The family home was known as 'The Ark', a house in Lambeth where the Tradescants created their own garden and housed a large number of curiosities from all over the world. They were both buried in a family box tomb at St Mary-at-Lambeth, which is a main feature of the Tradescant Garden – a fitting memorial to them.

The Trust was founded ten years ago by Rosemary and John Nicholson, who had been saddened by the sight of the then derelict church, a Thames landmark, and the irony of two great British gardeners lying in a churchyard knee-high with weeds. They managed to create enough interest in the church and proposed museum to form a charitable trust and launch a public appeal. Money remains a big problem, as the Trust does not have a regular income but relies on donations and fund-raising events. Likewise, there is a continual struggle against official red-tape, but the Trust seems to overcome all problems and goes from strength to strength, a credit to its founders.

The garden contains features common in seventeenth-century gardens and plants which were either introduced by the Tradescants or would have been known to them.

The central knot garden is outlined in a low hedge of box, and displays a lush collection of herbaceous plants. Germander (*Teucrium chamaedrys variegatum*), *Helichrysum virgineum* and pulsatilla are three of many. The paths of weathered red bricks add character to the garden, as do stone benches, a sundial on a wall and a stone wall-fountain with a trough beneath. At the north-west corner of the garden is the tomb of the Tradescants, which has an epitaph on top and carvings, representing their travels, around the sides; close by is the tomb of Captain Bligh of 'Mutiny on the Bounty' fame. Around the perimeter of the garden are shrub beds with plants like amelanchier, the

The Tradescant Garden in the churchyard of St Mary-at-Lambeth is crammed full of plants popularized by John Tradescant and his son, both keen seventeenth-century gardeners

smoke tree (*Cotinus coggygria*) and sweetbriar or eglantine (*Rosa rubiginosa*). The herbaceous plants are at their best in June but the garden has colour throughout the year. It is interesting to think that a lot of these plants came to be cultivated in this country because of the adventurous spirit of the Tradescants, who lie buried in the garden. They are credited with introducing or popularizing such familiar plants as walnut, plane tree, lupin, Virginia creeper, wandering Jew and many more.

Inside the church, the stonework has been cleaned and the remaining woodwork and monuments are lovingly cared for. This large space has a brightness and warmth which is very appealing. Permanent features are an exhibition on the life and work of the Tradescants, a collection of rare books about plants and gardening, a gift shop and a tea bar. A central space is used for temporary exhibitions, which change monthly; these include the works of artists specializing in botanical studies and aspects of garden history. The Trust organizes many fund-raising events throughout the year, including evening lectures and concerts. Most popular are the Spring Plant Fair, Autumn Craft Fair and Christmas Bazaar. Becoming a Friend of the Tradescant Trust gives you access to London gardens otherwise not open to the public and the opportunity to go on trips to gardens outside London. There is a newsletter giving advance notice of all events and an up-date of the Trust's work and connections with Friends in America and Australia.

Each year the Trust grows a little larger and a little stronger. Its roots are now firmly established and it is beginning to flourish. Plans for the future include a two-storey gallery along the north aisle to display the important collection of rare books, and a conference room. The Trust has always had the support of many interested parties from the Queen Mother down, but what makes it so inspiring is that all the work is done voluntarily. Everything you see at St Mary-at-Lambeth has been achieved by the courage, faith and hard work of people who wanted the idea to come to fruition. They should be proud. The Museum of Garden History is the most exciting and worthwhile venture in 'Green' London.

Heath and Common Land

Hampstead Heath and Wimbledon Common are two of London's wildest places, refreshingly natural and apparently untouched by Man. The Royal Parks apart, they are the two largest areas of open space in the city. Characterized by tracts of open grassland, woods, thickets of gorse, ponds and heath, they are the best places for long walks in areas where it is easy to avoid people and pretend that you are not in London. Bostall Woods, Oxleas Wood, and Barnes Common are some of London's other wild but smaller open spaces whose character is much the same as Hampstead and Wimbledon. Others like Blackheath, Peckham Rye, Streatham Common and Clapham Common have become cultivated and more like parks over the years, but are still valuable breathing spaces. Highgate Wood, Queen's Wood and Tooting Bec Common might also be included in this category as they are wholly or in part 'wild' places. But all these places are open spaces more valuable to their local communities than to casual visitors. This chapter concentrates on the biggest and best, Hampstead Heath and Wimbledon Common, which are worth making an excursion to explore.

HAMPSTEAD HEATH

Hampstead Heath is a sandy, elevated open space in north London. Having said that, it is impossible to describe, understand, or know it well if you are not a resident or a frequent visitor. Unlike a park, it has no easily definable boundaries; in fact, there does not seem to be an agreed figure for its size, accounts varying between 750 and 825 acres. It is divided by main roads and there are private houses in the middle of it. You cannot do a circuit of the perimeter fence because there is not one. A stranger can easily get lost or at best confused.

Of course, all this is part of the charm of Hampstead Heath. It is not a separate place which is simply visited; it is an integral part of life in the area. Ask a group of people who know London what Hampstead Heath is and you could get a variety of answers. Some will think of the village, with its trendy shops and restaurants, while others will think of its famous pubs like Jack Straw's Castle and The Old Bull and Bush. To others it is a wonderland for plants, birds and animals, or Kenwood with its art collection and concert bowl, or a good place to fly a kite or swim in a natural pond. The list could go on and on.

Here no attempt will be made to describe it fully or get to know it well, but below are suggested a few things to do and see there. It is the way all Hampstead's features come together which make it such a pleasurable place to visit. Golders Hill Park, The Hill, Fenton House, Kenwood and one or two of the pubs have been hived off and spoken of in other chapters. Where to begin?

Hampstead first came into the public eye in the early eighteenth century when chalybeate springs were discovered. They were thought to have medicinal qualities, and 'Hampstead Wells' became a popular spa. A lot of houses were built for fashionable people, who enjoyed being able to live in such a pleasant place so close to London. East Heath had always been common land and the rest of the countryside was enjoyed for riding, walking and views over the city. A racecourse was laid out on West Heath. When the spa declined, Hampstead continued to be a favoured place to live and a place of popular recreation.

In 1829 Sir Thomas Maryon Wilson, Lord of the Manor, decided that a fortune could be made by building an estate of villas on his land. Local residents were immediately up in arms, ready to fight any scheme to despoil what they considered their property. The Fenton family, owners of Fenton House, convened a meeting in the Hollybush Inn to protest against building on the Heath. For the rest of his life Wilson tried to defend in Parliament his right to build on his land. But he always failed against the local people, who had the force of usage on their side. Hampstead Heath had been used as a place of recreation for over a hundred years and it was not going to be given up easily. The problem was resolved in 1869 when Wilson died and his nephew and heir sold the land to the Metropolitan Board of Works for £47,000. Since then the Heath has been expanded by the following additions: Parliament Hill (1886), Golders Hill (1899), Hampstead Heath Extension (1906), Kenwood (1927) and The Hill (1963).

In 1889 plans by the London County Council to reorganize the Heath were met with stiff opposition. The result was the formation of the Hampstead Heath Protection Society, which is dedicated to preserving the Heath as a wilderness, albeit a well-used one. There has always been something about Hampstead Heath which people have thought worth fighting for.

The centre of Hampstead village, around the tube station, is a crowded, busy commercial area of cosmopolitan shops and restaurants. Leading off from here in all directions are quaint, irregular streets full of attractive old houses and pubs, dating mainly from the eighteenth and nineteenth centuries and many with literary associations. Lamb, Keats, Shelley and Leigh Hunt all lived in or visited Hampstead. The house in which Keats lived is now a museum to him and his friends. It is called Keats House and is in Keats Grove, near Hampstead Heath British Rail station. Other famous people to have enjoyed the fresh air and country atmosphere of Hampstead include Constable, John Galsworthy, George du Maurier, Sir Herbert Beerbohm Tree and, more recently, Charles de Gaulle. Hampstead and its neighbour, Highgate, are still known as something of a ghetto for the rich and famous.

Whitestone Pond is the highest point of the Heath, being 443 feet above mean sea level. On a clear day there are good views to the south over London, three miles away, which Wordsworth thought looked 'by distance ruralised'. To the north-west seven miles away is Harrow-on-the-Hill, with spired church and public school. The pond is not very attractive, being surrounded by tarmac and at a busy road junction. Model boats are sailed here, as they were by Shelley who used to entertain local children here.

Nearby is Jack Straw's Castle, one of the famous Hampstead pubs. It is named after a friend of Wat Tyler, leader of the Peasants' Revolt, who was hanged just outside the original pub. Dickens often frequented the pub; he had many friends in Hampstead. The pub was completely rebuilt in the 1960s and has an unusual weatherboarded front. On fine days there are good views from here, and drinks and food can be enjoyed in the large courtyard.

The whole of Hampstead Heath is, in fact, subdivided to add to the confusion. West Heath lies behind Jack Straw's Castle; Constable favoured this area and painted views from here several times. This is one of the lesser frequented corners of the Heath; it is thickly covered in oak and birch, with undergrowth of elder and bracken. The Leg of Mutton Pond is a good place to see birds such as Canada geese. The Heath here borders Golders Hill.

Walking east, Sandy Road brings you to North End Way, on which is another of Hampstead's famous pubs. The Old Bull and Bush is an attractive seventeenth-century building, once the home of William Hogarth, the painter and satirist. The pub was made famous in the song sung by music hall comedienne, Florrie Ford. This used to be a popular rendezvous for day trippers from the East End; 'appy 'ampstead on a bank 'oliday was something of a tradition around the turn of the century. The pub has paintings of Florrie Ford outside, and a lot of music hall memorabilia inside. The pub is part of North End, a charming old hamlet.

Sandy Heath was a favourite area of highwaymen such as Dick Turpin. There is no sand left because it was used in the last century to build the railway from St Pancras to the north, and in this century to fill sand-bags during the last war. What is left is a series of sometimes boggy hollows. The Sandy Road of West Heath continues here, ending at Spaniards Road. Being of a harder surface than most heath tracks, it is a good walk to take when the tracks over the Heath are too damp. As well as oak and birch, Sandy Heath has beech and fir trees.

To the north-west of Sandy Heath is an area with the uninspired name of Hampstead Heath Extension. This was acquired as part of the Heath by Dame Henrietta Barnett in 1906. Formerly agricultural land, some of its hedgerows still remain along with ponds, willows and fine oaks. This is another of the least frequented areas of the Heath. Surrounding it is Hampstead Garden Suburb, an idea conceived by Dame Henrietta Barnett and in part designed by Sir Edwin Lutyens.

The attractive-sounding Vale of Health was once a swamp. It lies to the east of Whitestone Pond, at the base of quite a steep hill. It is a small group of houses with many literary associations. D. H. Lawrence rented a room in a house here and wrote *The Rainbow*. There is only one road in and out of the Vale; it passes a large pond. One of the Heath's fairground sites is to the north of the houses.

More confusion, since East Heath is almost in the middle of Hampstead Heath. This is perhaps the most used part of the Heath because it is closest to the village and has a large car park in its southern corner, some pleasant walks near the lakes, and some good views. There are three lakes here, known as the Hampstead Ponds. The first two are used for angling; the third is the Mixed Bathing Pond. East Heath has more open grassland than a lot of the Heath. People come here to picnic, play games with the children or just sit, read, lie, talk, sleep or sunbathe. The car park is the Heath's other fairground site. The fairs are usually there at Bank Holidays and are another reason for this area being so popular.

On the eastern edge of the Heath, along the Highgate boundary, is a chain of six ponds. The second is Highgate Men's Pond, around which you often see boxers training. This is set aside for men to swim in, and sunbathe on its banks. Kenwood Ladies' Pond is the fifth in the chain; this is completely enclosed by trees and very private. The Mixed Bathing Pond on East Heath is also quite private. All three can be crowded throughout the week during the summer, and more so at weekends.

Hampstead Heath is not all scrubland; its ponds are also a beautiful feature and are often overlooked

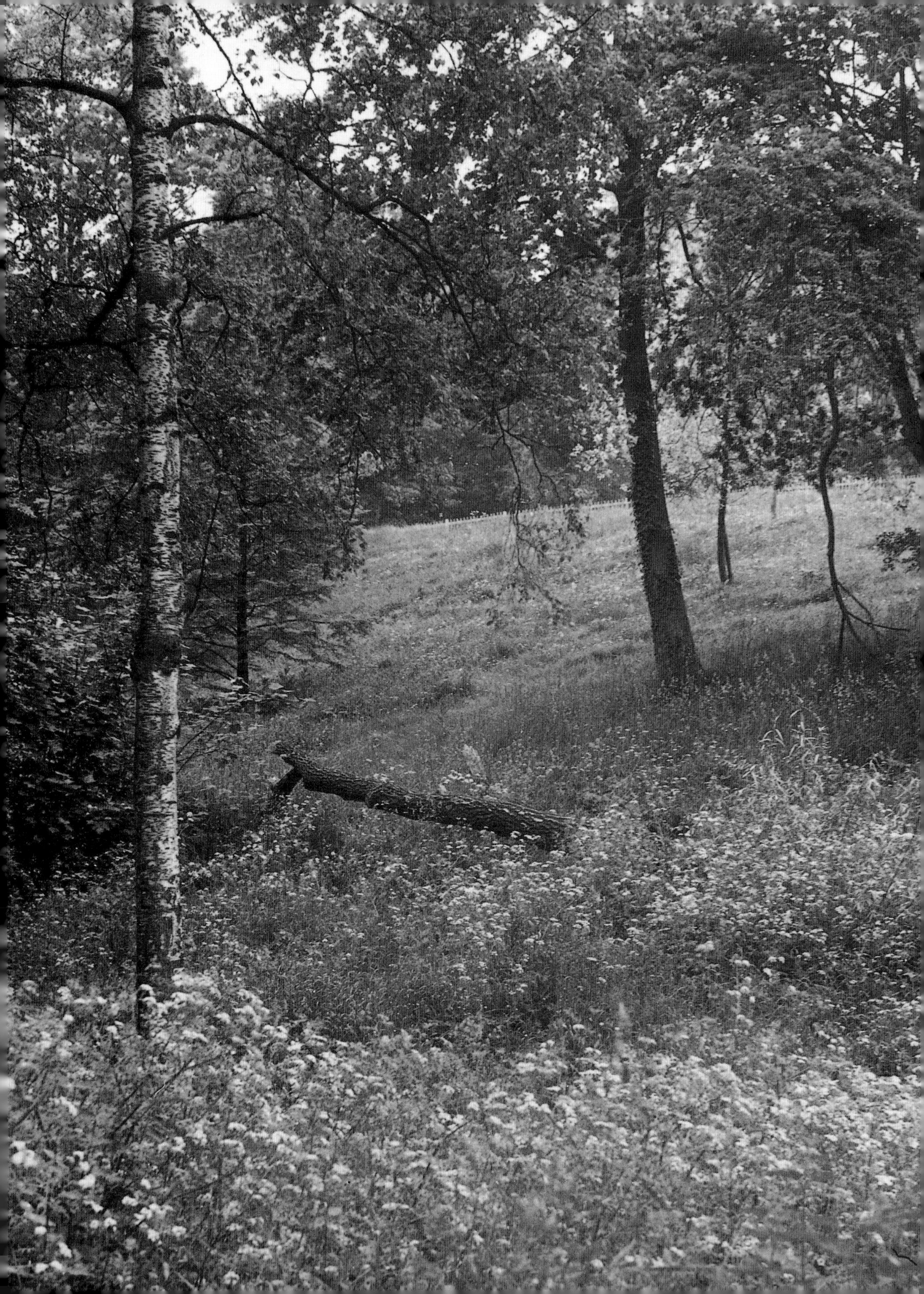

The Heath is keenly guarded by nature lovers; they do much to ensure it is kept as attractive as it is, both as lobbying pressure groups and as active conservationists. Conservation is a question of keeping a balance, without which the Heath could easily become a jungle of sycamore and bramble at the expense of more interesting plants, which in turn attract a greater variety of birds and animals. Likewise, keeping the ponds free of clogging weed and pollution is a full-time job, but necessary to ensure that a variety of aquatic plants, fish and waterfowl survive.

Verdant West Heath at Golders Hill

The GLC, who owned the Heath until 1986, were very responsive to public demand for nature conservation. The fourth lake in the Highgate group is set aside as a bird sanctuary. This very wild space can be seen from a path which divides it from the third lake. There are about eighty kinds of bird known to inhabit the Heath, including kestrels, tawny owls, woodpeckers and crested grebe. The Hampstead and Highgate ponds are full of every kind of fish, making them popular with anglers.

Ten small mammals have been recorded on the Heath, including squirrels, bats and foxes. The squirrels are easily spotted and can be quite tame. Grass snakes are a recent introduction. Plantwise, there are forty tree species and ninety smaller plants. In the sixteenth century the Heath was mostly open, heather-covered moorland, but over the centuries first scrub then trees took over and the heather completely died out. In 1986 heather was re-introduced to the Heath, so it is again complete and its name can be justified!

In 1886 Parliament Hill, sometimes known as Parliament Hill Fields, was added to Hampstead Heath. It got its name because it was the place where Oliver Cromwell regrouped his supporters after Charles I had dissolved Parliament. Kite Hill is a fine viewpoint, 320 feet above mean sea level; in summer there are nearly always people there flying kites, but in winter the hill is given over to ski-ing and tobogganing. At the base of the hill are facilities for organized sports, including an athletics track, a bowling green and tennis courts. There is also a lido and children's playground.

WIMBLEDON COMMON

Walking down Windmill Road towards Wimbledon village, I have to remind myself I am in suburban south London because what I see makes me think I am in the New Forest. I find it strange not to be able to see a building on the horizon; the only sign of civilization is the isolated windmill and its cluster of houses behind me. All around is grassland, heather, gorse and birch. But on Wimbledon Common you have to get used to this: it is possible to walk literally for miles without being reminded that Wandsworth is just up the road. These 1,000 acres are a glorious place to take a country walk.

It is good walking country because it is flat, and that is probably why surrounding suburbia does not intrude. At Hampstead or Richmond, although the land is wonderfully uncultivated, the hills make it possible to see beyond their boundaries – and that means London; not so at Wimbledon. Over most of the common the landscape has less features than Hampstead Heath and is quite unremarkable. But comparisons are invalid; Wimbledon Common is simply a great place to get away from London.

Wimbledon Common is like Hampstead Heath in that its boundaries are a little diffuse. At its north-east corner below the Kingston Road it becomes Putney Heath, the larger part of which is to the north of this road. To the west are un-commonlike playing fields, and Putney Vale Cemetery and Estate. To the south is the Royal Wimbledon Golf Course. Around Rushmere Pond, to the south-east, the common becomes more like a village

Wimbledon Common is famous for its windmill, built in the nineteenth century by a local carpenter. It is excellent walking and riding country

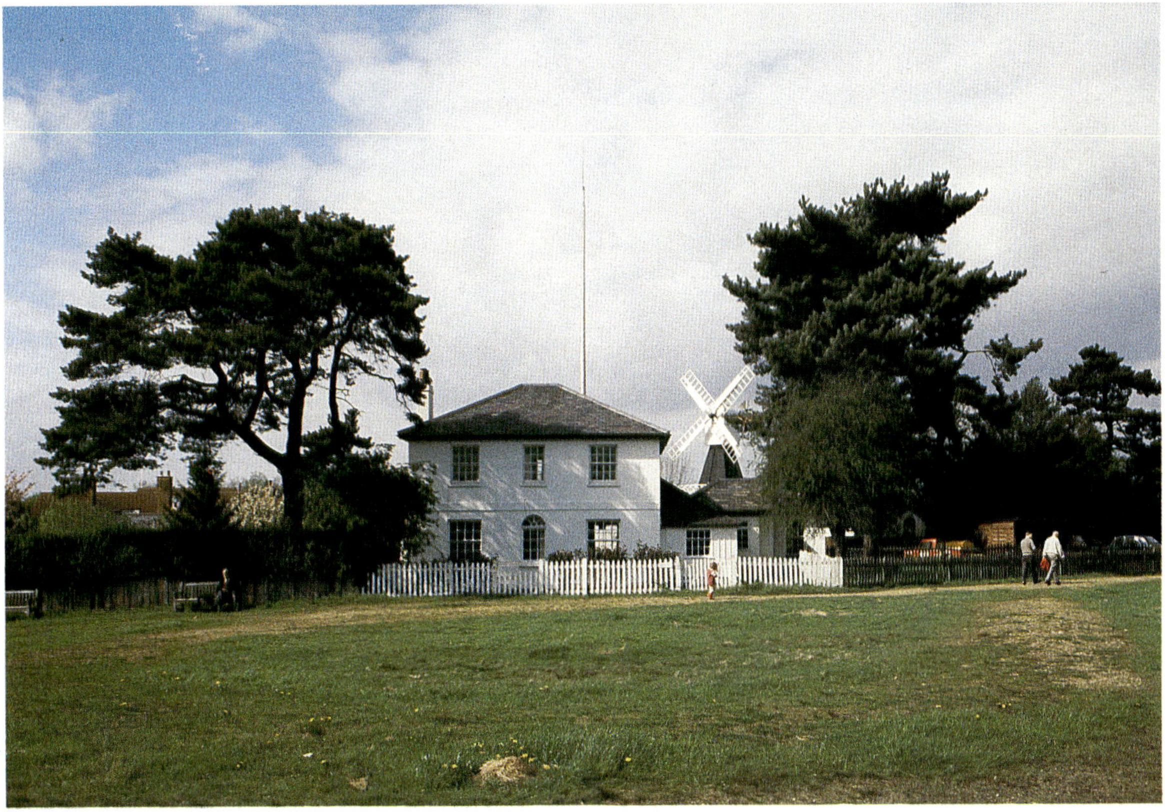

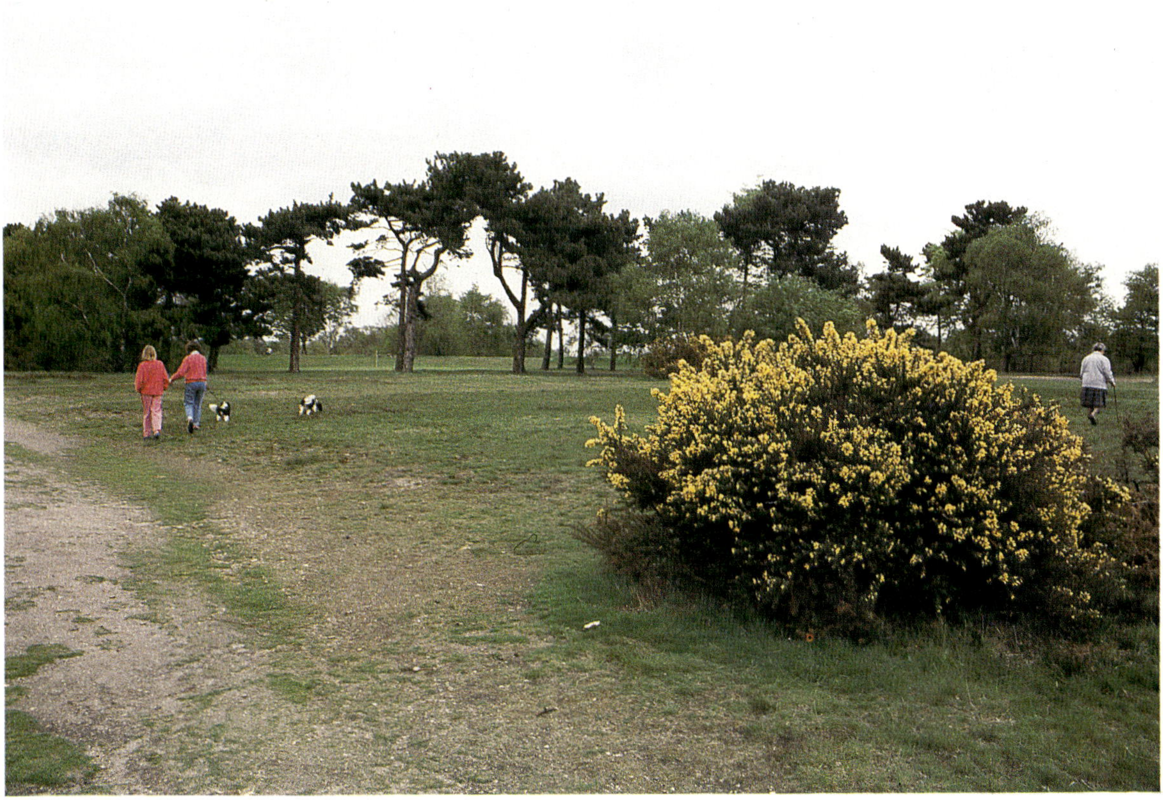

green. Here you will find the main entrance to Cannizaro Park, the grounds of a Georgian mansion, worth a look for its woodland garden and many unusual trees and shrubs.

Evidence of man's presence on Wimbledon Common has been uncovered dating back to the Neolithic Age (c. 3,000–1,000 BC), but it is the people of the Iron Age who have left the greatest mark from early times. 'Caesar's Camp' is a large earthwork on the northern corner of the Royal Wimbledon Golf Course. Its date of origin has been the subject of speculation for about 200 years, but it is now generally agreed to date from about 250 BC. Last century, without modern scientific techniques, the dating of such an earthwork would have been based on analogies, conjecture and probably a little romanticism. The name 'Caesar's Camp' dates from this time – although, like so many earthworks in southern England with this name, it has no connection with any Roman. The earthwork was probably built as a defence into which to retreat for safety from invaders.

Not much is known of Wimbledon Common until 1461, when the records of the Manor Court begin. The Manor Court, presided over by the Steward of the Lord of the Manor, met about three times a year to discuss all aspects of village life, make rules and administer justice. The regulations regarding the common applied solely to the Lord's copyhold tenants, the only people with the right to make use of it. The grazing of animals was monitored because the poor soil could only support a limited number. Other regulations related to the gathering of firewood and the digging of gravel. The records show that the Manor Court strictly administered the use of the common for about 200 years.

From the time of the Civil War in the 1640s, however, the rules and regulations were allowed to lapse and all people living in the area, not only the tenants, began to take advantage of the Common's resources. For the next 200 years it seems to have been ungovernable. Trees were felled without permission; land was enclosed and built upon; rubbish was dumped, and it became a home for gypsies and vagrants. This lonely isolated place was also notorious for highwaymen, and a favourite place for duels.

In 1807, eager to improve the situation, the Lord of the Manor tried to pass a Bill through Parliament giving him the right to enclose the Common. This was rejected because he did not consult the inhabitants. Learning a lesson from this, a later Lord of the Manor, Earl Spencer, first asked permission of the nine remaining copyholders. In November 1864, he won their support for selling Putney Heath and using the money to turn the common into a public park. Everything seemed cut and dried, but he did not count on the opposition presented by a large number of the area's middle-class inhabitants. The question of commons and open spaces was discussed in Parliament and led to a report against Earl Spencer's Bill, which he withdrew. In 1866 the inhabitants of the area formed a committee with the objective of preserving the whole of Wimbledon Common and Putney Heath for the benefit of the public. Lord Spencer continued to assert his rights as Lord of the Manor but by 1870 was beginning to have second thoughts. In 1871 the Wimbledon and Putney Commons Act was passed by Parliament. This placed the commons in the hands of the public in a body called the Conservators. Their responsibility was, and is, to protect the area as a wild open space in perpetuity. Money for preserving and improving the commons is raised by levying a rate on the occupiers of houses situated within three-quarters of a mile from them.

So Wimbledon Common, like Hampstead Heath, owes its existence to local inhabitants' concern for their environment. The Victorians could remember a less urban society and realized the importance to man's physical and mental health of contact with nature and, simply, space. They created new parks and fought bloody-mindedly to conserve heath and common land. Places such as Wimbledon Common do much to improve the quality of life in London.

It seems almost obligatory to begin a walk on Wimbledon Common from the windmill. Here there is a large car park, café and toilets, so not surprisingly most people are drawn to this focal point of the Common. The windmill is reached by a road of the same name, which is really no more than a short track off Parkside, which runs the eastern length of the Common. The road does a sharp left at the windmill and continues towards Wimbledon village. The road has restricted opening but is usually accessible during daylight.

The nineteenth-century composite smock-and-post-type windmill has been beautifully restored. It is open to view on Saturday and Sunday afternoons and contains a small but well-designed museum, with information about its own history and about milling in general. In 1816 Charles March, a Roehampton carpenter, made an application to the Manor Court for some land on which to build a windmill. A year later his request was granted, on condition that he provided a public corn mill for the use of the local people, and building began. The design of the windmill was quite unusual in this country, but seems to have served its purpose.

By the 1860s the March family of Kingston were working the mill. They had a successful business, running both wind- and water-mills in the area. In 1864 Earl Spencer began his campaign to enclose the Common and started to buy as many leasehold and copyhold properties as possible. The March family finally gave in and sold up, but took with them the mill machinery so that it could not be used in competition with their mills at Kingston. The Wimbledon mill ceased to be worked, and Earl Spencer converted it into six small cottages. The building which the Conservators inherited in 1871 was in a poor state of repair, and by 1890 was about to collapse; repairs were undertaken in 1893. In 1952 the mill needed further repairs and in 1974 a major restoration was begun. The Windmill Museum, on the first floor, was opened in 1976.

From the windmill it is possible to do a circular walk which gives a good impression of the Common, taking in open grassland, gorse thickets, dense woodland, the playing fields and one of the ponds – Queen's Mere – and extending as far as Putney Heath. As already mentioned, apart from the windmill there are no major features or places of interest; this is just a lovely place for a walk and some fresh air.

Going along Windmill Road towards Wimbledon village is the part of the Common that reminds me of the New Forest. You almost expect to see a group of ponies appear from behind the gorse and amble over the grass and heather. More likely, it is a group of horse riders along Windmill Ride South, which lies parallel to the road. This ride is one of several on the Common laid down specifically for riding, for which Wimbledon is a popular centre. Besides the rides, which total fifteen miles, there are exercise rings; the great attraction is that the Common adjoins Richmond Park, making an unbroken tract of land which is the best open space for horse-riding in suburban London. A surprisingly large number of people keep their own horses for use on the Common, and there are stables in the village where horses can be hired and lessons booked.

The first half of Windmill Road is one of the most open parts of the Common. Here in August the heather adds colour to the verdant landscape of birch and grass. The land is relatively flat. Interestingly, Wimbledon Common was chosen as an airport for flying in troops and equipment during the Germans' proposed siege of London in the last war. In fact, the area was well used by British forces as an ammunition dump, a practice ground for Bren-gun carriers and for army assault courses. Parts of the Common were planted with vegetables which were tended by Italian prisoners of war, who lived in a camp there. The Common has a long history of military uses; it was particularly favoured by George III, who reviewed his troops here on several occasions. Many volunteer regiments have also been based here, from the time of the wars with France at the end of the eighteenth century to the Home Guard of the last war.

Further south along Windmill Road the trees and scrub edge in and closely line its course. Gorse bushes abound, especially around the road's junction with the Memorial Ride. This shrub is very attractive in early summer when its brilliant yellow flowers are in full bloom. When the road turns to the right it becomes Robin Hood Ride. The exit for cars is to the left, into Camp Road and the village. Be careful, because this area contains a golf course; you may not see the balls but you should see the players who, by order of the Conservators, are obliged to wear a red garment. This rule was made during the last century, when fears were expressed for public safety. In fact, you are frequently reminded of the presence of a golf course by the smooth, perfectly maintained greens which seem so at odds with the woods and grassland.

Just to the south is Warren Farm Ride, which skirts the edge of Caesar's Camp. Robin Hood Ride ends at Beverley Brook, a stream which flows all the way to the Thames. Turning right, Beverley Ride follows the course of the brook. It is this ride which leads to Richmond. Before getting that far take Stag Ride, which marks the boundary of the playing fields, used for organized sports. It may seem strange to be using the horse rides as our guide, but this is the easiest way to get around the Common. They are simple to find and to follow. Of course, if you meet a horse it must have right of way but there is plenty of room so you do not necessarily have to step back into brambles. Besides, I have walked around here on a summer Sunday and not met a single rider. There are usually more people walking, though at this point of our tour even they are rare.

Along Stag Ride the wonderful woodland is a mix of oak, birch, holly, ferns and the odd hazel. In the woods on the right look out for a small railing on a slight rise. This is on the edge of Queen's Mere, one of the common's larger expanses of water. It is still, dark and uninviting, but last century it was apparently popular with gentlemen for naked early morning bathing. Around its edge are some fine beech trees, and at its far end a path that leads up to the windmill. Just to the south is a disused rifle butt, a reminder that from 1860 until 1889 the National Rifle Association had their headquarters on the common. They moved to Bisley because Wimbledon's population grew so dramatically over these years, which greatly increased the danger from stray bullets.

Stag Ride ends almost at Putney Heath. This area is generally more open than Wimbledon Common, there being less woodland and more gorse. It is unfortunately cut in two by the main Kingston Road. The route back is via Windmill Ride North.

The area around the windmill is always the busiest place on the Common. It is round here that most people walk, picnic, fly kites, sunbathe, kick balls and generally kill time. The café, in the shadow of the mill, is always busy, especially at weekends. It serves hot and cold drinks, ice cream, and a variety of rolls, pies and cakes. During the week there is a hot menu of things such as fish and chips and baked beans on toast. There is seating indoors and out. This is good dog-walking country, and the café always has several bowls of water for them on the patio.

Although busy Wimbledon Common always has a relaxed atmosphere; there is plenty of room for everyone. If you are feeling adventurous, stay off the main rides and take some of the seldom-trod paths which criss-cross the Common. It is easy to become disorientated here as there are few landmarks but it is a lovely place to be lost.

The Squares and Inns of Court

An essential characteristic of London is its squares. These formal gardens with iron railings enclosing shrubbery and lofty trees, surrounded by elegant town houses, have no exact counterpart in any foreign city. They have an aura of refined gentility which is very English. Likewise, the Inns of Court are dignified buildings around neat gardens that could be nowhere but England.

THE SQUARES

London's squares are still associated with their eighteenth- and nineteenth-century heyday, when their residential houses were the homes of the fashionable. Belgrave Square is mentioned in Oscar Wilde's social comedy *The Importance of Being Earnest*, when imperious Lady Bracknell is disappointed with Jack Worthing for owning a house on its 'unfashionable' side. Every square, or part of it, did have its day, but increasingly 'Society' vacated the squares and their character changed as homes became shops and offices, and the gardens were opened to the public. Such was the case with Soho Square and Golden Square. There are still traditional squares, however: Eaton, Belgrave and Bedford are classic examples. These all have a wealth of solid well-built houses, which seem to hold their own with dignity even though the streets before them are now busy with traffic. Their gardens are still private, and only the privileged residents have keys. But even though we are kept outside the railings, these squares are open spaces in otherwise monotonous streets and their trees exhale valuable oxygen.

The public squares are a mixed bunch. Some, like Leicester Square, have long since lost any claims which they may have had to gentility. Others, like beautiful, secluded St James's, are as splendid as they must always have been. All have fascinating histories, and provide much needed breathing spaces in congested central London. Here are descriptions of a few of the best.

Fitzroy Square
Not quite in Bloomsbury, an area of London famous both for its squares and for its Bohemian residents, because Fitzroy is on the west side of Tottenham Court Road in the shadow of the Post Office Tower. This handsome square has many fine buildings,

including an elegant terrace by the Adam brothers, built in the eighteenth century. The large garden is, in fact, private but can easily be seen because the railings do not have their usual partner of dense shrubbery. At the south-west corner is 'View', a sculpture by Naomi Blake. Nearby is a house which both G. B. Shaw and Virginia Woolf called home – though not at the same time.

Surrounding the garden is a large paved area where it is pleasant to sit and enjoy the peace of this relatively secluded square (fortunately vehicular access is limited to only the square's north side). Early in the morning I have seen a number of stray cats congregate here to be fed by a kindly American lady. Being out on a limb and free from main roads, Fitzroy Square has the time for such humane gestures. Its neighbouring streets have a friendly atmosphere, and this small London backwater has become to the locals' 'Fitzrovia'. The neighbourhood committee organizes a Fitzrovia Summer Festival, held on a Sunday in July. It is not widely publicized but it is a fun day for all the family, featuring music, street entertainers, food and drink, which is worth tracking down.

Gordon Square and Tavistock Square
To the east of Fitzroy Square and well into Bloomsbury are the twin squares of Gordon and Tavistock. Though built several years apart, they have the same shape and character. Gordon Square has a pretty garden full of flowering trees and roses. The trees around its perimeter have grown so close together that the buildings beyond can hardly be seen when they are in leaf. Though surrounded by roads, none of them is major, so this garden is a quiet haven in which to relax – but only during the week, as it closes at weekends. Lytton Strachey, friend of Virginia Woolf, lived at number fifty-one. Keep an eye open for blue plaques on buildings in Bloomsbury; there are plenty of them.

Just around the corner is Tavistock Square, which appears to have been devoted to peace on earth. At the centre of the garden is a memorial statue to peace-loving Mahatma Gandhi (1869–1948), leading campaigner for India's independence, who was assassinated by a Hindu extremist. Pandit Nehru, Prime Minister of India, on a visit to Britain in 1953, planted a copper beech tree here. In August 1967 the Mayor of Camden planted a cherry tree in memory of the victims of Hiroshima. In 1986 the League of Jewish Women planted a field maple opposite Nehru's copper beech to commemorate the International Year of Peace. There is also a pole with 'May Peace Prevail On Earth' written in German, French and Chinese as well as English. The garden is not unlike its neighbour, but it has a less dense covering of trees and is a little noisier because a main road runs along its eastern edge; a pleasant open space, none the less.

Russell Square
South of Gordon and Tavistock is Russell Square, one of London's largest. It contains a statue of Francis, Duke of Bedford, who built this square early in the nineteenth century and who owned much of Bloomsbury at the time. The garden contains large rose beds, flowering shrubs, evergreens, displays of bedding plants and, most notably, plane trees.

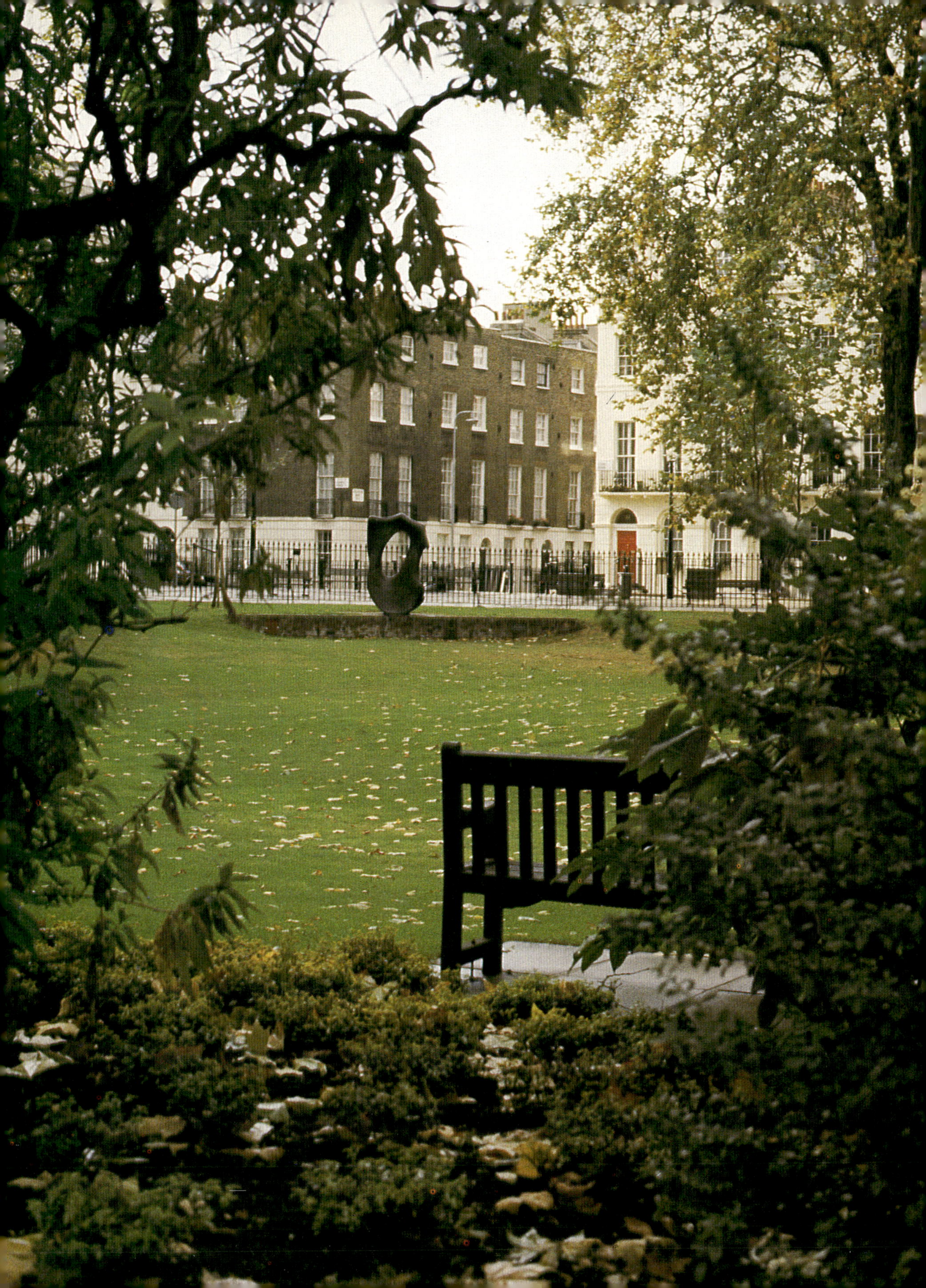

This square is busier than those already mentioned because it is nearer to offices at Holborn, and just round the corner from the British Museum; its best feature is a café.

Montague Place runs west from Russell Square to Bedford Square. Although the garden at Bedford Square is private, the surrounding buildings are well worth a look. In fact, the entire square has a preservation order on it, which means it cannot be altered and must be preserved in the style in which it was built. It is perhaps the most perfect eighteenth-century square in London, its elegant Georgian architecture having survived surprisingly well.

Grosvenor Square

We leave Bloomsbury now for the delights of Mayfair and St James's. Grosvenor Square, another of London's larger squares, was also one of its earliest, dating from 1725. It is dominated by the huge building of the United States Embassy, surmounted by an eagle with a 35-feet wingspan. This occupies the whole western side of the square. The six-acre garden was originally designed by William Kent, but nothing of his famous romantic Italian style remains. It is now an open greensward, criss-crossed by paths with some large plane trees around its edge. There is a bold memorial to President Roosevelt incorporating rose beds, pools and fountains. This is a very popular spot on warm summer days, when it seems that every shop and office worker in the area comes here for lunch. Because of its connections with the United States, the area is popularly known as 'Little America'.

Opposite: Standing in the shadow of the Post Office Tower, Fitzroy Square is one of London's quietest squares

Above: A statue of Gandhi dominates the centre of Tavistock Square, in the heart of Bloomsbury

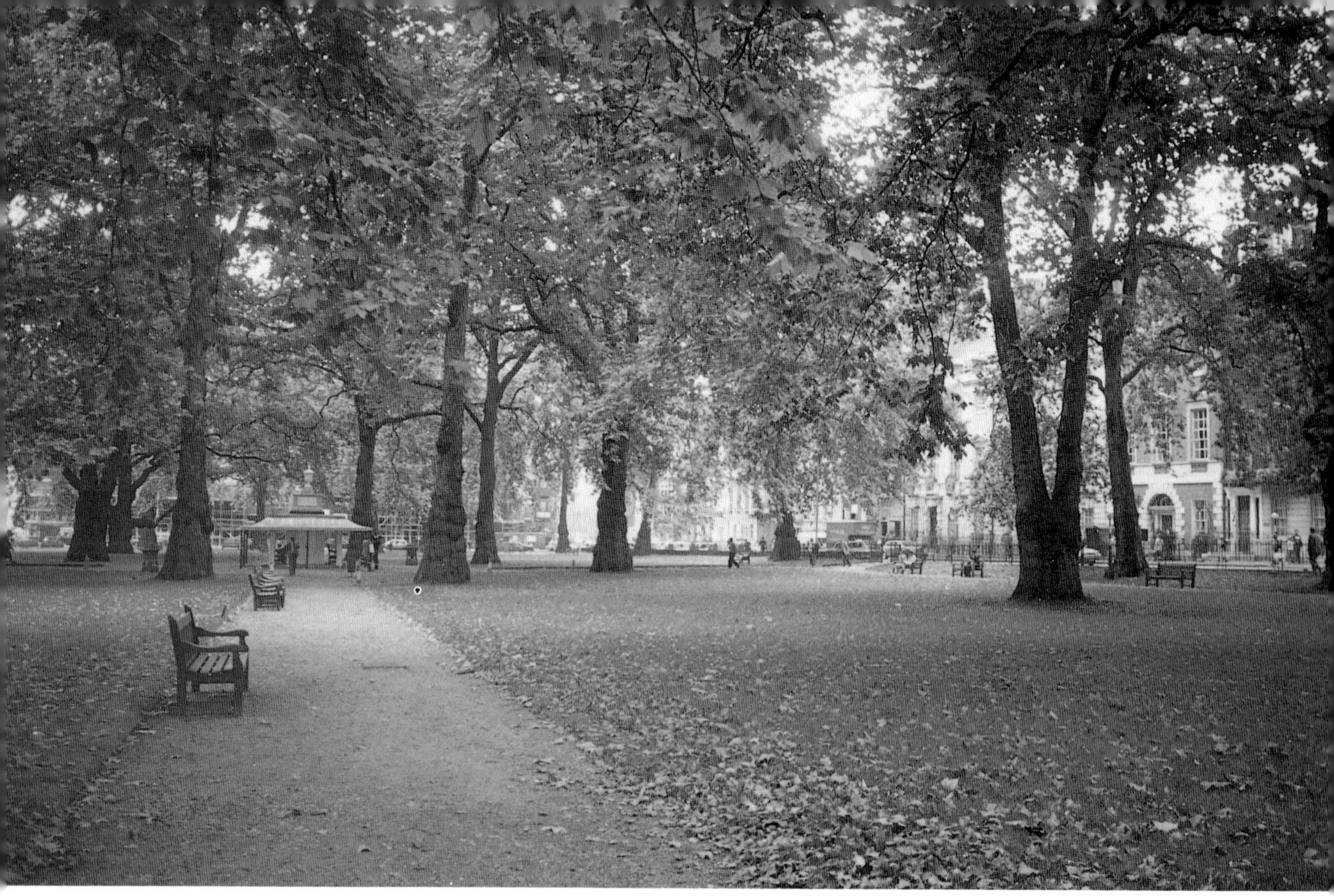

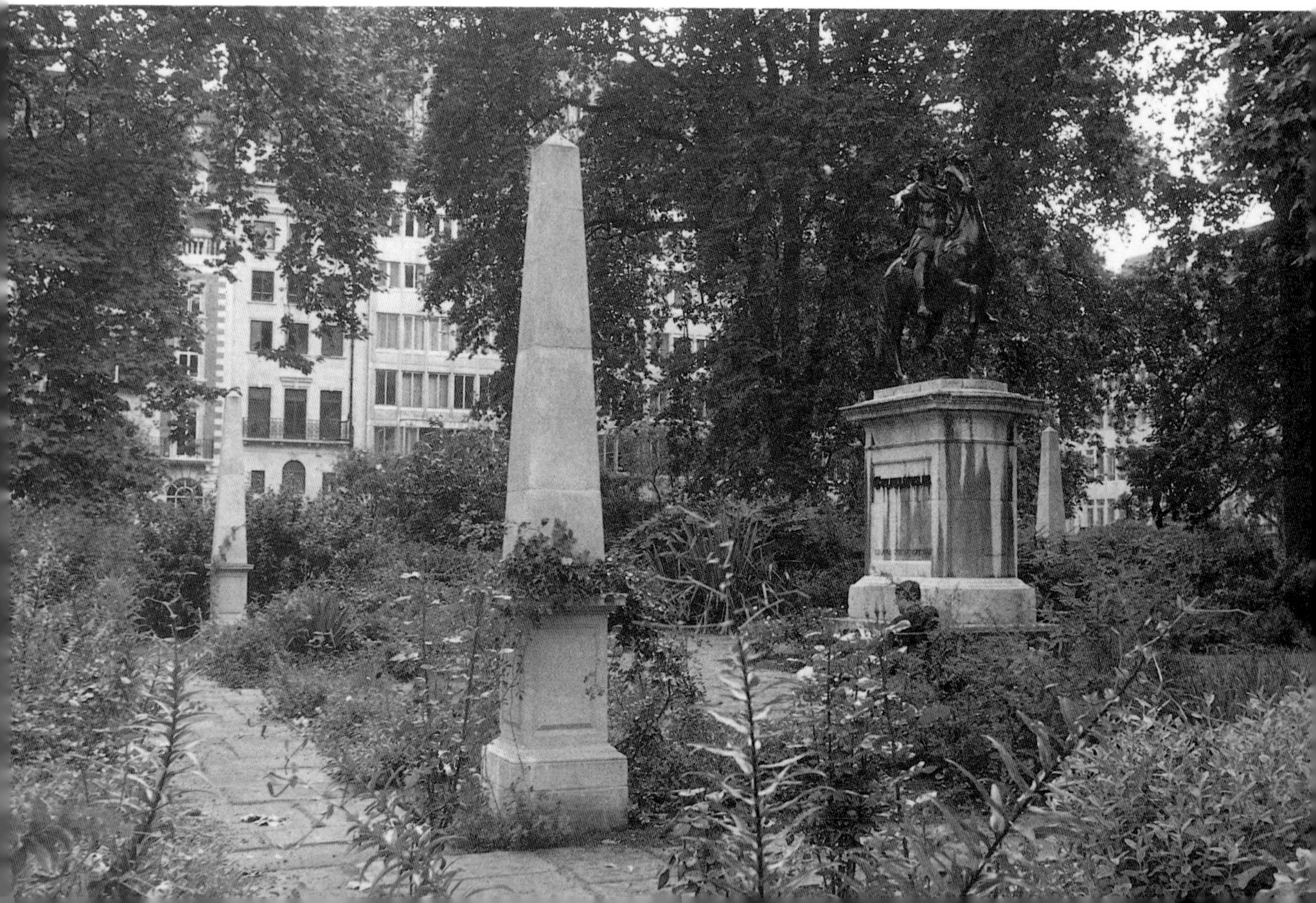

Berkeley Square
South-west of Grosvenor, but still in Mayfair, is Berkeley Square. Built in the late 1730s, this is another of London's earliest squares and it became one of its most aristocratic. Since the war it has been famous as the place where, according to a sentimental popular song of the time, 'a nightingale sang'. It is also well known for having some of the oldest plane trees in London, planted at the end of the eighteenth century.

Perhaps these were the inspiration for the horticulturist John Loudon, who advocated the wider use of plane trees in the city. In 1802 he published an article in the *Literary Journal* entitled 'Observations on Laying Out the Public Squares of London', in which he criticised the use of the then commonly planted yew and fir because smoke made their foliage extremely drab and they grew poorly. He suggested mixing deciduous species able to withstand the city smoke – such as planes, sycamore and almond – in with the evergreens. His idea was obviously popular because most of the squares have this mixture. Plane trees, such a feature of all the city's open spaces, were particularly suited to nineteenth century London because of their ability to exfoliate – shed bark – and thus survive the polluted and smoky atmosphere which choked other trees.

Planes are something of a tradition in London now, and no other tree will ever be able to take their place. Interestingly, they owe their introduction to Britain to John Tradescant the Younger. Berkeley Square has about thirty of these fine trees, which provide cool shade in the summer and plenty of leaves in the autumn! Never as busy as Grosvenor Square, this is a pleasant oasis, particularly on Sundays when the whole area is very quiet.

St James's Square
Saving the best till last, we arrive at St James's Square, a fair walk south-east of Berkeley. This is one of London's most attractive squares, public or private. It has a beautiful garden, with many fine trees and shrubs centred around an imposing equestrian statue of William III; the surrounding buildings are mostly eighteenth century and very elegant.

This square is a gem. Tucked in a corner between Piccadilly, Lower Regent's Street and Pall Mall, all traffic passes it by and so do a lot of people. You would expect it to be seething with people, going by the effect the sun has on Grosvenor Square, but you can always find a seat here even on the hottest summer's day. I assume everyone goes into St James's Park. This square is earlier than both its neighbours, as it was begun in 1665, although the Plague and the Great Fire meant it was not completed until 1676. A charming eighteenth-century poem details what would await a lady of quality who became a duchess:

> She shall have all that's fine and fair,
> And the best of silk and satin shall wear,
> And ride in a coach to take the air,
> And have a house in St James's Square.

Opposite above: **The eighteenth-century plane trees of Berkeley Square in Mayfair**
Below: **St James's Square is one of London's most attractive squares**

I do not think that any duchesses live in St James's Square today, but the gardens are kept to as high a standard as though they might. Lilac, cherry and laburnum are dwarfed by tall plane trees but nevertheless make a beautiful display in early summer. More unusual trees to be seen here include fig, mulberry and Indian bean. Around the statue is a formal garden of plants such as lilies, lavender, roses and flowering shrubs. An oval design, it is divided by flagstone paths with stone obelisks at key points. There are plenty of seats throughout the garden, including one in a shelter shaped like a classical temple. The best square in London.

THE INNS OF COURT

Some of the most peaceful gardens in all London are those among the venerable buildings devoted to the study of law – the Inns of Court. There is a sense of dignity and calm as soon as you enter from the noisy thoroughfares which surround the quiet courts. The most well known are the Inner and Middle Temple because they are visible from the Embankment, between Blackfriars and Waterloo Bridges. They also have an entrance from Fleet Street. To the north of these, beyond the Law Courts, is Lincoln's Inn, while

The Temple offers a retreat from the busy Embankment and Fleet Street

Gray's Inn is on the other side of Holborn. Linking them together can make a pleasant and interesting walk at any time of year, but be sure to go during the week as some of the gardens are closed at weekends; it is also better to see them in action. They were founded for the education and lodging of lawyers and today nobody can become a barrister without being accepted by an Inn of Court. Though access is allowed to the public to enjoy their courtyards, gardens and squares, the Inns of Court are in fact private property, in daily use by the people for whom they were originally designed.

The Temple
Despite being sandwiched between the busy Embankment and Fleet Street, the Temple is just as James Boswell described it in 1763 – 'a pleasant academical retreat'. Its groups of buildings of various ages arranged around courts and gardens and connected by alleys give it the feel of a college at Cambridge or Oxford. Leafy King's Bench Walk has some particularly attractive seventeenth- and eighteenth-century houses. Two are attributed to Sir Christopher Wren, who designed the gatehouse which opens from Fleet Street near Temple Bar. The oldest building in the Temple is its church, which dates from the late twelfth century and is one of only a few remaining round churches in England.

Although the large gardens of the Temple are unfortunately not open to the public, there is much to be enjoyed elsewhere – most notably Fountain Court. This delightful spot has a fountain and pool of goldfish, shaded by large mulberry trees, and a seat for you to enjoy it. The Temple is full of unexpected pleasures such as the manually operated gas-lamps in Middle Temple Lane. It is also steeped in history. Shakespeare's *Twelfth Night* was first performed here in 1601, and Oliver Goldsmith, Thackeray, John Evelyn and Dr Johnson all lived here. It is a fascinating place to explore.

Lincoln's Inn
Like the Temple, Lincoln's Inn has a mix of buildings of different periods and different architectural styles. The red-brick gatehouse was built between 1517 and 1521, the impressive classical stone buildings were begun in the 1770s, and the New Hall and Library date from the middle of last century. Eminent names associated with Lincoln's Inn include Sir Thomas More, Horace Walpole, Disraeli and Gladstone. New Square was built in the late seventeenth century but its central garden was not created until 1843. Within this attractive open space is a pool, roses and several trees including maples and cherries. Outside number twelve is an ancient fig and next door, at number thirteen, an equally aged wistaria.

North of the New Hall and Library is a garden, with a sign telling you that 'The Honourable Society of Lincoln's Inn' allows the public to use it between 12 and 2.30, Monday to Friday. Here you will find a row of seats under cherry trees, near a border of mixed shrubs and herbaceous plants, the most exquisitely maintained lawns, and large stately plane trees. All around is the Inn's gorgeous mix of architectural styles.

Inseparable is Lincoln's Inn Fields, a large square to the west of the Inn. This lays claim

Lincoln's Inn: dignified and calm

to some of the largest plane trees in London, which make it very shady and cool in summer. It is popular with local office workers, who come here for a peaceful lunchtime break. The more energetic can play tennis, and there is a busy netball league. Both activities provide entertainment for onlookers. The Figaro café does a roaring trade in rolls, cakes and drinks. There are plenty of tables and chairs on a large patio near the tennis courts at which to enjoy the refreshments. The square is well endowed with shrubbery, with bedding plants to provide the odd splash of colour. There are some interesting buildings around its perimeter, notably the Sir John Soane Museum with its sarcophagus of an Egyptian pharaoh, Hogarth's 'The Rake's Progress', and many other disparate objects.

Gray's Inn
A late seventeenth-century gatehouse leads off Holborn into South Square of Gray's Inn. In the central garden of standard roses, pinks, violets and sweet briar roses is a statue of Francis Bacon (1564–1626), one of the Inn's famous residents. Beneath the statue is a quote from his essay 'Of Gardens': 'God Almighty first planted a garden. And indeed it is the purest of human pleasures. . . .' The essay goes on, '. . . it is the greatest refreshment to the spirit of man' – a sentiment amply proven by this and all the Inns of Court, which are havens of peace amidst the noise of central London.

To the north is Gray's Inn Square, with its garden of well-kept lawn, lavender hedges and central sundial – very formal and in keeping with the square. An alley in the south-west corner leads into Field Court and the entrance to the Inn's largest open space. Beyond high railings and a gate are seats, gravel paths, lawns and mature plane trees, which cast plenty of shade in the summer months when this garden is open to the public for a couple of hours each weekday lunchtime. As with its neighbours, Gray's Inn has many interesting buildings and historical associations. The Inns are perhaps most attractive on a fine day in autumn, when this season of maturity, with its colouring trees and falling leaves, echoes the mellowness of these ancient establishments.

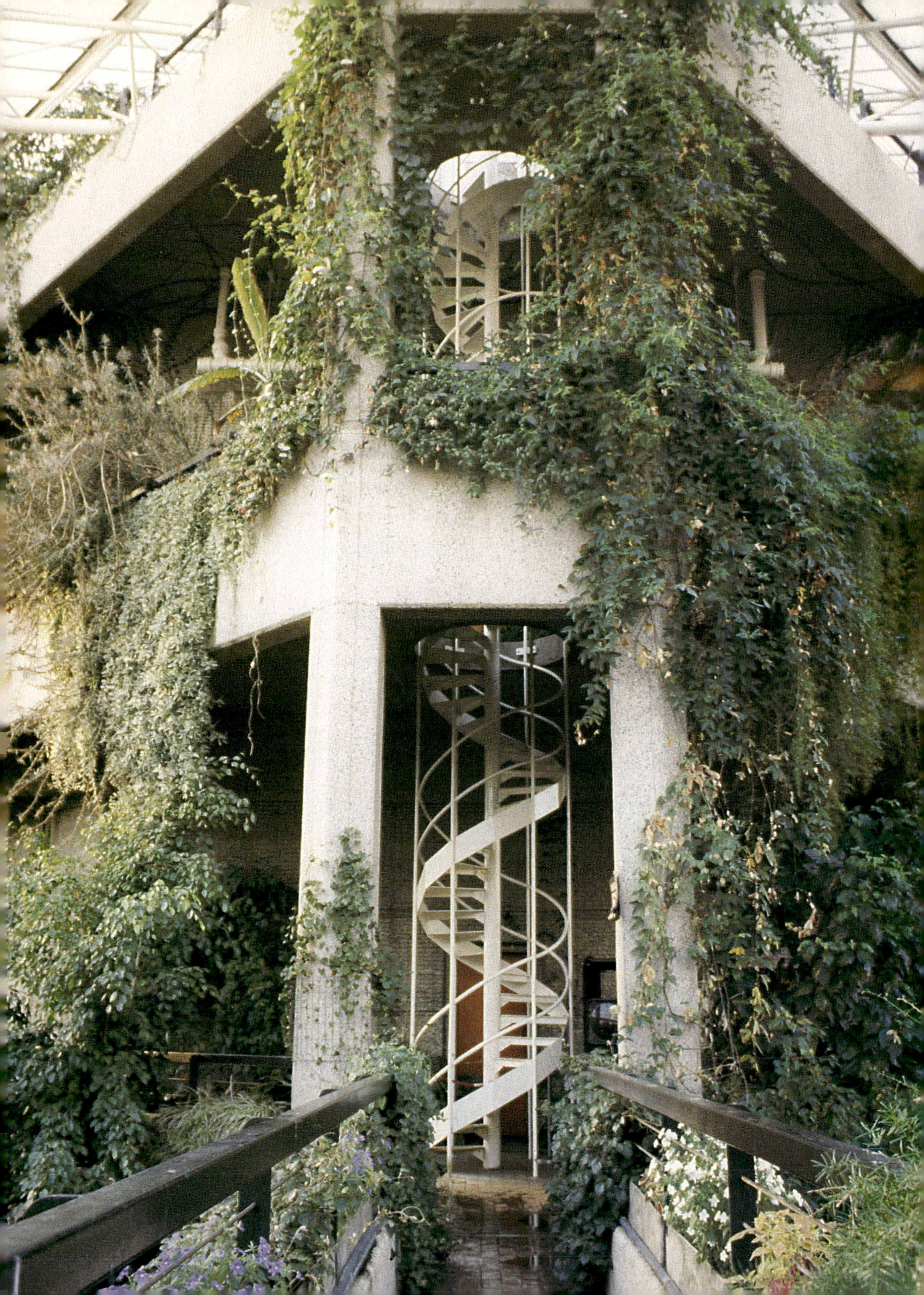

Roof Gardens and Landscaped Open Space

In recent years some of London's most impressive building developments have been designed with space for sympathetic planting or have actually made open space an important feature. In these ways architecture may be held responsible for making the city 'green'. Both roof gardens and landscaped open space owe their existence to the buildings of which they are an integral part. Roof gardens are planted on top of structures designed to take their weight and incorporate adequate drainage. Landscaped open space, as defined here, means an area which has been created to complement the architecture of surrounding buildings and is a significant feature of the complete development.

Land is inherently limited, and as population, urbanization, production and recreational needs increase, alternative uses for particular pieces of land begin to compete with each other. The scarcity of land in the centre of cities can lead to the sort of land-use that contradicts amenity and human values. A lack of urban open space reduces the quality of the environment and erodes some of the basic necessities of life. But it is difficult to justify the creation of new open space because, although the cost of provision and maintenance can be calculated, the value of the mere existence of such space cannot. The value of such space is based on very subjective and often personal views; hence it is not always easy to convince people of the need for it.

People today are increasingly aware that good health is not simply a question of freedom from disease but also of life-style in terms of eating habits, fitness and environment. The benefits of open space to people in inner cities are being realized, and architects and planners are designing accordingly. Hence, the Barbican incorporates both private gardens for residents and landscaped open spaces for visitors. Likewise, London's other great arts complex, the South Bank, has terraces and a promenade where people can enjoy magnificent views of the Thames. Further downriver is St Katharine's Dock, probably the best example of a landscaped open space in London, which provides a pleasant environment for recreation.

Using plants on roof gardens or sites divorced from the natural terrain is nothing new – witness Babylon. However, it is only recently that large-scale landscaped developments or 'roof landscapes' have been instigated. The latter are mainly private open spaces, existing as symbols of prestige, such as Arundel Great Court in the Strand. Here a

Opposite: **An impressive combination of architecture and open space: the Barbican Conservatory**

walkway leads from the pavement on to a lawn planted with specimen trees and shrub beds, a pleasant space for surrounding offices to look out on. Underneath the lawn is a car park – a good example of how architecture can be used for the benefit of the environment. The term 'roof garden' in fact describes more accurately the smaller developments such as Derry and Toms' 1930s fantasy in Kensington, or the incredible Barbican Conservatory, which is also reached by lift.

THE BARBICAN CONSERVATORY

This is a feature of the Barbican Centre for Arts and Conferences, the centrepiece of a 35-acre residential precinct on a site in the City of London, badly damaged during the last war. The Conservatory is built around the fly-tower of the Barbican Theatre, completely divorced from ground level. It has some fascinating views of the City's office blocks, such as the National Westminster Tower. They are all rather inhuman and forbidding compared with the lush, verdant Conservatory. This large, curiously shaped garden seems particularly welcome and familiar among these space-age buildings – a magnificent example of how architecture can be used to improve the environment.

The Barbican has been criticized for being a maze, or even a concrete jungle, but this is unfair. It is extremely 'green' with private gardens (many on roofs) and public open spaces for everyone to enjoy. What is more, over the whole estate elevated walkways

The Barbican Conservatory: a tropical jungle in the heart of the City of London

separate pedestrians and motorists, which must be an improvement in any city landscape. The Barbican Conservatory is undoubtedly unlike anything else in the City, or London come to that. As with Derry and Toms' Roof Garden, it is its location as much as its content which makes it worth visiting.

The Conservatory is on Level 8, easily reached by lift from the stalls foyer. There is a small charge for admission. You are immediately confronted by the bulk of the fly-tower, around which run three balconies. These are planted with tropical species, which have grown so luxuriantly that the tower is all but obliterated by a curtain of greenery. Around the entrance are placed seasonal displays of flowering plants – bulbs or chrysanthemums, for example. This area lies above the theatre's administrative offices, which have smoke outlets into the Conservatory. You can peer into these offices through their rooflights. It is all very strange, and definitely not like any traditional Victorian glasshouse.

The most striking plant here is *Cupressus cashmeriana*, a delicate blue conifer with a strange weeping habit. Also here is the rare adult form of *Ficus pumila*; looking like an elaeagnus, this shrub is more commonly known in its juvenile form as the houseplant creeping fig. Colour in the permanent displays is provided by such plants as the gingerwort (*Hedychium gardnerianum*), with its spikes of flowers disclosing brilliant red stamens in September, and the unique flowers of the bird of paradise plant (*Strelitzia reginae*), as well as more familiar plants such as coleus, fuchsias and flowering begonias. There is a small aviary here with finches and quail.

The path around the fly-tower becomes narrow and then broadens out around a bed of cacti from places as far apart as Bolivia and South Africa, but all doing well in the City of London. Beyond, the Conservatory becomes something of a tropical rain forest. All around are huge specimens of rubber plant and its relative the fiddle-back fig (*Ficus lyrata*), smaller shrubs like hibiscus and *Elettaria cardamomum*, the source of cardomom seeds, which are an ingredient of Indian curries. Other notable exotics include banana from South-East Asia and a tree tomato (*Cyphomandra betacea*) from Peru. This large tree in a small pot fruits in September; the tomatoes are edible and were grown by the Indians of ancient Peru for desserts and jams.

Among all this shrubbery is a stream leading into a pool and a path of tree sections with a handrail to guide you. First thing in the morning, when water is dripping all around and the air is humid, this place seems far away from London, but look out of the windows and you will have a harsh reminder of where you are. There is a flight of steps, well covered by a rampant climber, from which you get a good view of the forest around you. This leads on to the first balcony around the fly-tower. All the walls and pillars are literally smothered in plants. Wandering Jew seems to be in a race with *Asparagus sprengeri*, *Philodendron scandens* and a host of other climbers and trailers. One of the most interesting is the Dutchman's pipe (*Aristolochia elegans*). Its flowers appear in late summer, with a yellow tube and a purple-brown white-veined hood. From the balcony you can see the fish in the pool – golden orfe, goldfish, koi carp and rudd – and its bubbling spouts of water. You get the best views of the City from here too.

This is not the biggest conservatory in London, but in terms of maintenance and attention to detail (labelling, for example) it is second to none. It is certainly the most intriguing, and a great asset to the City of London.

DERRY AND TOMS' ROOF GARDEN

Possibly the most unusual garden in London is that on the roof of what was once Derry and Toms department store in Kensington High Street. Here, over 100 feet above ground level, can be seen Spanish, Tudor and Woodland Gardens, complete with a Moorish palace, fountains, a stream, flamingoes, and some stunning views over London. Visiting them is a strange experience and immensely enjoyable.

At the rebuilding of the department store in 1930 its director Trevor Bowen had the idea of incorporating a roof garden. Bernard George, FRIBA, was commissioned to redesign the store, with this unusual feature in mind. The new Derry and Toms was finished in 1933 and two years later the garden was begun, taking a further three years to complete. The concept of the garden as an integral part of the complete building meant that the structure was specifically designed and constructed for the needs of the garden. The soil, which is nowhere more than thirty inches deep, and averages eighteen inches deep, had to be taken into account along with the weight of masonry required for walls, arches, pergolas, paving and the restaurant. The floors below had to be waterproofed by having a bitumenized layer under the soil. Fresh artesian water is available from three wells below the neighbouring House of Fraser store (formerly Barkers). In addition to the ornamental use of water, large amounts are needed to compensate for that lost by evaporation.

Ralph Hancock was the landscape architect responsible for designing the three gardens. Considering their diversity, the visitor is gently led from one to another without any awkward changes. However, each does manage to make a very dramatic impact as the design is very forceful. Mr Hancock introduced over 500 varieties of trees and shrubs, and imported stone from Pennsylvania for the alpine plants. The whole garden was conceived on a grand scale, to impress and be admired.

The Spanish Garden is strongly architectural, being dominated by the Moorish palace with its campanile, fountains, pools and arches. Large palm trees are the most noticeable plants, but there are several beds of mixed shrubs and herbaceous plants. On a fine summer's day it takes little imagination to be far from central London. But that is only if you have your back to the perimeter wall, for the low walls reveal a view over the nearby shops and in particular the parish church, the spire of which looms over the garden and gives an almost surreal effect – a dramatic reminder of where you are. A plain red-brick arch leads into the courts and alleyways of the Tudor Garden; a much more intimate design this. The red brick is weathered and all but covered in climbing plants. There is a small fountain and several seats from which to enjoy the peace and tranquillity. A very secluded space.

A moorish garden one hundred feet above ground at Derry and Toms' Roof Garden

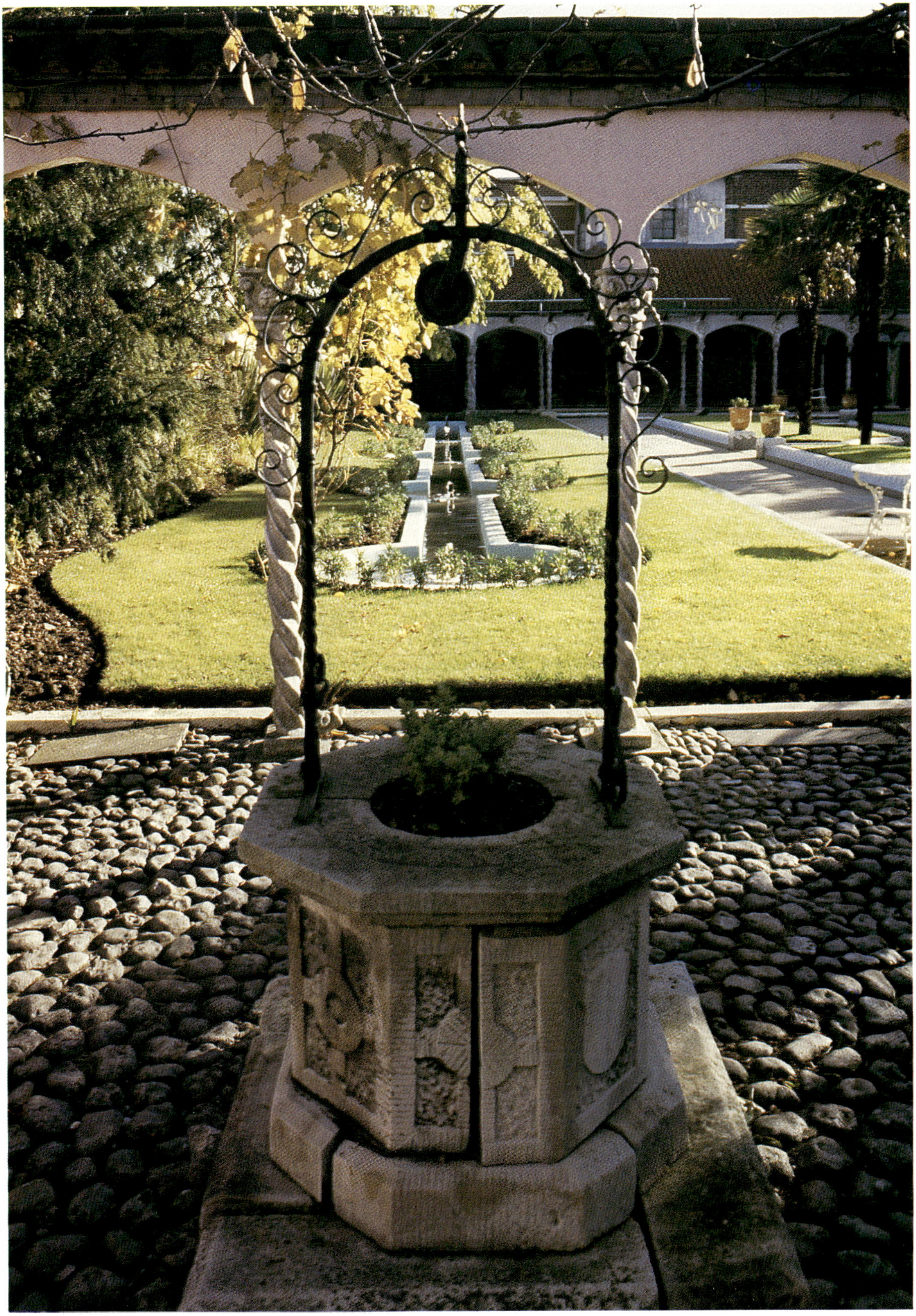

The third garden is the Woodland Garden, where the main feature is water. A meandering stream with pools and bridges is enjoyed not only by the garden's visitors but by a varied collection of waterfowl including flamingoes. The stream is edged with shrubs and trees including flowering cherry, maple and quickthorn. The trees do not seem to be stunted, which might be expected considering the shallow soil in which they grow. The perimeter wall here has several clair-voyées round portholes with metal bars which give glimpses over Kensington – again a reminder of where you are and the strangeness of the place. There is also a main viewpoint here, from which you can see several landmarks such as the Post Office Tower, the Royal Albert Hall, the museums in South Kensington and, on the horizon, the communications tower at Crystal Palace. However, unlike in the Spanish Garden, the surroundings of this garden do not intrude; the atmosphere is very secluded. Due to the garden's distance from the traffic below there is an uncanny silence; this, combined with the fact that there are no buildings rising above the skyline, gives one the impression of being in a country garden. Every visitor is amazed and intrigued by this garden 'fantasy'. Everyone should visit it.

ST KATHARINE'S DOCK

St Katharine's Dock is on the Thames, adjacent to the Tower of London; it is an exciting place and a lively rendezvous not only for people who like boats but for anyone who enjoys being out of doors and near water. It takes its name from a hospital and church,

Strange but true: mature trees in Derry and Toms' woodland garden

previously on the site, which were founded in the twelfth century by Matilda, wife of King Stephen.

St Katharine's was the last of a series of docks to be built at the beginning of the nineteenth century to cope with increased trade from America, the West Indies and Britain's expanding empire. It was completed in 1828 and became associated with long-term storage of wine and wool. Like all the docks, St Katharine's suffered from a dramatic decline in trade in the 1960s. As a result, in 1968, it became one of the first docks to close. Taylor Woodrow Ltd immediately stepped in to convert the dock into a residential area with a yacht marina, a commercial exhibition centre and an attractive open space.

The dock in fact consists of three areas of water: Central Basin, West Dock and East Dock. At the centre is St Katharine's most distinguished building, the Ivory House. This 125-year-old warehouse was used for trade with the Ivory Coast and handled ivory itself, which was in great demand at the turn of the century for piano keys. It now houses a variety of shops, serving local residents and visitors alike. At its eastern end is a continental-style patisserie serving drinks and delicious savoury or sweet snacks. You can eat indoors or, better still, on the paved area overlooking East Dock.

A pedestrian bridge between East Dock and the Central Basin leads to The Dickens Inn, a very popular pub. The building, a former brewery, was discovered among the bricks of a gutted warehouse. The 150-ton oak frame was jacked up and moved over 200 yards to its present position. Its exposed beams, antique furniture and sawdust on the floor give it a distinct atmosphere. The ground-floor Tavern Room does good 'pub grub' seven days a week. The exterior galleries of the pub are always richly planted with geraniums, ivy and the like each summer. The lower gallery and courtyard are always busy, particularly on weekdays in the summer when tourists, office workers and holidaying yachtsmen all meet here to drink. This is a very attractive location, facing as it does the Central Basin with East Dock and the Ivory House to its right. Nearby are poplar, willow and plane trees, while the Central Basin is edged with troughs and tubs of a variety of bedding plants and evergreen shrubs such as hebe, euonymus and elaeagnus. Not far away can be seen Tower Bridge. There is always a lively atmosphere, as one expects of anywhere connected with the sea. Another eating place is next to the pub, an old paddle steamer called the SS *Yarmouth*. Set in concrete on the edge of the Central Basin, this is now a café.

Walking towards Tower Bridge, the large building in the foreground is the luxury Tower Hotel, in front of which is a wide promenade along the river, which leads to the bridge and beyond to the Tower of London. A favourite stopping point here is at the much-photographed statue, 'Girl with a Dolphin'. This is a good place to sit and look at the river.

Returning to the Central Basin, walk to the right towards West Dock. You will see a strange 'temple', which looks as if it should be at Chiswick House, or perhaps The Hill. It is the Coronarium Chapel, made of seven cast-iron columns from a former dock

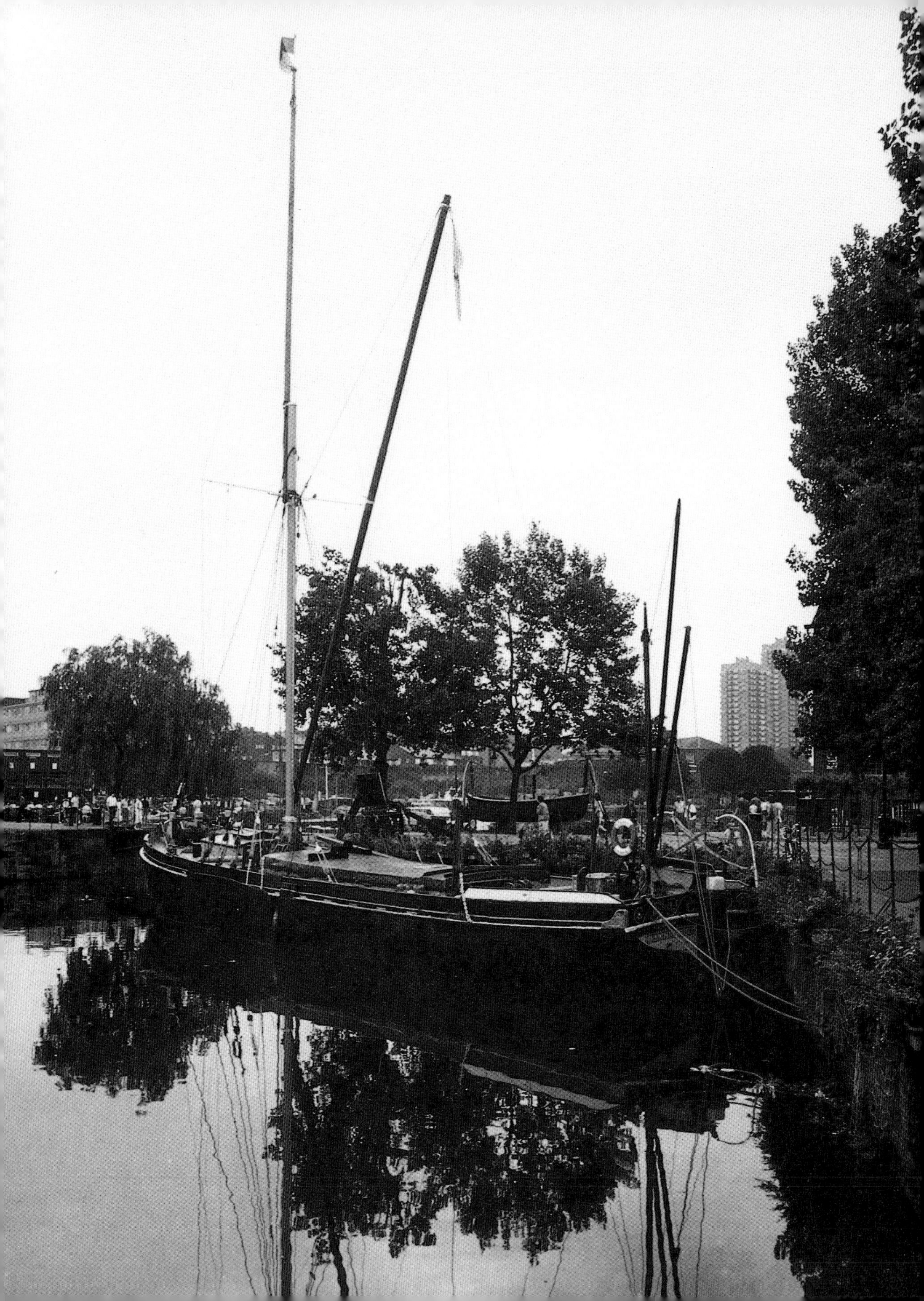

warehouse. At its centre is an altar and above the door a large block of perspex, depicting the Imperial Crown. The building was unveiled by the present Queen, to celebrate her Silver Jubilee in 1977, and stands approximately on the site of the original church of St Katharine. On the far side of West Dock is the World Trade Centre. From the Coronarium Chapel a bridge spans the gap between West Dock and the Central Basin and leads to the Ivory House where we began.

St Katharine's Dock has been beautifully adapted to serve yachtsmen and visitors of all kinds. There are, in fact, ten acres of open space here – West Dock, East Dock and the Central Basin – making a considerable area in the heart of London. St Katharine's is as relaxing as any park and more interesting than some, with its comings and goings of yachts and other craft such as the famous Thames barges. It is a fascinating place in which to kill time, especially around noon when there is most activity or at either end of the day when it is more tranquil. An evening stroll here is a particular delight as the Ivory House is stunningly illuminated. St Katharine's is a good example of a commercial development which still leaves much-needed space for human beings. It can be done.

THE SOUTH BANK

The South Bank is an area around the south end of Waterloo Bridge, with a complex of buildings used for the arts. The open space begins as a wide, tree-lined promenade outside the National Theatre, to the east of the bridge, and continues on the other side (the National Film Theatre is under the bridge) past the Hayward Gallery and the three concert venues – the Purcell Room, Queen Elizabeth Hall and Royal Festival Hall. It then borders Jubilee Gardens and ends at County Hall, by Westminster Bridge, though a riverside walk continues to Lambeth Bridge near the Tradescant Trust garden.

What makes the area so attractive is that it is on a curve of the Thames and has magnificent views both upstream to Westminster and downstream to the City. The National Theatre and Royal Festival Hall take full advantage of these views with raised terraces where you can eat and drink and enjoy the space. After all, the Thames must be London's biggest open space and the South Bank is one of the best places to appreciate it. In fact, this and Battersea Park are the only two places in central London where you can take a decent walk by the river, free of traffic noise and pollution. There are plenty of riverside walks, but you are always accompanied by a main road.

The 4½-acre site between Waterloo Bridge and County Hall was reclaimed from mudflats for the Festival of Britain in 1951, which was an exhibition to celebrate the country's economic recovery after the war. It was as big a success as its predecessor, the Great Exhibition of 1851 in Hyde Park. The biggest and most important building of the exhibition was the Royal Festival Hall, the beginning of the arts complex which has become such a magnificent addition to London's cultural life. The buildings themselves are not very attractive from the outside, although inside they perform their various functions extremely well. However, it is the uses to which they are put and the

Opposite: **St Katharine's Dock: after the dock closed in 1968, it became a yacht marina, a commercial exhibition centre and an attractive open space**

atmosphere created which makes the South Bank such a lively place. Along the promenade and on the wide terrace outside the Royal Festival Hall there is always a lot of activity in fine weather. There are occasional theatre performances, street entertainers, exhibitions, and a regular book market under Waterloo Bridge at weekends. This is also a favourite place for young people with roller skates and skateboards. At the Festival Pier you can take a one-hour cruise up as far as Westminster and down as far as the Tower of London.

The Jubilee Gardens on the Festival of Britain site were opened by the Queen in June 1977 to commemorate the twenty-fifth year of her reign. This open space has a large grassed area which is used for special events such as the annual 'Thamesday', an open-air festival based around the river, and political rallies. There is also a decorative walled garden, with seasonal bedding and a fountain. The gardens include memorials to William Morris, the socialist designer and craftsman, Spanish Civil War heroes, and Peace Year

The South Bank's wonderful promenade takes full advantage of London's biggest open area: the Thames

1983. A children's play area features modern equipment such as a tent-shaped climbing frame, wooden bridge and animals, set among trellises of climbing plants which form enclosed spaces which children seem to enjoy. Next to the gardens is County Hall, built for the London County Council in 1908 and later home of the GLC until its abolition in 1986.

Like the Barbican, the South Bank has been criticized for its maze of tunnels and stairways but at both places these serve to keep people and cars separate – which is a distinct advantage. At the South Bank it is possible to leave a train at Waterloo Station, go to a performance and return without crossing a road. (Likewise at the Barbican, via Moorgate Station.) There is much to be said for modern architecture which creates space for people, especially in cities where it is at a premium. The redesigning of this river frontage has created an attractive open space, right in the heart of London, which takes full advantage of its greatest natural asset, the Thames. The spacious promenade with its trees, seats and Victorian lampstands is a great place to admire London, at any time of day or night.

Eating Out

Eating out-of-doors is a lovely idea – and one being increasingly taken up by people wanting to bring a little continental *'joie de vivre'* to dear old London town. It is not all that easy, though. Accepting that a summer here is never uninterrupted sunshine and warmth, London does not have boulevards with wide pavements as in France, or tiny informal squares as in Greece or Italy; there is just not the room. However, there are places in London where you can eat (or drink) out-of-doors in very pleasant surroundings which are far more relaxing than any pavement café.

Many London restaurants advertise gardens but these tend to be courtyards or patios, though very prettily planted. I have chosen three very different restaurants which actually have sizeable gardens. Pubs with gardens are more numerous. Here I mention some where you can combine lunch with a visit to one of the parks or gardens described earlier in the book. It seems that most of London's bigger parks and gardens have cafés, but most are quite basic. This chapter picks out a few of the better ones, with the most beautiful settings. All are self-service. Finally, some of London's most attractive places for a picnic. Considerations here should be a sense of space, not too many people gawping at you, toilets nearby, and a good view of something to look at. For addresses, opening times and means of access see pp.170–5.

It is worth remembering that, British weather being what it is, we can have beautiful hot, sunny days in April or September so do not think of eating out-of-doors as something restricted to July. Whenever there is fine weather, make use of it. A bonus is that places are less busy in early or late summer.

RESTAURANTS

The Gardens

This is the name of the club in the middle of the spectacular roof garden in Kensington, already described. It is open to the general public for lunch, Sunday to Friday. There are set prices for two or three courses of *nouvelle cuisine*-inspired food, and on Sunday there is a choice of traditional roast and salads. Be sure to book and ask for a table outside; a stroll round the gardens is a must.

Lauderdale House, on the edge of Waterlow Park, has a very good café

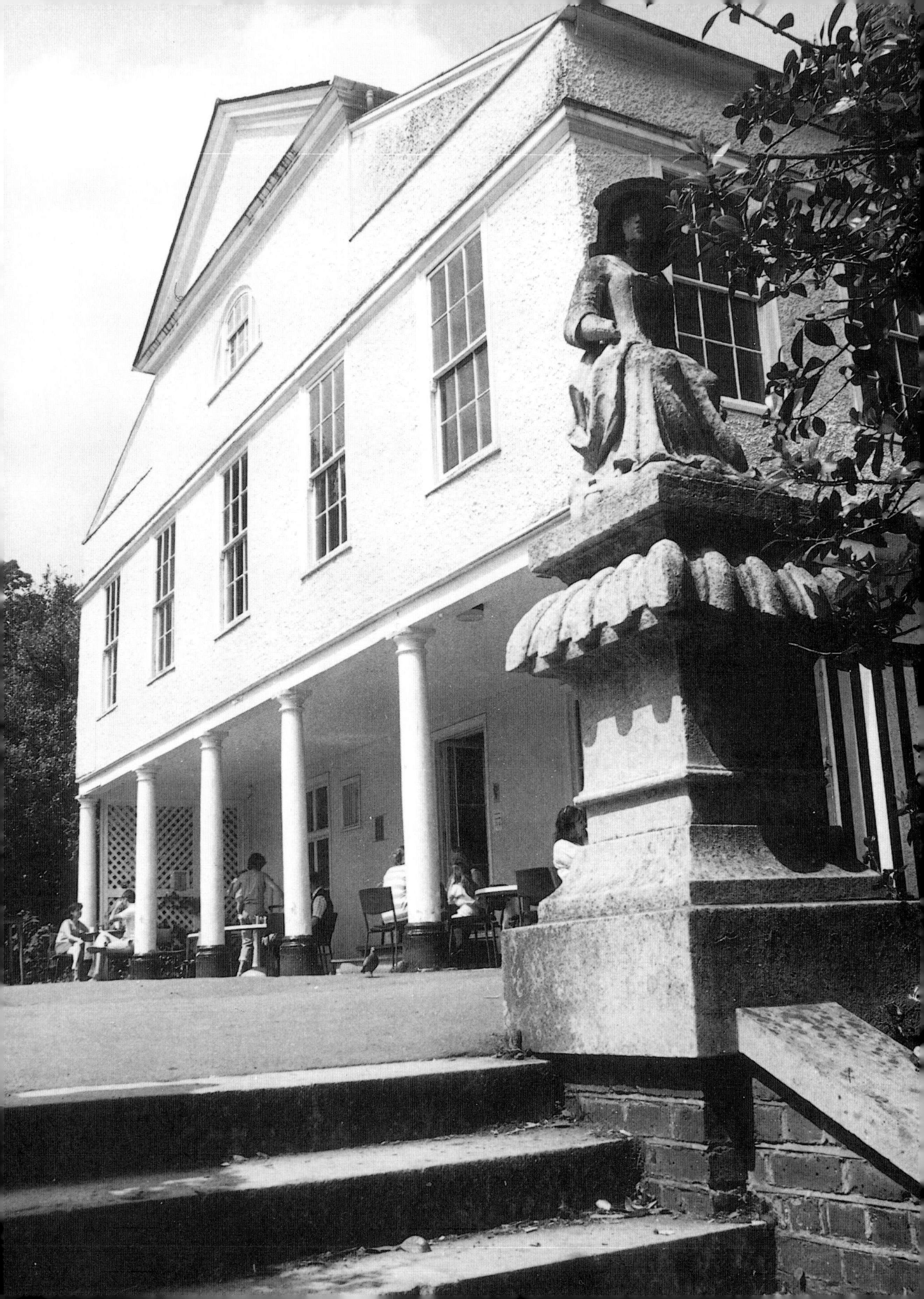

Henry J. Bean's (But His Friends All Call Him Hank) Bar and Grill
Obviously American. The garden of this popular Chelsea haunt is very long, mostly paved and full of tables, so there is usually room for anyone who wants to eat outside. The furniture is traditional wooden 'park-like' seats with solid tables. Some are sited under wooden pergolas covered in climbing plants. The finest tree is a mulberry near the entrance to the restaurant, while side borders contain an assortment of shrubs, herbaceous plants and bedding plants. As a retreat from the hectic King's Road this large garden, shaded by trees and the surrounding buildings, is very welcome, although it can become almost as busy as the street outside.

The interior is pure Americana with its huge, glass-backed bar, vintage posters and ephemera. Likewise the limited menu, which includes hot dogs, burgers, potato skins and nachos, with ice cream, pecan pie and chocolate cheesecake to follow. A 'fun' place, where it is possible to relax out-of-doors with a drink and a meal in pleasant surroundings. At the far end of the garden is a large gravel-covered play area for young children.

The Old Rangoon
This popular, colonially inspired restaurant and bar is just south of Hammersmith Bridge. The interior, a cool green, has wicker furniture, lots of palms and ceiling fans. Lunch and dinner are served on an impressive colonnaded terrace decked with 'tropical' cordyline, phormium and yucca; more British is the honeysuckle, and geraniums in hanging baskets. Eating here, you overlook a paved terrace where people may just drink, and beyond is the huge walled garden complete with pond and ducks. All around are trees and beds of mixed shrubs and herbaceous plants. The lawn is dotted with wooden tables and in one corner is a children's play area. During the summer a marquee is erected, which may be hired for private parties.

The menu offers mainly Indian-inspired dishes as well as char-grilled food and salads; tea is served throughout the afternoon. A pleasant place to enjoy a summer's day – or night, when the whole garden is floodlit.

PUBS

The Duke of Clarence
From the outside this is an unremarkable pub. The entrances open into a traditional public bar, complete with darts. A step down leads into a lounge area, and beyond this is a very impressive large conservatory with arched roof and paved floor. Artificial plants are used over the beams and to hang from the roof, but there are large ground displays of exotic plants which all look very healthy and well cared for. The atmosphere is very tropical, added to by the bamboo tables and matching padded chairs and prints of unusual plants. Blinds on the roof arches can be lowered for shade in the summer, and the conservatory is heated in winter. There is a large barbecue here too.

A door leads out into a very pleasant garden. The traditional wooden seating is on a paved area among well-maintained beds of roses, shrubs and bedding plants. The whole garden is walled, and shaded in part by cherry and ash trees. What makes the garden particularly attractive is the lighting by mock-Victorian lamps and the fact that it has its own purpose-built bar. Much nicer than trekking through the conservatory and lounge every time you want a drink.

This well-organized pub also has a good food bar; the traditional ploughman's lunch is supplemented by lasagne, pizza, a range of salads and suchlike. Also tea and coffee. A very pleasant pub which should please everyone, especially those who enjoy outdoor or semi-outdoor living. A good retreat after exploring Holland Park.

The Freemason's Arms
Said to have the largest garden of any pub in London. The Freemason's Arms is conveniently close to Hampstead Heath, so can be your reward after a healthy walk. The sloping site has been properly landscaped to provide two terraces, both paved and with plenty of seating. The garden has shade from ash and sycamore trees; it is surrounded by shrubbery, with a lot of roses and a fountain.

Food such as quiche, ploughman's lunch, salads and some hot dishes like lasagne can be bought indoors, but the garden has its own drinks bar. There is also an 'à la carte' restaurant indoors. This pub does get very busy at weekends, so unless you do not mind crowds get there early, or avoid it.

The Hand and Flower
Close to Richmond Park and Ham House, this small pub has a delightful newly created garden and covered patio. A lot of thought obviously went into its making. The garden's main feature is a goldfish pond with a small waterfall in a rockery and a weeping willow; it is floodlit at night. The surrounding lawn, edged with beds of flowering shrubs, conifers and herbaceous and bedding plants, has lots of tables with umbrellas and chairs. Off to one side is a cubby-hole with a wooden table enclosed by arches of climbing plants and there is also a summerhouse with seats inside. The garden is very well cared for. The patio, next to the pub itself, is prettily decorated with hanging baskets of fuchsias and nasturtiums, and bedding plants in raised beds, incorporated into low surrounding walls.

The pub has a good atmosphere and the staff are very friendly. A menu of homemade hot dishes, such as macaroni cheese and pies, and salads is available.

The Hare and Hounds
In the heart of suburban west London is this lovely 'country' pub, part of the semi-rural enclave of Wyke Green with its hedgerows, greensward, sports grounds, garden centre and the neighbouring parkland of Osterley. The pub's garden consists of a large lawn with tables set among roses, flowering shrubs and trees, including eucalyptus. At one end is a children's play area with swings, slide and see-saw. It is best to get here early at

weekday lunchtimes because it is popular with office workers from the surrounding factories, who come for the unusually large choice of hot and cold food.

The Spaniard's Inn
This is an old pub on Hampstead Heath with a pretty garden, full of roses. It has been a 'local' for the likes of Byron, Shelley, Keats and Dickens – and Dick Turpin is still sometimes seen here! About a lawn are beds of bush roses and a large pergola of climbing roses. Cherry trees and bluebells provide colour earlier in the year. There is a special bar for the garden, which has plenty of tables and chairs, but they soon get full up on sunny days.

This is one of Hampstead's most famous and popular pubs; typical 'pub grub' is available.

The Victoria
Another pub close to Richmond Park, with a garden so good that it has won awards. Lawn, roses, herbaceous plants, masses of hanging baskets, fine wall shrubs and a paved area full of wooden tables make this a good place to eat out. There is also a large canopy in case the weather is doubtful.

Good food is available throughout the week; on Friday and Saturday evenings and all day Sunday there is a barbecue serving very good chicken, burgers and steaks. A busy, friendly pub popular with all ages.

CAFÉS

Golders Hill
This café in Golders Hill gives north London a little taste of Italian al fresco living. It certainly deserves its very good reputation. There is a small indoor seating area, decorated with mementos of Italy and 'I Maestri del Colore', a set of booklets about artists hung on hooks for the customers to read – a nice touch. The large terrace outside has good views over much of the park as it sweeps down hill. To the south can be seen the woodland of West Heath, with paths leading to the romantic gardens of The Hill.

The food is delicious and temptingly displayed. Large filled rolls (salami, of course), apple pie, cheesecake, fresh melon, good cappuccino and espresso coffee and Italian ice cream are the sort of things you can get here. The café is very popular, and always busy throughout the summer.

Ham House
The café here is part of the old orangery; it is situated in the walled rose garden. In the summer there are always plenty of tables and chairs laid out on the smooth, well-kept lawns in front of the café (for a description of the garden see pp.92–8). The interior of the café is decorated with pot plants and old posters for exhibitions at the Victoria and Albert

Opposite above: **The popular Golders Hill Café**
Below: **The Refreshment Pavilion on the Broad Walk, Regent's Park**

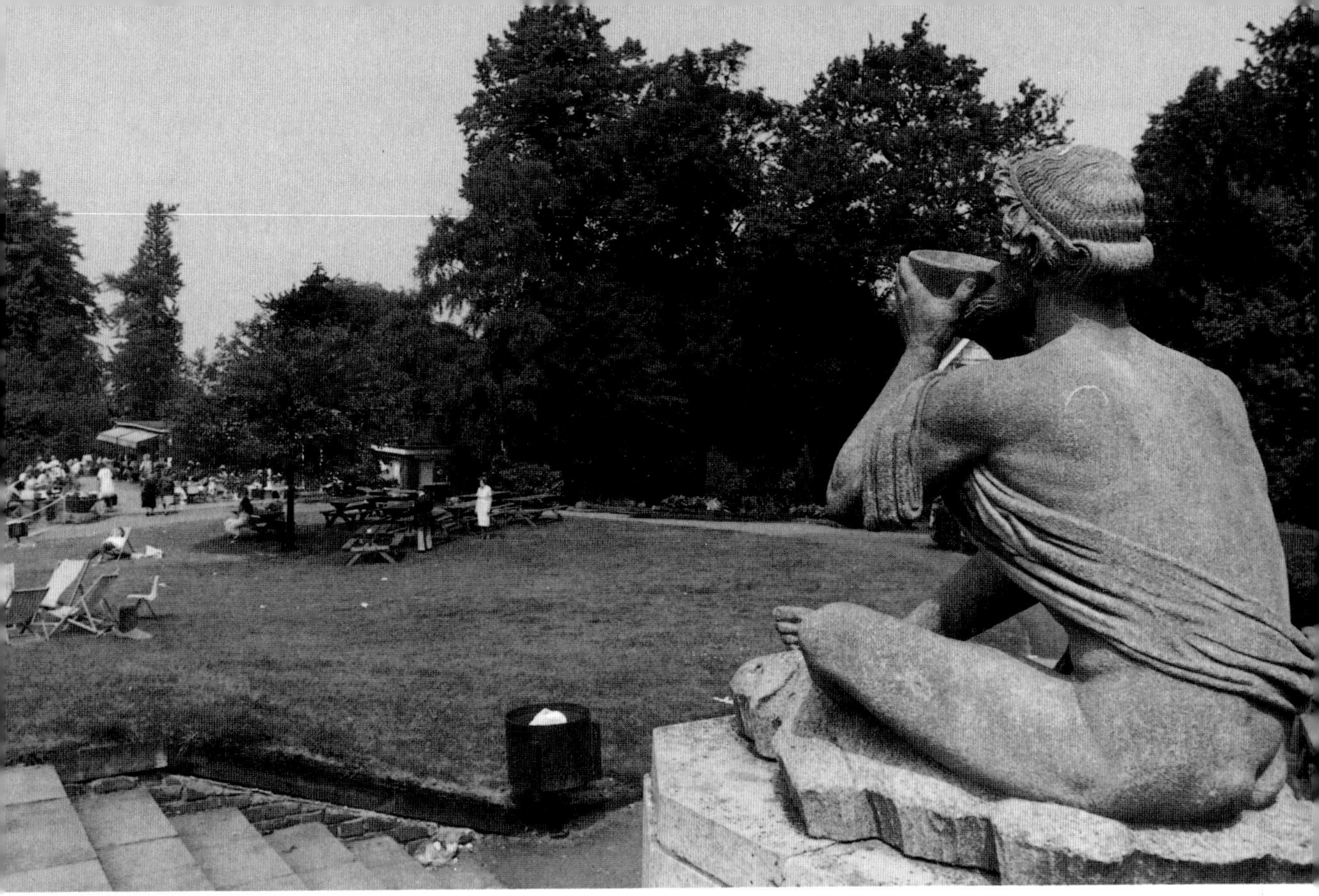

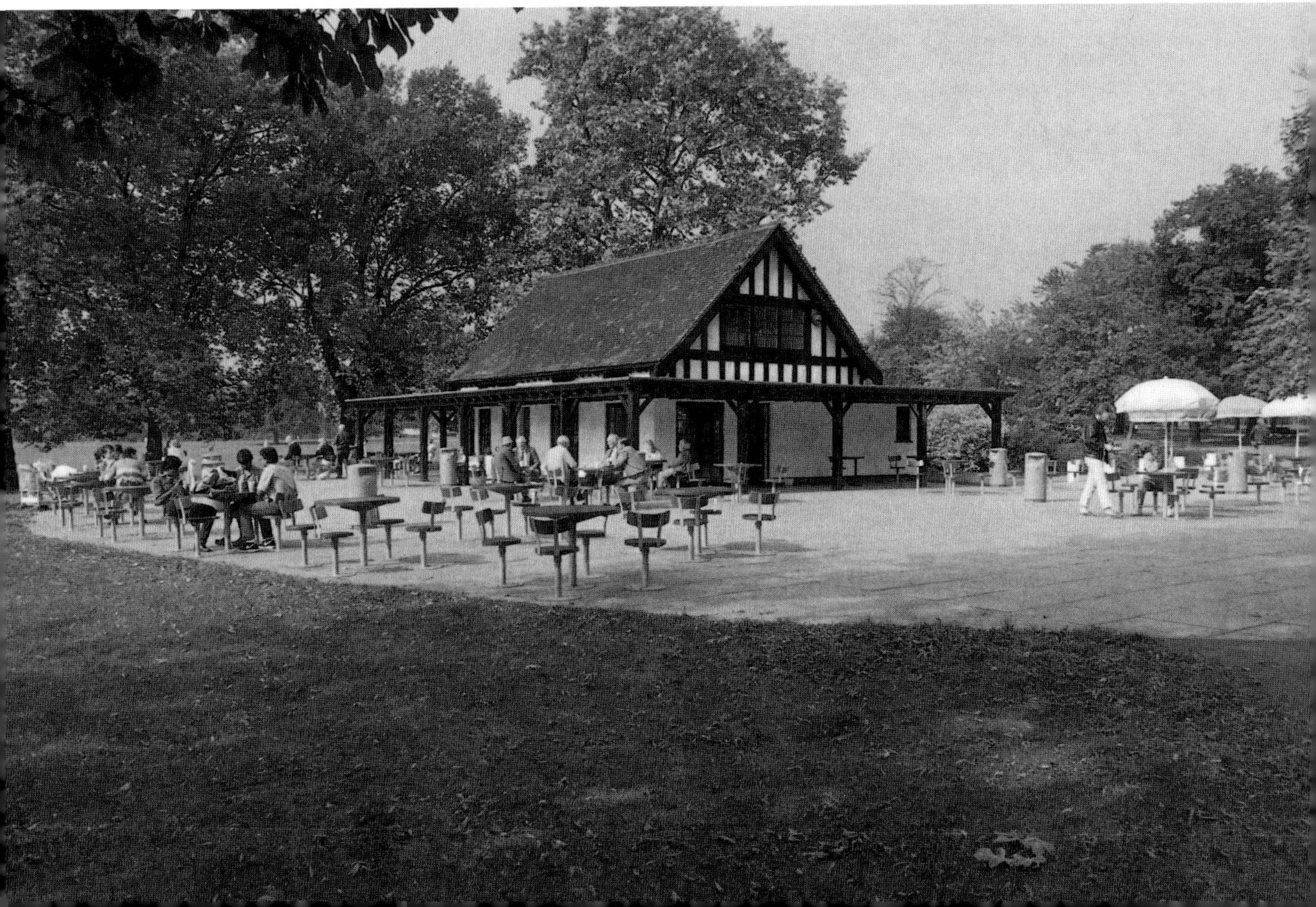

Museum. This café is the perfect place to have afternoon tea (they have lovely cakes). The service is very friendly. The best time to visit is during the week because the garden is never too busy.

Kew Gardens

The main café at Kew is in the south-east of the gardens near the pagoda. It can get very busy on fine summer days – or even wet ones, when everybody has to crowd indoors. At less busy times it is a very pleasant place to linger over a cup of tea, or even have lunch. The food includes meat and two veg., fish and chips, salads, sandwiches, and a range of cakes. The large outdoor area is in part covered by a pergola of climbing plants, but the great attraction of eating here is that only a low iron railing separates you from the gardens themselves. All around you can see the magnificent trees and shrubs of London's very best gardens. This is the ideal place to go on one of those fine days in April or September. Kew also has a smaller refreshment kiosk near the palace, with seating under a large canopy.

Regent's Park

The Rose Garden Buffet is situated in Queen Mary's Gardens. The outside seating area is surrounded by roses, with a background of trees – a lovely location. Food includes soup and freshly prepared pasta dishes as well as a choice of salads; cakes are a speciality.

Also in Regent's Park is a Tea Pavilion, just opposite the old Bedford College and facing the tennis courts. An assortment of savoury snacks, cakes and drinks is available. It is well used by people waiting to play tennis or recovering from a game. There are a few tables indoors, but more outdoors from where you can watch the tennis. The whole site is surrounded by trees, and if you like watching tennis can be a very pleasant place to rest a while.

About half-way along the Broad Walk is a Refreshment Pavilion serving the same selection of food and drinks as the Tea Pavilion. The attraction here is the sense of space as it is sited at the top of a slight hill with magnificent views over the surrounding greensward and playing fields. Only slightly obscured by the trees of the Broad Walk to the east can be glimpsed the splendid architecture of Cumberland Terrace, on the park's perimeter.

It is worth mentioning that the food served at the Open Air Theatre is also very good. You can choose between a varied salad table or barbecued burgers and sausages; all the food is freshly prepared.

Russell Square

A good haven in central London. At the north-east corner of this large square is a café where you can buy a variety of rolls, cakes and drinks. You can enjoy them at seating provided on a small paved area in the shade of enormous plane trees. It is a popular lunchtime venue for office workers, but never overcrowded. Anyway, you can always go and sit in another part of the square, which lots of people do to avoid the scavenging pigeons and sparrows, which are tame enough to eat out of your hand.

PICNIC PLACES

Greenwich Park
The magnificent views over London are the prime reason for suggesting Greenwich Park as a picnic place; below or to the east of the Wolfe statue is a good spot. From here, the park slopes away down the hill to the gracious buildings of the Royal Naval College; beyond, the Thames meanders eastwards to the sea. The skyscrapers of the City and the immense dome of St Paul's Cathedral are all clearly visible.

There are also several fairly secluded corners of the park where you may prefer to picnic: One Tree Hill and near the tumuli at the Croomshill Gate are both worth a try. Fortunately, the toilets are located at the centre of the park, near the Planetarium, so they are never very far away.

Hampstead Heath
Well, if you want to avoid people you should be able to do that on Hampstead Heath, though you may do a lot of walking while trying to decide on the best place to stop. There are some good views from Parliament Hill and on East Heath to the west of the Mixed Bathing Pond. One of the most 'rural' areas is Cohen's Fields, to the east of Kenwood. This gentle hillside is covered in long grass, with the odd tree and shrub, and seems miles from London. Kenwood itself is also worth considering because it has toilets and that large sweep of lawn in front of the house, where – summer weekends aside! – you should be undisturbed.

Primrose Hill
One of London's great viewpoints is the south side of Primrose Hill, but for privacy go to the north side. There is plenty of room here and it has the friendly feel of a local park. It must be the least frequented of the Royal Parks.

Richmond Park
Spankers Hill Wood or Prince Charles Spinney are the best places to picnic here. You can admire the handsome park from these viewpoints and be prepared for any advancing deer. Like Hampstead Heath, there is plenty of room here to avoid people.

Wimbledon Common
A lot of Wimbledon Common is taken up by dense woodland and the golf courses so your best bet is near the windmill, which is not such a bad idea as there are toilets here. If you search a bit, you can find some secluded pockets of grass, where the gorse and birch begin to thicken along Windmill Road. The greensward near the village is another good place.

Buying Plants

Gardening in London has never been more popular. People realize the benefits of creating their own 'green' haven and have more leisure time in which to care for it. In recent years garden centres have been opening throughout the city to cater for an ever-increasing market. Many are aware that some people who want a nice garden regard caring for one as a necessary evil; information desks, advisory leaflets and careful labelling of plants, stating their requirements, are all intended to reduce the hardship. Some go as far as to have landscaping and maintenance services for those who are willing to pay for someone else to do the work. Reluctant gardeners can take heart from one of the greatest, Gertrude Jekyll, who said: 'In garden arrangement, one has not only to acquire a knowledge of what to do, but also to gain some wisdom in perceiving what is well to let alone.'

Often people try too hard to keep a garden neat and tidy when a little less work may

The Chelsea Gardener offers a flamboyant approach to gardening

lend an element of informality which can be very welcome in town gardens. But there are many keen gardeners in London with a real love of gardening who are well catered for by the capital's excellent garden centres. However, all gardens should be enjoyed and not be just sources of work; as Osbert Sitwell said, 'Physical action is inimical to the green lethargy we seek, and sweat is a mighty foe to peace.' Likewise, visiting garden centres these days is not necessarily a chore but can be a real pleasure. Here are descriptions of a few which are worth visiting, with a good selection of quality plants and sundries for the urban gardener.

Also covered in this chapter are a few specialized shops – one selling seeds, one garden ornaments, and another, Chattels, a beautiful array of garden-related products such as wood and thatch bird houses, besom brooms, dried flowers and pot-pourri. It is one of those shops where looking is more than half the pleasure. Likewise, New Covent Garden and Columbia Road Markets are fascinating places to browse. For addresses, opening times and means of access, see pp.174–5. The chapter concludes with a couple of London's best florists, both long established and renowned for the quality of their flowers and the expertise of their staff.

GARDEN CENTRES

Alexandra Palace Garden Centre
Opened in 1986, this north London garden centre caters specifically for the needs of town gardeners. It was also set up with the laudable aim of providing jobs and training for unemployed young people – as were the Camden Garden Centre and Fulham Palace Garden Centre. Two good 'local' centres, the former has an interesting water feature and the latter a mini-Crystal Palace.

The one at Alexandra Palace is much bigger and incorporates a conservation area, café, children's play equipment and show gardens. The large impressive main building is reminiscent of a country house conservatory, complete with weather vane. Inside are sundries and up a ramp an area with a good selection of houseplants including some large specimens – for example, a five-foot weeping fig (*Ficus benjamina*) and standard hibiscus. Beyond this is a semi-enclosed area where plants of seasonal interest are displayed. When I went, in summer, it was full of bush and trailing geraniums, standard fuchsias and planted hanging baskets. The whole garden centre is on a hillside, which gives it great character. That is why there is a ramp within the building and outside display tables seem to be perilously close to the vertical. The shrub beds are less dramatic but you are still aware of the sloping site.

The garden centre stocks many plants which grow well in poor light – a problem for a lot of town gardeners. There are also plenty of climbing plants for people with limited space who can exploit trellises and pergolas. The garden centre is well stocked with quality plants of all kinds. There is a good selection of herbs, including some larger plants. Specimen shrubs include wistaria and magnolias.

While here, you should walk up the hill to see Alexandra Palace itself, a famous landmark and venue for concerts and exhibitions. The first regular television service was inaugurated here by the BBC on 2 November 1936. It is now being restored after a devastating fire in 1980, but when it opens in 1988 it will feature a newly landscaped Great Hall Palm Court and the East Hall, consisting of a sports and indoor athletics stadium – a very exciting development. The surrounding park was opened in 1863 to celebrate the marriage of the Prince of Wales to Princess Alexandra of Denmark; the palace was not completed until some years later. The park features a rose garden, large children's play area, boating lake, animal enclosure and, best of all, fine views over London.

The Chelsea Gardener
This is an up-market garden centre, popular with Chelsea's artistic and media community, and suitably flamboyant. It immediately strikes you as being well organized, selling quality goods in a very 'Chelsea' manner. The outdoor area is divided by an elaborate redwood trellis and pergola. On the roof of the offices are some fanciful white pavilions, one complete with pink drapes. This could only be Chelsea.

The Chelsea Gardener is well organized and teams with good ideas for the city dweller

The plants here are displayed on tables, thus taking the backache out of inspection. Bold signs tell you how the plants are grouped – Winter Shrubs, Scented and Aromatic Plants, Plants for Shaded Sites, and so on. It is easy to see what choice is available for your particular purpose. There is a good selection, but they are more than willing to order anything which is not in stock. The displays of seasonal interest are always bold, especially their superb range of Christmas trees, garlands and wreaths. They stock some interesting plants such as the herb purslane, box clipped into globes and pyramids, orange trees complete with oranges, variegated rhododendrons and tulip trees (*Liriodendron tulipifera*). Gardeners will enjoy exploring here and finding the unusual and exotic.

The 'hardware', like trellis and large decorative pots, is also outdoors. The large, uncluttered shop sensibly keeps chemicals and sundries to a minimum – though any new product is sure to be found here – in favour of books, quality furniture, an extensive range of seeds and floristry. A room of houseplants includes rarities like indoor bonsai, pistachio and weeping fig (*Ficus benjamina*).

The Chelsea Gardener is associated with several designers for those who want the full treatment, and can also arrange for the services of related craftsmen and a horticulturalist. The staff here are helpful and efficient, showing an interest both in the plants and in the people who buy them. There is much here to interest the keen gardener and inspire the reluctant one.

The garden centre is part of the pleasant Chelsea Farmer's Market, a group of small buildings selling things like fruit and vegetables, good cheese, fresh fish and pet supplies. There is also a good café.

Clifton Nurseries
Similar in style to the Chelsea Gardener, Clifton Nurseries also has a rather colourful approach to selling plants. Down a passage between large terraced houses you will find this well-organized garden centre, where goods are displayed in an interesting group of buildings and 'spaces'. It is fun to explore because you are never sure what you are going to find. A central feature is a large classical stone column supporting a climbing rose. About this are a shop of sundries; a garden full of antique and reproduction furniture and ornaments; an area specifically for shade-loving plants, overhung by large trees; a glasshouse of indoor plants; a semi-conservatory with furniture and terracotta; beds of trees, shrubs and other plants in season, and a section for items like peat, compost and trellis. The low glasshouse is particularly interesting as it has a large selection of specimen houseplants such as spathiphyllum, yucca and dracaena, and a good display of large cacti, something not often seen. An adjoining room has some unusual plant pot covers and basket work.

The outdoor plants are of good quality, with a bias towards those most suitable for the small urban garden. There is a particularly good range of climbers and plenty of clipped specimen bay and box. Emphasis is placed here on seasonal interest, so bedding gives way to heathers, then fruiting shrubs and so on. The main shop has all the necessary bits and pieces and a good selection of books displayed in glass cases; an elaborate Indian-style cage of canaries completes the homely image. Aware of the lack of space which is a problem for most gardeners in London, the garden centre stocks a wide range of pots and containers in wood, terracotta and stone, as well as the more unusual and elaborate antique items. There are landscaping and maintenance services available here.

The staff are very helpful but usually have a queue of people behind them, all demanding attention. The garden centre is especially busy at weekends, when a lack of parking adds to the frenzy, so try to go during the week. The same company owns the Colonnades Garden Centre in Bishop's Bridge Road, W2, and a shop, Clifton Nurseries, in Russell Street, WC2.

Syon Park Garden Centre
This is one of numerous attractions set in the landscaped parkland estate of the Duke of Northumberland, which make it a popular place for a weekend outing. Huge, well-stocked and efficiently managed, Syon Park Garden Centre is in the supermarket style of those found in the provinces, but fortunately for Londoners is not very far out of town.

Clifton Nurseries is full of interesting corners like this one, displaying furniture and ornaments

The sheer size of the place means that you can spend a lot of time browsing over a bewildering range of outdoor plants, seeds, peats and composts, sundries, houseplants, books, flower-arranging materials, tools, furniture, barbecues, mowers and electrical equipment such as propagators. A separate area has larger items like sheds, greenhouses, summerhouses, fencing and paving. They do not have a particular bias towards urban gardeners with limited space, but stock a comprehensive range of items for outdoor living. Of course, anything the city dweller needs is bound to be here; the staff are very helpful.

Syon House is a sixteenth-century mansion, improved by Robert Adam, with some magnificent rooms. The gardens are divided in two, and both have a charge for admission. The six-acre rose garden is best seen in June; the other garden features a large lake created by 'Capability' Brown, a woodland area and herbaceous beds. The Great Conservatory built in the 1820s is quite impressive – from a distance. It has for many years been in need of fundamental repair, but this has only recently been undertaken and progress is slow. The whole garden is somewhat overshadowed by its neighbour across the Thames, Kew, and Richmond, too, is only a little way upriver. The London Butterfly House, a motor museum, the park, a café, the house and gardens all make Syon something of a funfair on summer weekends, but the garden centre is well worth a visit.

SHOPS

Chattels

This is the sort of shop you go to just to look at, but always end up buying something. Being in the Chalk Farm Road, it is close to the markets of Camden, so avoid it on Saturday and Sunday as it is always packed with people.

What do they go to see? Well, the shop door leads into a room of dried flowers; they are stacked in baskets on the floor, piled up the walls, and hanging in bunches from the ceiling. Mixed in among them might be the odd thatched bird house or Sussex trug (a gardener's shallow wooden basket). The flowers are not only the common statice, sea lavender and everlasting flowers (helichrysum) – though they are there. Here you will find roses, sweetcorn, dainty little xeranthemum with their wiry stems and small daisy blooms; there are dozens to choose from. Beyond, down a couple of steps, is the area where you pay for the flowers, the delicious scents of pot-pourri filling the air. This is Chattels' other speciality, and there are several varieties, all with suitably old-fashioned and wholesome-sounding names.

Beyond this is a passage leading to a backyard, carefully calculated to give an impression of a rustic idyll. Through the locked gate you can see grass and cow parsley; a shed is covered in Russian vine and a mangle stands rusting. The scene thus set, it is dressed with items for sale such as terracotta pots, besom brooms, wooden tubs and trellis. Throughout the shop are all manner of useful country items now meant purely for decoration in trendy London homes, often incorporated in floral arrangements. There is a lot of basketwork, pressed flower greetings cards, walking sticks, corn dollies and rope quoits. A fascinating shop in which to browse.

Garden Crafts

If you want an ornament to decorate your garden, to give it interest or focus, go to Garden Crafts in Fulham, specialists in ornaments and furniture; they have been there for over sixty years. You will probably be surprised at the choice you have. In the main display area there are the obligatory classical figures in all shapes, sizes and poses, plus dogs carrying baskets, Japanese lanterns, a bust of Shakespeare on a column, small Buddhas, and even some gnomes. Pots, troughs and urns are everywhere. There are three working fountains, showing another dimension which can be added to your garden. There are also some bird-baths. For walls there are Greek drama masks, medallions and friezes, and even a mirror with a surround of moulded concrete. House signs are made to order.

These reproduction garden ornaments are mostly in cast concrete and thus come a lot cheaper than antique originals. There are a few in other materials, such as marble, which do cost more. In separate bays are unusual terracotta pots and ornaments and a selection of furniture in wood and metal. Garden Crafts should have what you are looking for; they advertise themselves as having the largest and most impressive selection in London.

Sutton's Seeds

This is London's only specialist seed shop. It is small, but then you do not need a lot of room to sell packets of seeds. In fact there is room enough to stock the whole of Sutton's considerable catalogue. This shop is something of a showplace for the firm, who are 'By Appointment to Her Majesty the Queen – Seedsmen'.

The range of seeds will appeal to the traditional horticulturalist because it includes everything which is established and well liked. They are, however, always extending their range to include new introductions as they increase in popularity, but without pandering to the 'avant-gardener' with lots of exotica, as some firms do. The small packet seeds are on the ground floor; in the basement are grass seed, peas, beans and sundries such as soil, pots, fertilizers and insecticides.

Clifton Nurseries shop is just around the corner in Russell Street, on the Covent Garden piazza.

MARKETS

Columbia Road Market

Columbia Road is a gently curving street of regular, terraced, one-storey Victorian shops and houses in the East End. On Sunday mornings it is transformed by thirty or more stalls into the most beautiful street market in London. It is a fun place to go, whether you like plants or not. People here are always friendly and ready for a laugh, which must say something for the merchandise which is being sold. Depending on the season, you will find cut flowers, shrubs, bulbs, houseplants, artificial and dried flowers, trees, bedding plants, herbs, seeds, Christmas trees and wreaths, and there is always a sprinkling of flower pots, tools, compost and the like. Everything is much cheaper than in the shops. Adding to the atmosphere are men flogging plants off the backs of lorries, a sea-food stall, a pub on the corner; traditional English breakfast is served at 'Quinns' restaurant.

Also worth a look is a shop just off Columbia Road in Ezra Street. S. & B. Evans have an impressive range of clay pots, which they make at their Dalston workshop. They mix sand with the clay, thus making the pots frost-proof and more suitable for the British climate – a distinct advantage over the imported Italian terracotta found at most garden centres, which soon begins to flake after its first exposed winter.

Columbia Road is a must for those who like to see the 'real' London. Though smaller, it is a much pleasanter and more good-humoured place to visit than Camden or Petticoat Lane Markets are these days.

New Covent Garden Market

This is the largest horticultural market in Britain. From here fruit, vegetables and flowers are distributed all over the country. It is big business, run efficiently from this purpose-built site in a wasteland of railway sidings and warehouses at Nine Elms, Battersea. Unfortunately, when the market moved south of the river in 1974 it left behind all its glamour and ease of access for the casual visitor. There is no theatre for miles and definitely no Professor Higgins or Eliza Doolittle. But there are some workers who knew the old market, and in their own way they have brought with them some of its character. I wonder what they think of the old market now with its tourism and tat?

The flower market is separate from that selling fruit and vegetables. It is worth visiting just for the sight of the massed cut flowers, with exotic blooms fresh from halfway across the world, and pot plants, both flower and foliage. You will also have the opportunity to buy very cheaply.

What you must remember when visiting New Covent Garden is that in theory it is a wholesale market where the majority of customers buy in bulk. Having said that, the traders selling more unusual items such as protea blooms will only expect people to buy in small quantities. There is always a preponderance of lady florists on the look-out for something a bit different for an arrangement, or shop owners stocking up with half a dozen of this and that. However, they are there specifically to buy and this is a place of business, so idlers who get in the way are not going to be greeted with a smile – especially so on Thursday morning, when all the weekend business is being done.

Wednesday is probably the best day for a casual look around but there will not be quite as much on show. Cut flowers and houseplants are the mainstay but there are a few stalls with dried flowers and florists' sundries, and bulbs and Christmas trees in season. This is all housed in a huge open market hall with a translucent roof, automatic doors and a constant temperature of 14°C all year. The area is divided by aluminium screens into bays for the various traders.

1923
TRUMAN
HANBURY
BUXTON
& Co Ltd.
THE
ROYAL
OAK
EZRA ST.
AL OAK
THE ROYAL OAK

What gives the building some of the old market's character is the 'ant-like' activity of the porters taking the goods here and there. Some use the wooden sack-barrows brought from north of the river, and I remember seeing one old-timer carrying an incredible amount on his head. Lightweight metal trolleys seem to be more popular though. After rush hour – that is, early in the morning – the porters and the people selling the plants are usually more relaxed and easily strike up a conversation. I assume they can recognize a stranger or non-buyer, or whatever they call us. New Covent Garden is a fascinating insight into one of those aspects of London life which we take for granted.

FLORISTS

Felton and Sons

Established in 1900 and founder members of Interflora, Felton and Sons are highly respected London florists. Their services are excellent, and they use only best quality blooms which are in season and never anything which has been forced. This large shop on a corner site along the Brompton Road has picture windows which give an enticing view of the display inside. The shop is packed full of the most beautiful fresh cut flowers, and some dried ones.

Moyses Stevens

Moyses Stevens have been in business for 100 years. The quality of their flowers is excellent, as you would expect from the Queen's florist. The shop's displays are suitably lavish but discreet enough to suggest that nothing is actually 'bought' here. The company is famous for its arrangements of fresh, dried and artificial flowers, which are incorporated among lush drapes and displayed on a large stone table and in stone troughs and vases. The dried arrangements always seem particularly intricate, making use of unusual materials such as dried conifer formed into globe-headed trees.

Columbia Road. A typical east-end street becomes London's prettiest market every Sunday morning

For Children

In this chapter I have picked out the places already described which have features particularly attractive to children. Apart from zoos, playgrounds and the like there are simpler pleasures such as feeding ducks and squirrels. Perhaps the greatest is just having room to run, play games and kick a ball without having to worry about doing any damage. Many of the parks have special events in the summer, such as children's entertainers. Although I have not included them here, some children may also enjoy exploring places such as the garden at Chiswick House or the woodland at Lesnes Abbey.

KEW GARDENS
Not an obvious place, but I have often seen children enjoying this magnificent open space in their own way. I suppose it is something of an adventure to explore this huge garden and find surprises like the pagoda and lake and ponds with their fish and waterfowl. The 'jungles' inside the houses are always popular with children, especially the Temperate House which has spiral staircases to climb and a gantry running around the roof.

The Royal Parks

GREENWICH PARK
Greenwich Park has the largest playground in any Royal Park, with a variety of traditional equipment; next to this is a boating lake. Young children may enjoy seeing the deer in the Wilderness, while the older ones could explore the old Royal Observatory. This is a good place to fly kites and go sledging in winter. Children could also have a ride on a donkey at nearby Blackheath, or a look at the *Cutty Sark* and the other sights of Greenwich.

HAMPTON COURT
The Maze is always popular with children.

BUSHY PARK
Here there is a playground with a large sandpit, swings and slide and a pond on which to sail model boats. The roaming herds of deer are tame, though they should not be fed.

HYDE PARK
Children, like everyone else, will be drawn to the Serpentine for its boating, swimming and waterfowl. There is also a small playground near the Edinburgh Gate.

KENSINGTON GARDENS
'The' Royal Park for children, with a playground, waterfowl, the Round Pond (for model boats), Elfin Oak, and of course the Peter Pan statue.

REGENT'S PARK
The Zoo is the big attraction here. There is also a playground and small boating pond near Hanover Gate, two other playgrounds – at Gloucester Gate and near Park Square – and the large boating lake with waterfowl.

PRIMROSE HILL
Ideal for kite flying and sledging.

RICHMOND PARK
There are lots of deer here. Adam's Pond, near Roehampton Gate, is used for sailing model boats and there is a small playground near Ham Gate.

ST JAMES'S PARK
The great numbers of waterfowl here like to be fed. The pelicans are always fun to watch, though they should not be fed. Tame sparrows eat out of your hand on the bridge. There is a playground with refreshment kiosk near Wellington Barracks. You can also watch the Changing of the Guard at nearby Buckingham Palace.

Parks

BATTERSEA PARK
Lots of animals here, as a small zoo is open throughout the year, and there is an enclosure with wallabies, deer and other animals; the lake attracts geese and other waterfowl. There is boating on the lake.

GOLDERS HILL
More animals here, with enclosures for goats, deer and exotic birds such as rhea and Sarus crane; there are also flamingoes near the flower garden. There is a small play area, especially for younger children, with a sandpit and wooden animals. It is enclosed and thus free from dogs.

HOLLAND PARK
There is woodland here to explore, and unusual birds like peacocks. Three play areas cater for children of various ages. Just down the road on Kensington High Street is the Commonwealth Institute. This is an instructive and colourful collection of artefacts, photographs and produce provided by all the nations of the Commonwealth, showing their varying cultures. The Institute has a lively and varied programme of events which includes theatre, dance and music. Worth a visit, as it puts a strong emphasis on work with children.

WATERLOW PARK
Good slopes for sledging. There are waterfowl on the lakes and more exotic birds in the aviary. Highgate Cemetery is the place for children who like to be scared.

A school party enjoying the Waterhouse Woodland Garden, Bushy Park

Heath and Common Land

HAMPSTEAD HEATH
Plenty of scope here to have fun exploring. Whitestone Pond is used for sailing model boats, while ponds on the Heath itself have lots of different birds. Kite flying at Parliament Hill. Sledging all over the place. Often has special events and regular fun-fairs.

WIMBLEDON COMMON
Again, a great place to explore. Special attractions are kite flying, the windmill and two power-boat clubs practising their model craft each Sunday morning at Rushmere Pond. Also has special events.

Roof Gardens and Landscaped Open Space

DERRY AND TOMS' ROOF GARDEN
'Fun' garden with flamingoes and ducks.

THE SOUTH BANK
Jubilee Gardens has modern play equipment in a specially created area. River boat trip to Westminster and the City from Festival Pier.

Eating Out

HENRY J. BEAN (But His Friends All Call Him Hank) Bar and Grill
A good place to take children. The food should appeal, also the amusing décor which includes such things as a kangaroo in a chair suspended from the ceiling. At the far end of the garden is a large play area for younger children. It is covered in gravel and has small items of play equipment.

THE OLD RANGOON
Plenty of room here for children to play. There is a special area set aside for them, and a pond with ducks.

THE HARE AND HOUNDS
Play area with swings, see-saw and slide.

CAFÉS
The best cafés in the parks most suitable for children are at Golders Hill, Kew Gardens and Regent's Park.

PICNIC PLACES
Everywhere suitable.

Buying Plants

ALEXANDRA PALACE GARDEN CENTRE
There is a small area of play equipment here for young children. Up the hill behind the palace is a large play area and boating lake, with an enclosure for llamas, ponies and deer nearby.

SYON PARK GARDEN CENTRE
You can appease the children here with the Butterfly House and the motor museum.

For People with Disabilities

This chapter is intended as a rough guide for people with disabilities visiting the places already described. It mentions good and bad points. Band concerts in St James's and the scented blooms of the Regent's Park rose garden may make those places particularly attractive to people with a visual handicap, whereas steps may make a place inaccessible for someone who uses a wheelchair. People and their disabilities vary greatly, and the chapter does not claim to help everyone. In my experience people would rather go out somewhere and risk being frustrated on arrival than not go out at all.

Highlighted are three places of particular interest to people who enjoy gardening but have a disability.

KEW GARDENS
Allocated parking near main gate on Kew Green. Wheelchairs (W.) are available for hire and can be reserved in advance.
W. toilets.
Gardens basically flat with plenty of even paths. Temperate House, Palm House, Princess of Wales Conservatory and Wood Museum all have ramped access, though there may be awkward corners inside. Orangery is ramped and easier inside. General Museum, Kew Palace, Marianne North Gallery and Queen Charlotte's Cottage all have steps.

CHELSEA FLOWER SHOW
Access generally good. A few kerbs and slight slopes.
W. toilets.
Beware the crowds – go early or late.
Guide dogs not allowed but the organizers will provide an escort if contacted in advance.

RHS Exhibition Halls in Vincent Square
Old Hall: flight of steps at front but attendants will carry chairs up. New Hall: ramp at back door; wheelchair users should make themselves known for it to be opened. Library: in same building as Old Hall so steps have to be overcome. Once inside it is reached by lift and accessible for W.

The Royal Parks

GREENWICH PARK
Partly on a steep hill. Tarmac paths throughout. Tea house accessible for W. indoors and out.
W. toilet.
Band concerts on summer Sundays.

HAMPTON COURT
Generally flat but some paths are rough gravel. Allocated parking.
W. toilets.
Maze rough and narrow. Vine accessible. Café and restaurant both up a step. Area outside café flat.

BUSHY PARK
Rough grassland apart from roads. Paths in Waterhouse Woodland Garden a bit rough.
W. toilet.

HYDE PARK
Flat with tarmac paths.
W. toilet.
Dell Restaurant accessible indoors and out. Ser-

pentine Restaurant: waiter-service accessible; self-service accessible, though entrance to food counters is through the exit. Flat access to boats and Lido at Serpentine. Speakers' Corner no problem.

KENSINGTON GARDENS
Flat with tarmac paths.
W. toilets in Hyde Park.

REGENT'S PARK
Generally flat with tarmac paths.
W. toilet.
Theatre accessible. Band concerts at summer lunchtimes. Queen Mary's Rose Garden highly scented.

PRIMROSE HILL
Steep hill but well served by tarmac paths.
W. toilet in Regent's Park.

RICHMOND PARK
Rough grassland and gravel paths apart from roads. Hilly.
W. toilets.
Slope into café near golf course at Roehampton Gate. Flat access into outdoor seating area at same place.
Pembroke Lodge café flat access indoors and out. Plenty of space at both cafés.

ST JAMES'S PARK
Flat with tarmac paths.
Cake House accessible inside and out. Band concerts early evening in summer.

GREEN PARK
Slightly undulating. Tarmac paths.

Parks

BATTERSEA PARK
Flat with good paths. Steep ramp into glasshouses, which are cramped. Café accessible inside and out.
W. toilet.
Large collection of herbs.

GOLDERS HILL
Undulating grassland with tarmac paths. Disabled given priority use of small car park. Glasshouse awkward.
Band concerts summer Sunday afternoons.
Toilet for disabled should be built by summer 1987.

HOLLAND PARK
Decorative areas have tarmac paths. Woodland undulating with gravel/dirt paths.
Café accessible but a bit awkward due to lack of space.
W. toilet.

KENWOOD
Cars may be parked in front of the house.
Garden next to house flat with level paths. Lawns and woodland undulating.
Ground floor of house easily accessible. Concert bowl accessible down sloping grass. Tea room and adapted toilet reached by a small step.

LESNES ABBEY WOOD
Decorative area has flat tarmac paths. Woodland steep with very rough grass.
W. toilet.
Café accessible indoors and out.

OSTERLEY PARK
Mainly rough grassland but reasonably flat.
W. toilet.
Café in stable block has flat access. House reached by many steps.

WATERLOW PARK
Quite a steep site but plenty of good paths.
W. toilet.
Outside of café accessible. The inside of Lauderdale House is in the process of being made entirely accessible for W. users; this will include a toilet.

Gardens

CHELSEA PHYSIC GARDEN
Gravel paths. Generally flat. Steps down into the garden.
Plenty of scented plants.

CHISWICK HOUSE
Gravel paths but quite flat and the whole garden generally level.
Conservatory ramped. House accessible on ground floor but many steps to first floor.

FENTON HOUSE
Gravel paths and steps. Lots of scented plants.

HAM HOUSE
All on the flat. Gravel paths. House has steps at its entrance but there is a lift inside – though this is

only really suitable for small chairs.
W. toilets.

THE HILL
Gravel and cinder path from main road to the entrance.
Pergola full of steps. Lower garden has tarmac paths but is on a slope.

THE TRADESCANT GARDEN

Heath and Common Land

HAMPSTEAD HEATH
Steep slopes and gravel paths or rough grassland. Area around Highgate Ponds and Parliament Hill most easily accessible.
W. toilets at Kenwood and Parliament Hill.

WIMBLEDON COMMON
Generally flat but the tracks can be hard going as some are sandy and others can be muddy.
Windmill has many steps. Café flat outside and in.

The Squares and Inns of Court

Being in central London there are a lot of roads and kerbs to negotiate, and it is not always easy to park nearby.

FITZROY SQUARE
The paving surrounding the garden is a bit bumpy due to exaggerated rainwater channels.

GORDON SQUARE
Slight step down. Gravel paths quite level.

TAVISTOCK SQUARE
Easy access on three sides. Tarmac paths.

RUSSELL SQUARE
Easy access. Tarmac paths.
W. toilet – pay-as-you-enter cubicle opposite Hotel Russell.

GROSVENOR SQUARE
Easy access. Tarmac paths.

The Demonstration Garden at Battersea Park is well used by people of varying abilities

BERKELEY SQUARE
Accessible but gravel paths rough.

ST JAMES'S SQUARE
Sloping tarmac ramp up into this square. Tarmac paths.

THE TEMPLE
The odd kerb but generally good flat surfaces.

LINCOLN'S INN
Again kerbs, but generally trouble-free. Lincoln's Inn Fields has flat tarmac paths. The café is all on the level.

GRAY'S INN
Kerbs. Flat.

Roof Gardens and Landscaped Open Space

THE BARBICAN CONSERVATORY
Lower area accessible. Lift access easiest from Level 3.
W. toilets in Barbican.
Reserved spaces in Barbican car park.

DERRY AND TOMS' ROOF GARDEN
Ramp on ground floor gives access to large lift. The garden has single and double steps throughout. Surfaces are flat paving or flagstones.

ST KATHARINE'S DOCK
Cobbled sections and the odd kerb in a generally flat area.
Dickens pub is inaccessible but there is plenty of room to sit outside in good weather. Patisserie also has an outdoor area which is accessible.

THE SOUTH BANK
Generally very accessible.
W. toilets in all main arts buildings.
Braille description of the Jubilee Gardens next to commemorative plaque on a wall near children's play area.

Eating Out

THE GARDENS
Ramp on ground floor gives access to a large lift. In the restaurant there are three or four steps to the main eating area. Otherwise flat. Flat areas outside for eating, but the whole garden has single and double steps throughout. Surfaces in the garden are flat paving or flagstones.

HENRY J. BEAN (But His Friends All Call Him Hank) Bar and Grill
Flat access into bar off street. Steps into garden but emergency exit is a slope from street.

THE OLD RANGOON
Garden accessible for W. from car park. Restaurant up several steps.

THE DUKE OF CLARENCE
Couple of steps between bars, conservatory and garden.

THE FREEMASON'S ARMS
Garden reached by several steps down out of pub. The pub itself is entered by a step.

THE HAND AND FLOWER
Garden easily accessible. Large flat lawn. Pub itself full of steps and odd angles.

THE HARE AND HOUNDS
Garden accessible but pub more difficult. Flat paving and grass.

THE SPANIARD'S INN
Garden easily accessible. Flat paving. Pub reached by steps.

THE VICTORIA
Garden accessible through side gate. All concrete and flat. Plenty of room. Pub up steps.

GOLDERS HILL (Café)
The café terrace is easily accessible. Slight step to interior, which is small.

HAM HOUSE (Café)
Outdoor seating area accessible. Two steps into café. The seating area is a little cramped.
W. toilet.

KEW GARDENS (Café)
Tables inside and out are accessible.
W. toilets.

REGENT'S PARK (Café)
Rose Garden Buffet has plenty of room for W. The indoor areas of the other two cafés are a little cramped though accessible.

Outdoor areas accessible.
W. toilets.

RUSSELL SQUARE (Café)
All flat and totally accessible though indoors small.
W. toilet just outside, opposite Hotel Russell.

PICNIC PLACES
Down to you to choose the most suitable sites. See descriptions in relevant chapters.

Buying Plants

ALEXANDRA PALACE GARDEN CENTRE
Sloping site. Gravel and tarmac paths. Steep climb to the palace (you can drive).
Ramps in shop. Generally plenty of room. Slight lip into café which is small, but room to sit outdoors.

THE CHELSEA GARDENER
Both inside and out are flat and accessible to W.

Access for the disabled varies greatly in 'green' London. St Katharine's Dock is relatively trouble-free

Outdoors many of the plants are displayed on low tables, making selection from a W. easier. Can be a bit cluttered and awkward for W.

CLIFTON NURSERIES
Accessible but cluttered outdoors. Indoor areas also crowded, with only narrow paths and some steps.

SYON PARK GARDEN CENTRE
Plenty of space and all on flat concrete. Access generally good to all the attractions, apart from a few steps at the house.
Reserved parking near the garden centre.

CHATTELS
Very cramped; narrow with steps.

GARDEN CRAFTS
Up a few steps and very cramped.

SUTTONS SEEDS
Up steps and cramped.

NEW COVENT GARDEN MARKET
All on the flat. Have to be quick to get out of the way of men at work.

COLUMBIA ROAD MARKET
Ordinary street with kerbs and may be a little uneven. Can be quite crowded.

FELTON AND SONS
Step into the shop. Just about room to turn around in a W.

MOYSES STEVENS
Step into the shop. Enough room to look around in a W.

Horicultural Therapy and Demonstration Gardens

Horticultural Therapy is an organization which promotes gardening for people with special needs. In London it manages three demonstration gardens adapted for people with disabilities and used by special schools, residential homes, social services establishments and individuals. All the gardens are designed to show how absorbing and beneficial gardening can be to all people, regardless of disability, handicap or infirmity. Visitors can participate in gardening activities, watch demonstrations, see a range of special tools and equipment, and get ideas of how they can enjoy gardening in their own homes.

BATTERSEA DEMONSTRATION GARDEN
This garden is in a pleasant location in the northeast corner of Battersea Park near the café. A full-time demonstrator is employed here who takes classes and organizes workshops in the garden and lecture room, which are totally accessible for wheelchair users. The centre of the garden is a large tarmac area dotted with beds of varying heights, shapes and sizes. There is also a raised pool. Close by are some commercially produced movable plant containers and a few innovative and cheaper ones made from tyres, a mangle and a sink.

The area shows that outdoor gardening does not necessarily involve a lot of backache. The garden is raised for the benefit of people who use wheelchairs and those who cannot bend over. Likewise, not everyone can stretch up to tend fruit trees. The garden has trees trained on cordons growing to a height of no more than five feet and also low bush varieties of a similar size. The perimeter of the garden has beds used for demonstrations of how to handle lightweight tools and other specially adapted tools.

A wide variety of plants is grown in the garden, and the demonstrator can advise visitors on the most suitable types for their needs. Every aspect of indoor gardening is also covered, from bulbs to bottle gardens.

DULWICH DEMONSTRATION GARDEN
The demonstration garden in Dulwich Park, south London, was begun in the autumn of 1986. It is particularly exciting because it has been conceived, planned and in part built by people with handicaps for the benefit of others. It is an undulating site with mature trees and shrubs close to the park's café. It will be fully accessible for people who use wheelchairs, with plenty of seats for those who tire easily. Some of the seats will be specially high for people who have difficulty getting up from a traditional low seat. Raised beds will allow people in wheelchairs to work in the garden, and there are other work areas planned. Special emphasis is being placed on making the garden attractive to people with a visual handicap. Different types of path surface will be used to act as a guide around the garden. The 'feel' through shoes is an excellent

guide to those who have difficulty seeing. Scented plants will be planted in groups but spaced out around the garden so fragrances do not blur. Raised beds will allow people to touch as well as smell the plants. Sound beacons such as fountains and plants with leaves that rustle will be incorporated. The garden will also have a picnic area under one of the large trees. A full-time demonstrator will be employed here when the garden is completed.

Dulwich Park is noted for its spectacular display of rhododendrons in spring; it also has a pretty boating lake, aviary and many sports facilities. Being on the flat it is particularly suitable for wheelchair users. There is a toilet for the disabled and a braille map of the park.

SYON PARK DEMONSTRATION GARDEN

Being part of the formal garden at Syon Park, it is open the same hours. Here are raised beds, including a water garden, ground level beds covered with plants which smother weeds and reduce maintenance, displays of evergreen plants suitable for raised beds and containers, and cordon fruit trees. There is also a fully equipped greenhouse. Like those at Battersea and Dulwich, this garden is full of good ideas. A demonstrator is available on Wednesday afternoons and Friday mornings.

The garden centre at Syon Park is excellent for users of wheelchairs.

HORTICULTURAL THERAPY

If you would like to know more about this type of gardening please contact Horticultural Therapy who are always willing to help. They are in touch with dozens of organizations in London who have gardens and use them for the benefit of people with special needs.

Address Horticultural Therapy, Goulds Ground, Vallis Way, Frome, Somerset BA11 3DW.
Telephone (0373) 64782.

ACCESS IN LONDON – *The Unique Tourist Guide for Disabled People and Those Who Have Problems Getting Around* is published by Robert Nicholson Publications (1984) and well worth a look.

Information

KEW GARDENS
Address Kew, Richmond. Entrances: Kew Green; Kew Road opposite Lichfield Road.
Telephone 940 1171.
Open Daily 10 a.m.–dusk.
Admission 50p.
Transport British Rail: Waterloo–Kew Bridge; North London Link: North Woolwich–Kew Gardens. Tube: District Line to Kew Gardens. Bus: 27, 65. River-boat from Westminster. Parking on Kew Green and Queen Elizabeth Lawn.

CHELSEA FLOWER SHOW
Address The Royal Hospital, Chelsea, SW3. Entrances: Chelsea Embankment; Royal Hospital Road opposite Franklins Row.
Open Late May. Wed. 8 a.m.–8 p.m., Thur. 8 a.m.–8 p.m., Fri. 8 a.m.–5 p.m.
Admission Price drops each day, and there is a reduction after 4 p.m. on the first two days.
Transport Tube: District or Circle to Sloane Square. Bus: 11, 39, 137. Parking at Battersea Park from where there is a free minibus service to the show.

Other RHS Shows
Addresses Old Hall, Vincent Square, SW1. New Hall, Greycoat Street, SW1.
Shows monthly. Prices vary.
Transport Tube: Victoria, District or Circle to Victoria. Bus: 10, 76, 88. Parking meters.

LINDLEY LIBRARY
Address Third floor of RHS offices, Vincent Square.
Open Mon.–Fri. 9.30 a.m.–5.30 p.m. Till 6 p.m. on first day of shows in Halls. All enquiries to RHS.
Telephone 834 4333.

The Royal Parks

GREENWICH PARK
Address Greenwich, SE10. Entrances: either side of National Maritime Museum, Romney Road, and Chorlton Way, Blackheath.
Telephone 858 2608.
Open Daily 5 a.m.–dusk.
Transport British Rail: Charing Cross–Greenwich. Bus: 53, 188. River-boat from Westminster. Car park.

HAMPTON COURT AND BUSHY PARK
Address East Molesey. Entrances: Hampton Court Road, also Park Road, Teddington, for Bushy Park.
Telephone 977 1328.
Open Daily dawn–dusk. Waterhouse Woodland Garden daily 9 a.m.–dusk.
Transport British Rail: Waterloo–Hampton Court, Teddington, Hampton Wick. Bus: 111, 131, 216, 218, 267. River-boat from Westminster. Car parks.

HYDE PARK
Address London W1.
Open Daily 5 a.m.–dusk.
Transport Tube: Central Line to Marble Arch. Piccadilly Line to Hyde Park Corner or Knightsbridge. Bus: 2B, 6, 7, 8, 9, 12, 14, 15, 16, 16A, 19, 22, 25, 30, 36, 36B, 52, 73, 74, 82, 88, 137.

KENSINGTON GARDENS
Address London W8.
Telephone 937 4848.
Open Daily 5 a.m.–dusk.
Transport Tube: Central Line to Lancaster Gate or Queensway. Bus: 9, 12, 33, 49, 52, 52A, 73. Parking near Serpentine Restaurant.

REGENT'S PARK AND PRIMROSE HILL
Address London NW1.
Telephone 486 7905.
Open Daily, Outer Circle 5 a.m.–dusk. Inner Circle 7 a.m.–dusk.
Transport Tube: Circle, Bakerloo, Jubilee or Metropolitan to Baker Street. Circle or Metropolitan to Great Portland Street. Bus: 3, 13, 53, 74, 82, 137. Car park near Gloucester Gate.

RICHMOND PARK
Address Richmond. Main entrance: junction of Richmond Hill and Star and Garter Hill.
Telephone 948 3209.
Open Daily 7 a.m.–half an hour before dusk.
Transport British Rail: Waterloo–Richmond; North London Link: North Woolwich–Richmond. Then bus. Bus: 65, 71, 72, 264. River-boat from Westminster. Car parks.

ST JAMES'S PARK AND GREEN PARK
Address London SW1.
Telephone 930 1793.
Open Daily 5 a.m.–midnight.
Transport Tube: District or Circle to St James's Park. Victoria, Jubilee or Piccadilly to Green Park. Bus: 3, 11, 12, 24, 29, 53, 77, 88, 159. Parking meters.

Parks

BATTERSEA PARK
Address Albert Bridge Road, SW11.
Telephone 228 2798.
Open Daily 7.30 a.m.–dusk.
Transport British Rail: Victoria–Battersea Park. Bus: 44, 137. Car parks.

GOLDERS HILL
Address North End Road, Hampstead, NW3.
Telephone 455 5183.
Open Daily 7.30 a.m.–dusk.
Transport Tube: Northern Line to Golders Green or Hampstead. Then bus. Bus: 268. Small car park. A larger one is up the hill beside Jack Straw's Castle.

HOLLAND PARK
Address Abbotsbury Road, Kensington, W8.
Telephone 602 2226.
Open Daily 8 a.m.–dusk. Floodlit gardens around restaurant remain open much later.
Transport Tube: Central Line to Holland Park. District Line to Kensington High Street. Bus: 9, 12, 27, 28, 33, 49, 73, 88. Car park.

KENWOOD
Address Hampstead Lane, NW3.
Telephone 340 5303.
Open Daily dawn–dusk.
Transport Tube: Northern Line to Archway or Golders Green. Then bus. Bus: 210. Car parks.

LESNES ABBEY WOOD
Address New Road, Abbey Wood, SE2.
Telephone 310 2777.
Open Daily 7.30 a.m.–dusk.
Transport British Rail: Charing Cross–Abbey Wood. Bus: 99, 269. Parking in surrounding residential areas or at Bostall Heath.

OSTERLEY PARK
Address Jersey Road, Osterley, Isleworth.
Telephone 560 3918.
Open Daily 10 a.m.–dusk.
Transport Tube: Piccadilly Line to Osterley. Bus: 91(Mon.–Sat.) or 111. Car park.

WATERLOW PARK
Address Highgate High Street, N6.
Telephone 435 7171.
Open Daily 7.30 a.m.–half an hour before dusk.
Transport Tube: Northern Line to Highgate or Archway. Then bus. Bus: 210, 271. Parking around Highgate.

Gardens

CHELSEA PHYSIC GARDEN
Address Swan Walk, Chelsea, SW3.
Telephone 352 5646.
Open Mid-Apr. to Mid-Oct. Wed., Sun., Bank Holiday Mon., 2–5 p.m. Tue.–Fri. of Chelsea Flower Show week, 12–5 p.m.
Admission Adults £1.50, students and children £1.
Transport Tube: Circle Line to Sloane Square. Bus: 39, 137. Parking in residential streets nearby.

CHISWICK HOUSE
Address Burlington Lane, Chiswick, W4.
Telephone 994 2861.
Open Daily dawn–dusk.
Transport British Rail: Waterloo–Chiswick. Tube: District Line to Chiswick Park or Turnham Green. Bus: 290. Car park off Hogarth Lane.

FENTON HOUSE
Address Hampstead Grove, Hampstead, NW3.
Telephone 435 3471.
Open Mar., Sat. & Sun. 2–6 p.m. Apr.–Oct., Sat.–Wed. 11 a.m.–6 p.m.
Transport Tube: Northern Line to Hampstead. Bus: 268. Parking in residential streets or car park beside Jack Straw's Castle.

HAM HOUSE
Address Ham Street, Richmond.
Telephone 940 1950.
Open Daily 8 a.m.–5 p.m.
Transport British Rail: Waterloo–Richmond; North London Link: North Woolwich–Richmond. Then bus. Tube: District Line to Richmond. Then bus. Bus: 65, 71. Car park.

THE HILL
Address Inverforth Close, North End Way, Hampstead, NW3.
Telephone 455 5183 (Golders Hill number).
Open Daily 9 a.m.–dusk.
Transport Tube: Northern Line to Hampstead. Then bus. Bus: 210, 268. Small car park at Golders Hill. Larger one beside Jack Straw's Castle.

THE TRADESCANT GARDEN
Address Lambeth Palace Road, SE1.
Telephone 261 1891.
Open Mon.–Fri. 11 a.m.–3 p.m. Sun. 10.30 a.m.–5 p.m. Closed from second Sun. in Dec. to first Sun. in March.
Transport Tube: Circle or District to Westminster. Bus: 3, 44, 77, 159, 170. Limited parking in front of the church.

Heath and Common Land

HAMPSTEAD HEATH
Address Hampstead, NW3.
Telephone London Residuary Body (successor to GLC) 930 0613.
Open Daily all hours.
Transport Tube: Northern Line to Hampstead. Bus: 210, 268. Car park near Hampstead Ponds; another beside Jack Straw's Castle.

WIMBLEDON COMMON
Address Wimbledon, SW19. Windmill approached up Windmill Road off Wimbledon Parkside.
Telephone 788 7655.
Open Daily all hours.
Transport British Rail: Waterloo–Wimbledon. Tube: District Line to Wimbledon. Bus: 80, 93. Car park at the windmill.

The Squares and Inns of Court

Use parking meters, or a car park if you are sightseeing all day.

FITZROY SQUARE, W1
Transport Tube: Northern or Victoria Line to Warren Street. Bus: 14, 18, 24, 27, 30, 73.

GORDON AND TAVISTOCK SQUARES, WC1
Open Gordon 8 a.m.–8 p.m. Mon.–Fri. Tavistock open daily during daylight.
Transport Tube: Circle or Metropolitan Line to Euston Square. Piccadilly Line to Russell Square. Bus: 68.

RUSSELL SQUARE, WC1
Open Daily, during daylight.
Transport Tube: Piccadilly Line to Russell Square. Bus: 5, 7, 8, 19, 22, 25, 38, 55, 68, 77, 77A, 153, 171, 188, 196, 501.

GROSVENOR SQUARE, W1
Open Daily dawn to dusk.
Transport Tube: Central or Jubilee Line to Bond Street. Bus: 6, 7, 8, 12, 13, 15, 30, 73, 88, 137.

BERKELEY SQUARE, W1
Open Daily dawn to dusk.
Transport Tube: Victoria, Jubilee or Piccadilly Line to Green Park. Bus: 9, 14, 22, 25, 38.

ST JAMES'S SQUARE, SW1
Open 10 a.m.–4.30 p.m. Mon.–Fri.
Transport Tube: Bakerloo or Piccadilly Line to Piccadilly Circus. Bus: 9, 14, 22, 25, 38.

THE TEMPLE
Address Fleet Street, WC2. Gatehouse near Temple Bar.
Open Daily during daylight.
Transport Tube: District or Circle Line to Temple. Bus: 6, 9, 11, 15.

LINCOLN'S INN
Address Lincoln's Inn Fields, WC2. Entrances also in Carey Street and Chancery Lane.
Open Main gate: 8 a.m.–7 p.m. Mon.–Fri. Garden: 12–2.30 p.m. Lincoln's Inn Fields daily all hours.
Transport Tube: Central Line to Holborn. Bus: 6, 8, 9, 11, 15, 22, 25.

GRAY'S INN
Address Holborn, EC1. Gatehouse opposite Chancery Lane.
Open Daily during daylight. Garden: 12–2.30 p.m. Mon.–Fri. 1 May–30 Sept. inclusive.
Transport Tube: Central Line to Chancery Lane. Bus: 8, 22, 25, 45.

Roof Gardens and Landscaped Open Space

THE BARBICAN CONSERVATORY
Address The Barbican, EC2.
Telephone 638 4141 (Barbican – General Enquiries).
Open 10 a.m.–6 p.m. Sat. 12–6 p.m. Sun. and public hols.
Admission Adults 50p. Senior citizens, unemployed and children under 14, 20p.
Transport Tube: Circle or Metropolitan Line to Moorgate or Barbican. Bus: 9, 11. Car park in Barbican.

DERRY AND TOMS' ROOF GARDEN
Address 99 Kensington High Street, W8 (entrance in Derry Street).
Telephone 937 7994.
Open Daily 10 a.m.–6 p.m.
Transport Tube: Circle or District Line to High Street Kensington. Bus: 9, 27, 28, 31, 49, 73. Parking meters.

ST KATHARINE'S DOCK
On the Thames next to Tower Bridge.
Open Daily all hours.
Transport Tube: Circle or District Line to Tower Hill. Bus: 15, 56, 78. Car park next door.

THE SOUTH BANK
On the south side of the Thames between Waterloo and Westminster bridges.
Open Daily all hours.
Transport Tube: Northern or Bakerloo Line to Waterloo. Bus: 1, 68, 171, 181. Car park at National Theatre.

Eating Out

RESTAURANTS

THE GARDENS
Address 99 Kensington High Street, W8 (entrance in Derry Street).
Telephone 937 7994.
Open 12.30–3 p.m. Sun.–Fri.
Transport: Tube: District or Circle Line to High Street Kensington. Bus: 9, 27, 28, 31, 49, 73. Parking meters.

HENRY J. BEAN (But His Friends All Call Him Hank) Bar and Grill
Address 195–197 King's Road, SW3.
Telephone 352 9255.
Open 11.30 a.m.–11.45 p.m. Mon.–Sat. 12–10.30 p.m. Sun.
Transport Tube: District or Circle Line to Sloane Square. Bus: 11, 19, 22. Parking meters.

THE OLD RANGOON
Address 201 Castlenau, SW13.
Telephone 741 9655/6.
Open 12–11.30 p.m. daily.
Transport Tube: Metropolitan, District or Piccadilly Line to Hammersmith. Bus: 9. Car park.

PUBS

Usual London opening hours are 11 a.m.–3 p.m. and 5.30–11 p.m. with minor local variations.

THE DUKE OF CLARENCE
Address 203 Holland Park Avenue, W11.
Telephone 603 5431.
Open 7 p.m. Sat. eve. Otherwise normal hours. Food available daily. Barbecue Wed.–Fri. 8–10.30 p.m.
Transport Tube: Central Line to Shepherd's Bush or Holland Park. Bus: 12, 88. Parking in residential streets nearby.

THE FREEMASON'S ARMS
Address 32 Downshire Hill, NW3.
Telephone 435 4498.
No food Sun.
Transport Tube: Northern Line to Hampstead. Bus: 268. Parking in residential streets nearby.

THE HAND AND FLOWER
Address Upper Ham Road, Ham Common.
Telephone 940 1377.
Food available daily.
Transport British Rail: Waterloo–Richmond; North London Link: North Woolwich–Richmond. Then bus. Tube: District Line to Richmond. Then bus. Bus: 71, 65. Parking nearby.

THE HARE AND HOUNDS
Address Windmill Lane, Wyke Green, Isleworth, Middlesex.
Telephone 560 5438.
Food lunchtimes all week.
Transport Tube: Piccadilly Line to Osterley. Bus: 91. Car park.

THE SPANIARD'S INN
Address Hampstead Lane, NW3.
Telephone 455 3276.
Food available daily.
Transport Tube: Northern Line to Golders Green or Archway. Then bus. Bus: 210. Car park.

THE VICTORIA
Address 10 West Temple Sheen, East Sheen, SW14.
Telephone 876 4238.
Food available daily. Barbecue at weekends.
Transport British Rail: Waterloo–North Sheen or Mortlake. Bus: 33, 37. Parking in residential streets nearby.

CAFÉS

GOLDERS HILL
Open Mar.–Oct. daily 10.30 a.m.–6 p.m.
Directions, see under 'Parks'.

HAM HOUSE
Open Apr. (or Easter, if earlier)–Oct. Tue.–Sun. 12–5 p.m. (often later if fine). Also weekends in Nov.
Directions, see under 'Gardens'.

KEW GARDENS
Open Apr.–Oct. daily, all day.
Directions, see under 'Gardens'.

REGENT'S PARK
Open Rose Gardens Buffet and Tea Pavilion open daily all year. Refreshment Pavilion closed during the week in winter months. They all open at 10 a.m. and close between 5 and 8 p.m., depending on the season and the weather. Directions, see under 'The Royal Parks'.

RUSSELL SQUARE
Open Daily all year 8 a.m.–6 p.m.
Directions, see under 'The Squares and Inns of Court'.

PICNIC PLACES

Directions under relevant headings.

Buying Plants

ALEXANDRA PALACE GARDEN CENTRE
Address Alexandra Park, Wood Green, N22.
Telephone 883 6477.
Open 9.30 a.m.–5.30 p.m. Mon.–Fri. 9.30 a.m.–6 p.m. Sat. 10 a.m.–6 p.m. Sun. May close at 5 p.m. in autumn and winter.
Transport British Rail: King's Cross–Alexandra Palace. Bus: W3, 29, 134. Car park.

THE CHELSEA GARDENER
Address 125 Sydney Street, SW3.
Telephone 352 5656.
Open 10.30 a.m.–6 p.m. Mon.–Sat. Till 7 p.m. on Wed. 10.30 a.m. till 5 p.m. on Sun. and Bank Holidays.
Transport Tube: District or Circle Line to Sloane Square. Bus: 11, 19, 22, 49. Parking in neighbouring streets.

CLIFTON NURSERIES
Address 5A Clifton Villas, W9.
Telephone 289 6851.
Open Mon.–Sat. 8.30 a.m.–5.30 p.m. Sun. 9.30 a.m.–1.30 p.m.
Transport Tube: Bakerloo Line to Warwick Avenue. Bus: 6, 8, 16, 18. Parking in neighbouring residential streets.

SYON PARK GARDEN CENTRE
Address Syon Park, Brentford, Middlesex.
Telephone 568 0134.
Open 9.30 a.m.–5 p.m. daily Oct.–Mar. Till 5.30 p.m. Apr.–Sept.
Transport British Rail: Waterloo–Syon Lane. Tube: Piccadilly, District or Metropolitan Line to Hammersmith. Then bus. Bus: 237, 267. Car park.

CHATTELS
Address 53 Chalk Farm Road, NW1.
Telephone 267 0877.
Open 10 a.m.–5.30 p.m. Tue.–Sat. 12–5 p.m. Sun.
Transport Tube: Northern Line to Chalk Farm. Bus: 24, 31, 68. Parking in neighbouring streets.

GARDEN CRAFTS
Address 158 New King's Road, SW6.
Telephone 736 1615.
Open 9 a.m.–6 p.m. Mon.–Fri. 9 a.m.–5 p.m. Sat.
Transport Tube: District Line to Putney Bridge. Bus: 22. Parking in neighbouring streets.

SUTTONS SEEDS
Address 33 Catherine Street, WC2
Telephone 836 0619.
Open 9.30 a.m.–5.30 p.m. Mon.–Fri.; Jan.–Easter 10.30 a.m.–3.30 p.m. Sat.
Transport Tube: Piccadilly Line to Covent Garden. Bus: 6, 9, 11, 15, 68. Parking meters.

COLUMBIA ROAD MARKET
Address Columbia Road, E2.
Open 8 a.m.–noon Sun.
Transport Tube: Northern Line to Old Street. Bus: 6, 22, 35, 55. Parking in neighbouring streets.

NEW COVENT GARDEN MARKET
Address Nine Elms Lane, SW8.
Open 3–11 a.m. Mon.–Fri.
Admission £2 entry to car park.
Transport Tube: Victoria Line to Vauxhall. Bus: 44, 170, N88.

FELTON AND SONS
Address 220–224 Brompton Road, SW3.
Telephone 589 4433.
Open 8.30 a.m.–5.30 p.m. Mon.–Fri. 8.30 a.m.–noon Sat.
Transport Tube: Piccadilly, District or Circle Line to South Kensington. Bus: 14, 30, 45, 49, 74. Parking meters.

MOYSES STEVENS
Address 6 Bruton Street, W1.
Telephone 493 8171.
Open 8.30 a.m.–5.30 p.m. Mon.–Fri.
Transport Tube: Piccadilly, Victoria or Jubilee Line to Green Park. Bus: 9, 14, 22, 25, 38. Parking meters.

For the Disabled

THE SOUTH BANK
Jubilee Gardens has modern play equipment in a specially created area. River boat trip to Westminster and the City from Festival Pier.

BATTERSEA DEMONSTRATION GARDEN
Address Battersea Park, SW11.
Telephone 720 2212.
Open Daily 7.30 a.m.–dusk. Demonstrator usually on site Mon.–Fri. If you wish to take part in an activity or see the tools and equipment phone to make an appointment.
Directions, see under 'Parks'.

DULWICH DEMONSTRATION GARDEN
Address Dulwich Park, College Road, SE21.
Open Daily 7.30 a.m.–dusk.
Transport British Rail: Victoria–West Dulwich. Charing Cross–North Dulwich. Bus: 12, 37, 63, 78, 185. Car Park.

SYON PARK DEMONSTRATION GARDEN
Address Syon Park, Brentford, Middlesex.
Telephone 560 0882.
Open Daily 10 a.m.–dusk. Demonstrator available Wed. 2–4 p.m. and Fri. 10 a.m.–noon.
Directions, see under 'Buying Plants'.

Overleaf: Maps showing all green areas featured in this book.
Above: Greater London. *Below:* The central area enlarged

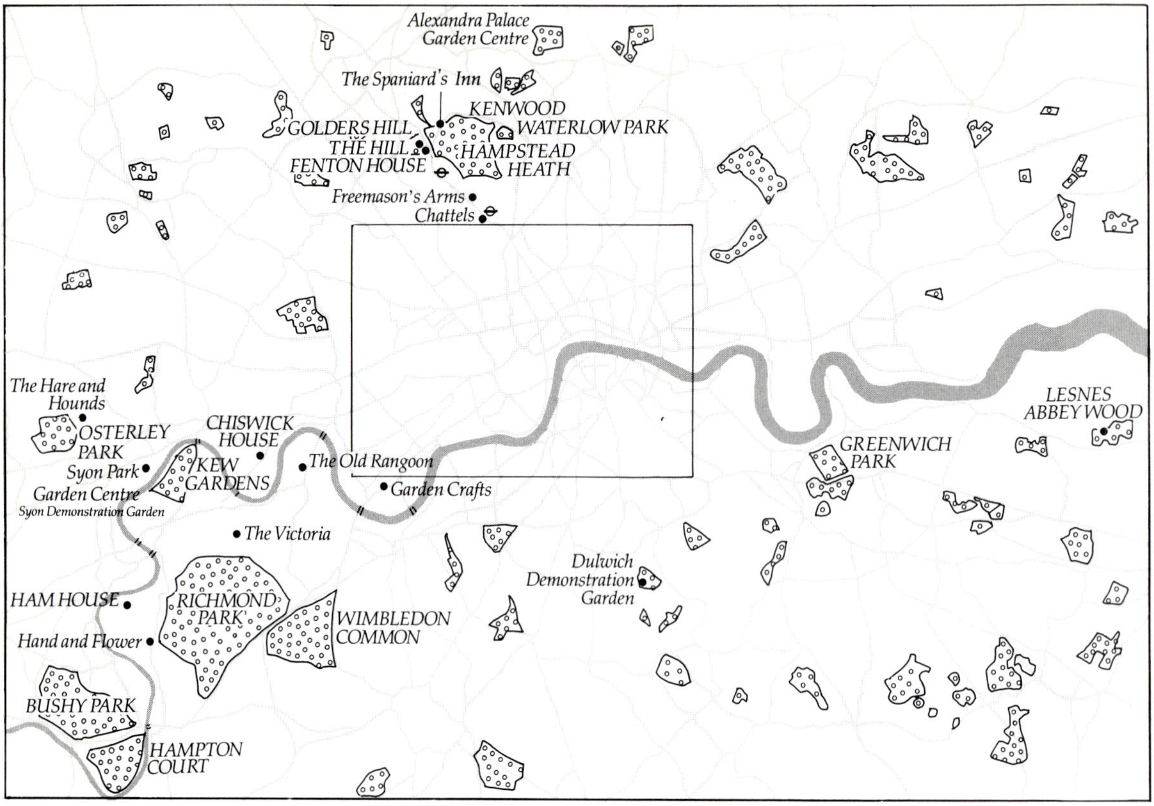

Alexandra Palace Garden Centre
The Spaniard's Inn
KENWOOD
GOLDERS HILL
WATERLOW PARK
THE HILL
HAMPSTEAD HEATH
FENTON HOUSE
Freemason's Arms
Chattels
The Hare and Hounds
OSTERLEY PARK
CHISWICK HOUSE
Syon Park
KEW GARDENS
The Old Rangoon
Garden Centre
Syon Demonstration Garden
Garden Crafts
The Victoria
LESNES ABBEY WOOD
GREENWICH PARK
Dulwich Demonstration Garden
HAM HOUSE
RICHMOND PARK
WIMBLEDON COMMON
Hand and Flower
BUSHY PARK
HAMPTON COURT

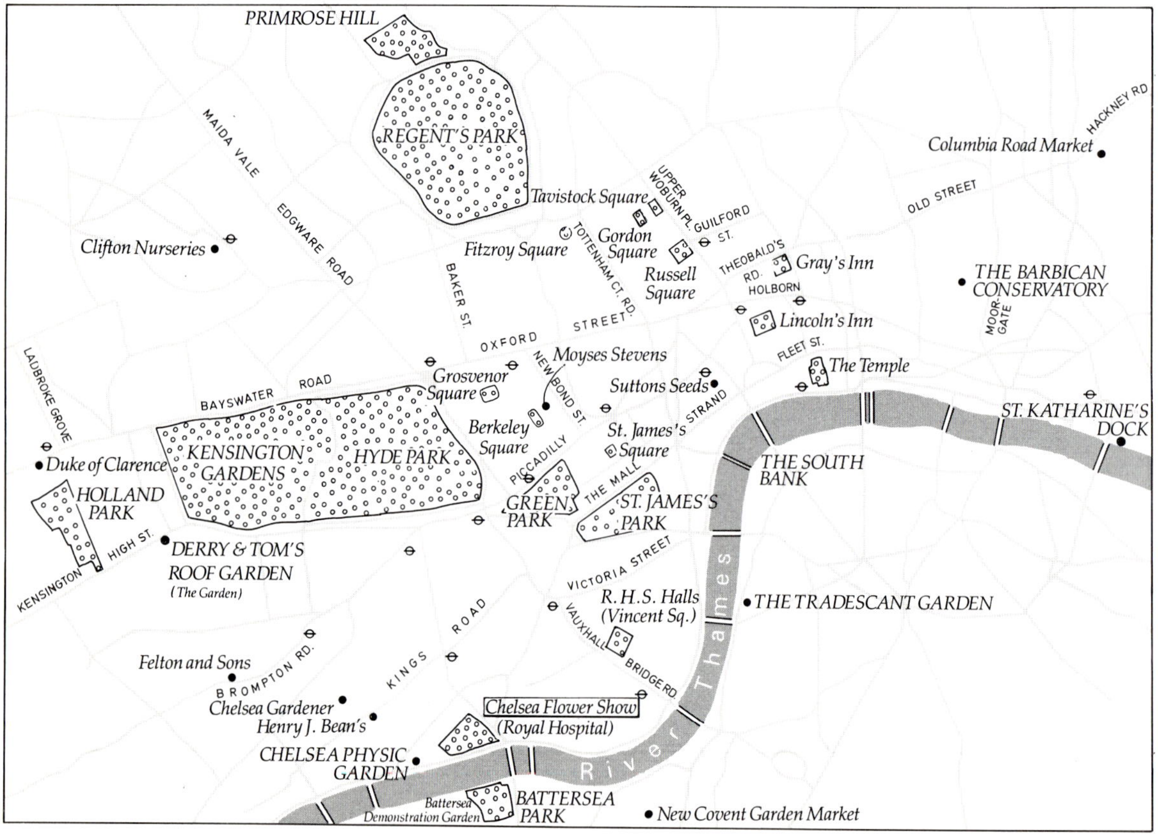

PRIMROSE HILL
REGENT'S PARK
MAIDA VALE
EDGWARE ROAD
HACKNEY RD
Columbia Road Market
OLD STREET
Tavistock Square
UPPER WOBURN PL.
GUILFORD ST.
Clifton Nurseries
Fitzroy Square
TOTTENHAM CT. RD.
Gordon Square
Russell Square
THEOBALD'S RD.
Gray's Inn
HOLBORN
THE BARBICAN CONSERVATORY
MOOR-GATE
BAKER ST.
Lincoln's Inn
OXFORD STREET
LAUDBROKE GROVE
Moyses Stevens
FLEET ST.
The Temple
BAYSWATER ROAD
Grosvenor Square
NEW BOND ST.
Suttons Seeds
STRAND
ST. KATHARINE'S DOCK
Berkeley Square
St. James's Square
Duke of Clarence
KENSINGTON GARDENS
HYDE PARK
THE SOUTH BANK
PICCADILLY
THE MALL
HOLLAND PARK
GREEN PARK
ST. JAMES'S PARK
KENSINGTON HIGH ST.
DERRY & TOM'S ROOF GARDEN
(The Garden)
VICTORIA STREET
R.H.S. Halls (Vincent Sq.)
THE TRADESCANT GARDEN
VAUXHALL BRIDGE RD.
ROAD
KINGS
Felton and Sons
BROMPTON RD.
Chelsea Gardener
Henry J. Bean's
Chelsea Flower Show
(Royal Hospital)
River Thames
CHELSEA PHYSIC GARDEN
Battersea Demonstration Garden
BATTERSEA PARK
New Covent Garden Market